MIDDLESEX CCC
THE CHAMPIONSHIP YEARS

MIDDLESEX
CRICKET

JON BATHAM
BEN KOSKY

To my dad, without whose sporting passion, passed on to me with great joy,
this book would never have been written.

First published 2023 by DB Publishing, an imprint of JMD Media Ltd,
Nottingham, United Kingdom.

ISBN 9781780916484

Printed in the UK

CONTENTS

ACKNOWLEDGEMENTS — 6

FOREWORD BY
MIKE SELVEY (MIDDLESEX PRESIDENT) — 8

INTRODUCTION — 11

CHAPTER 1
1878 AND 1903 — 14

CHAPTER 2
1920 AND 1921 — 25

CHAPTER 3
1947 AND 1949 — 47

CHAPTER 4
1976 — 72

CHAPTER 5
1977 — 89

CHAPTER 6
1980 — 105

CHAPTER 7
1982 — 124

CHAPTER 8
1985 — 142

CHAPTER 9
1990 — 161

CHAPTER 10
1993 — 180

CHAPTER 11
2016 — 198

ACKNOWLEDGEMENTS

Much as I loathe 'Oscars speeches' with their tendency towards 'I'd like to thank my mother for having me', there are several people who deserve my thanks for enabling this book to come to fruition.

Firstly, to my co-author Ben Kosky, who I am lucky enough to call my friend. Thank you for your writing, not to mention all the phone calls to check progress, and texts of encouragement, providing assurance in the darker moments this last winter that we would get there in the end.

Steve Caron and Michelle Grainger at JMD Media, thank you for keeping us on track, being in it with us at every step and for believing in the book enough to commission the idea in the first place.

Another man whom this would have been impossible without is Alan Rees at the Lord's library. Thank you Alan for digging out all sorts of material and facilitating my visits this winter – it has been a pleasure to meet you and other members of your team.

Middlesex County Cricket Club – there would be no story to tell if it were not for the county's rich sporting history, to which I hope I've done even a modicum of justice. Thank you to Steve Fletcher for facilitating some of the interviews and for providing photos from the Middlesex CCC archive.

Speaking of photos, thanks too to Matt Bright for the use of his Toby Roland-Jones image from 2016 for the jacket cover. It's a great picture and the only one I really wanted for that position. Hope you're enjoying life down in the south-west.

Thanks to each of the Middlesex legends who gave their time and shared their stories and especially to Mike Selvey for agreeing to write the foreword – I'm in your debt, gentlemen.

Wisden, thank you for agreeing to waive copyright on material from the relevant *Almanacks*, still the cricket lover's bible. All quotes from *Wisden* are with kind permission of John Wisden & Co.

This seems the time to acknowledge all those who have especially enriched me on my sports journalism journey over the last 18 years. Dave Watters, for giving me my first opening. We still work together when we can at the *Non-League Paper* as I'm a great believer you should never forget where you've come from and the debts of thanks that you owe.

Speaking of those to whom I'm in debt, David Waterhouse, Paul Warburton, Tim Street, John Whitbread, Matt Lewis, Tom Moore and Jake Murtagh. I hope you guys know what a huge influence you all were in those early days learning on the job at the office in Hounslow. All those times when you, Warbo, in particular shouted across the sports desk at me, 'What's the top line?' every time I put the phone down on an interview. It drove me nuts at the time, but you knew what you were doing. Sixteen years on my love for all you guys is undiminished.

I must not forget Steve Clare of Prost International, whose presence I have missed in the Lord's press box since he has gone back over the other side of the pond. Thanks for being your persistent 'dog with a bone' self, without which this book would have never seen the light of day.

And finally, to my wife Anne, the very best Jamaican woman ever, who despite her general lack of interest in sport has been a cheerleader through this whole process when I've been welded to my laptop for long periods to her detriment.

As my dear dad told me on the phone the day after meeting Anne for the first time, 'Son, there's never been anything wrong with your taste in women.' I'd have loved it if he stopped there, but he followed up with, 'You're just lucky she has a shocking taste in men.'

FOREWORD BY
MIKE SELVEY (MIDDLESEX PRESIDENT)

Do cricket followers really care now about the County Championship? We have the glitz and, at times, gimmick (looking at you The Hundred), and increasing riches of white-ball cricket, and global franchises. You won't find 30,000 filling Lord's to watch a four-day county game as there were for Blast matches immediately before the pandemic. From when I first started playing county cricket, more than half a century ago, the game has developed into one of bombastic hitting, aided by nuclear bats but hugely skilful nonetheless, flicks and ramps, dot balls and slow-ball bouncers, and out-fielding of an athletic standard that boggles the mind compared to us sedentary boundary-grazers of old.

White-ball cricket is the game's cash cow. Only recently it took a concerted effort by the chairs of the 18 first-class counties to ward off what was not even a disguised attempt by the England and Wales Cricket Board, the governing body of cricket in this country, to dilute further the programme of red-ball cricket, pushing it to the margins of the season, with the clear ultimate intention of forcing some counties to the fringes and eventually into irrelevance, all the while spending freely (and recklessly in my opinion) promoting a spurious competition played in a format played by no one else in the world. All under the guise of a supposed High-Performance Review.

And yet. Ask any professional county cricketer in this country in their heart of hearts whether they feel their careers and the status of their team is a function of white-ball success or by winning the County Championship and I'd strongly argue that they would say the latter. Put the same question to the members of clubs who are the lifeblood of the county game and you would get the same answer. Each would say the Championship defines them as a county; just ask those at Northamptonshire, Gloucestershire or Somerset, each of which has come within reach of the summit without quite getting there, what it would mean to win the title now.

Although my first-class career as a player began, while still a student, with Surrey and finished with two seasons as captain of Glamorgan, it is Middlesex, the county of my birth, to which I gave my best years. And as I sit here writing this foreword, I can see on a shelf four small silver goblets, each one denoting the County Championships that I helped the county win – 1976, 1977 (albeit shared with Kent), 1980, and 1982 – the

The Championship Years

genesis of a period of success that saw seven titles in 17 seasons. I also have two Gillette Cup winners' medals, but I don't see them on display. One-day titles were achievements without doubt but we all craved the Championship.

What prompted the cultural change that saw, by the early 1980s, arguably one of the finest of all county sides? We can start with ambition. By 1971, when Mike Brearley took over as Middlesex captain, the club had been 22 years since the twin postwar successes of 1947 and 1949, and a further 26 years before those since a previous title. In other words, one win and one shared title in almost half a century. In our dressing room, the frequent visits of Denis Compton and Bill Edrich, with their tales of the success and excess of their memorable 1947 summer (which included, by the way, an amazing season for the more understated Jack Robertson, as 'best supporting actor' if you will) actually started to rankle. There were some superb players for the county in the intervening years but the dominance of Surrey in the 1950s and Yorkshire in the '60s, with 14 out of 17 titles, restricted winning opportunities. We wanted our own legacy.

But how do you go about building a Championship side, especially in the days where freedom of movement of players between counties was restricted? It is true that a definitive season for an individual batter or bowler can in itself be a major factor. And yet in the last 50 years, only eight times has the leading run-scorer in the competition played for the winning county, and only nine times the leading wicket-taker.

It took Brearley five years of gradual progress to get together a side that played as a team, better than the sum of its parts, one that evolved almost by osmosis. Perhaps you start (and here I claim vested interest) with the premise that for all the importance of runs on the board, it is the role of batters, with their badge-kissing, bat-waving celebrations, to get no more than sufficient for the bowlers to do their job, for ultimately it is they who win the matches by taking 20 wickets. A quality all-round bowling side started to emerge. Two high-class spinners in Phil Edmonds and John Emburey developed, first as foil to and then as replacement of Fred Titmus. Allan Jones, a multi-county maverick bowler of genuine pace and some notoriety, was recruited, tamed, and proved an inspired signing. The young Wayne Daniel was in the pipeline, and I was gaining experience all the time. Later was to come the phenomenal Vintcent van der Bijl, almost an accidental signing, and Jeff Thomson and further international pacemen in Norman Cowans and Neil Williams. The signs were there then when Middlesex reached, if lost, two Lord's finals in 1975. We began to believe. With the bat, the system developed in Mike Gatting, and later Mark Ramprakash, two of the county's greatest ever players. Once you learn how to win, you thirst for more, resenting it when you didn't come out on top, a winning culture created that was carried on under Gatting's leadership. Two brilliant leaders in two decades and more lent that continuity.

9

The last match report I was to write after 30 years as chief cricket correspondent of *The Guardian* was, for me, appropriately from Lord's, on the final day of the 2016 summer when Toby Roland-Jones's last-ditch hat-trick scuppered Yorkshire to clinch the title after another barren period, this time 23 years, and I exulted in it. I know from the four years I have spent subsequently as club president in the company of today's Middlesex players how much that meant after hearing us old-timers banging on about our time and I was so happy for them. That triumph was the monkey off their back just as ours had been. They have created their own legacy.

INTRODUCTION

'You should write a book.' Five words spoken by someone else which triggered the autumn-and-winter-long journey leading to the manuscript you are now embarking on.

At the time I was sitting in a press marquee in the surrounds of Merchant Taylors' School, its art deco structure imposing itself on the landscape. My focus though was the afternoon's play between Worcestershire and hosts Middlesex, whose on- and off-field adventures I was now reporting for a 16th season.

The five words were ones I'd heard before a few times, though not in a cricket context. The suggestion this time came from Steve Clare of Prost International. We'd met a couple of years before in the media centre at Lord's. You don't get many new faces there for a county match, so it was only right to say hello.

From that day, Steve would regularly embarrass me by telling other newcomers that if they wanted to know anything about Middlesex cricket, myself and Ben Kosky were the ones to ask. Always a slightly awkward moment in truth and one Nick Friend from *The Cricketer* – always great company in a press box – would be more than entitled to dispute.

I initially brushed off the suggestion with, 'Of course I should,' but anyone fortunate enough to meet Steve will know he is something of a force of nature, so, over the next few weeks those five words would slip into the conversation on a regular basis.

Eventually, I consulted Ben Kosky, my friend and co-conspirator writing on Middlesex for the ECB Reporters' Network, who'd spent lockdown in 2020 penning his first book, *Are you Rangers in Disguise?*, a story of his adventures covering Queens Park Rangers as both reporter and fan.

Unfortunately for me, Ben thought I was more than able to produce my own tome, even offering to help write it and to introduce me to his publisher, Steve Caron at JMD Media Ltd.

'That's OK,' I told myself. 'Steve won't want a book on county cricket.' However, Steve jumped at it and here we are.

It has felt like the next step on a long journey. I came to sports journalism late by a circuitous route. A creative writing course run by the Arvon foundation was the catalyst. The house of the former Poet Laureate Ted Hughes in Hebden Bridge, surrounded by old cotton mills, formed a great setting and journalists Anthony Clavane and Will Woodward were encouraging and inspirational.

Nearly a year later and now a freelance sports journalist having ditched mind-numbing work as a market researcher to give my dreams a chance, I got some shifts providing cover at Trinity Mirror Hounslow, so getting some on-the-job training. It's impossible to say how much I owe to Dave Waterhouse, Paul Warburton, Tim Street, John Whitbread and others for those days, though I lost count of the number of times I finished a phone interview to hear Warbo's dulcet tones call out, 'What's the top line?' as soon as the receiver was down. If I couldn't immediately answer him, the suggestion would come, 'I suggest you ring him back.' Can't say I welcomed those interventions at the time, but they taught me so much.

It was while I was at Trinity that I first met Ben, who was working for the opposition Archant titles. We shared interviews, mainly at Wealdstone FC and occasionally QPR, both of which were on our respective patches. I soon learned he was a journalist of huge integrity whose word was his bond and who I could trust not to put his story out before the time we had agreed. Such journalists are all too rare and we became firm friends.

It was also while at Trinity that I got the chance to cover Middlesex County Cricket Club. I guess you could say I was in the right place at the right time when on a shift one afternoon the staffers were discussing their desire for a new Middlesex reporter, yet feeling none of them were quite right for the role.

I'd been a cricket fan for over 30 years by then, having fallen in love with the sport aged eight, watching the first day of the 1973 England versus West Indies Test, and Middlesex were the county I watched whenever finances and time allowed.

So, never one to be a shrinking violet, I piped up, 'I'll do it.' It was 2007 and Middlesex had just signed Tim Murtagh from London rivals Surrey, so I was tasked with getting a line from the then CEO Vinny Codrington on the new recruit. A few hours later, story filed, I got the gig.

I've therefore been lucky enough to call Lord's my summer office for 16 years, firstly as Trinity Mirror Southern's correspondent and in more recent times as part, along with Ben Kosky, of the ECB Reporters' Network.

So, it seems only right my first, and perhaps last, venture into authorship should centre on the history of Middlesex's County Championship triumphs, currently 13 in number, though we have included a nod to the class of 1878, who were the top county before a championship was ever an official thing.

Despite the early mornings and late nights from January to April in particular racing the copy deadline, this has largely been a labour of love, researching and writing on legends of Middlesex folklore as well as meeting and interviewing some heroes of my own boyhood. They say to never meet your heroes, but after a pleasant hour or so in the company of several of them, I beg to differ.

It goes without saying that Ben and I would have loved to have interviewed more of the legends, but being self-employed we've had to produce the book in a certain time window while keeping food on our respective tables amid the current cost of living crisis.

Nevertheless, we hope to give you at least the essence of the greatest days in Middlesex CCC's history.

There will be stories of stalwarts who went from performing heroics on the cricket field to the trenches of the battlefield, some never to return, while others resumed their sporting passion with a zeal determined to pour every last drop of the life they had been spared into the game they loved.

Serious topics will be raised, such as racism in the sport and the demise of the role of spin bowling in longer forms of the game.

But don't fret; there will be laughs too with tales of travel disaster, life advice, a legend known to another legend only as 'Thingy', and a recount of a somewhat steamy championship celebration among them.

So, we, that is Ben and I, wish you several happy evenings with your beverage of choice, dipping into tales of Middlesex's finest players of summers past and present.

Enjoy!

CHAPTER 1
1878 AND 1903

Toby Roland-Jones's hat-trick ball of 2016 didn't signal the only 'lucky 13' of Middlesex County Cricket Club's history. For that you have to travel back some 144 years to a committee meeting in the club's infancy, the outcome of which, had it been different, would have meant none of the 13 triumphs yet to unfold would ever have happened.

The club arose out of a meeting at the London Tavern – a hostelry in Bishopsgate renowned for its business meetings over food and drink – on 15 December 1863, thanks in large part to the Walker family of Southgate. Yet only nine years on from that night of sporting hopes the club faced up to the hardest of questions. Were all those dreams about to die? Middlesex had begun life at the Cattle Market Ground in Islington, winning their first game there against Sussex back in 1864 by an innings with Vyell Walker, one of the founding fathers taking nine wickets in an innings and 14 in the match.

When the hotelier who owned the ground sold up in 1868, the club upped sticks to the Lillee Bridge Road Ground on the border of Fulham and Chelsea. It was a venue synonymous with sporting events and perhaps for that reason suffered more than its fair share of wear and tear. After three seasons Middlesex made the decision to cut ties with the venue due to the poor quality of the turf and the termination of the relationship provoked the question of whether or not the club should fold.

The committee meeting must have been a vociferous one with strong views held on both sides of the argument and a proposal was put to the room that the club should continue and seek a third home elsewhere. That vote was carried 7-6. Middlesex supporters through time have potentially one wavering voter to thank for holding on to his sporting dreams and so casting his vote one way and not the other. Sir, whoever you may have been, we the Middlesex faithful raise our bat, or should that be doff our cap in acknowledgement.

They didn't move far, to the Princes Cricket Ground in Chelsea, where first visitors Yorkshire somewhat spoiled the beginning of the new adventure, winning by two wickets.

Middlesex stayed for five seasons at the ground, which was also used for lawn tennis and badminton with a permanent roller skating rink also installed. However, the Cadogan & Hans Place Improvement Act saw more and more of the site sold off for development, leaving Middlesex to move again to what has been their home ever since, Lord's, as tenants of Marylebone Cricket Club.

They made an inauspicious start; all four games hosted there in the summer of 1877 were lost, giving little indication success was around the corner.

However, the following summer, this corner of north-west London would begin to feel more like home.

Fulham-born Robert Henderson, in what proved his last year in first-class cricket, returned 6-21 to secure the hosts a first-innings lead of 21 over Surrey in the opening game of the season, the men from south of the river routed for only 84.

If Henderson bamboozled Surrey with spin, they were ultimately undone by pace courtesy of James Robertson, whose figures of 6-22 in the second innings secured victory for Middlesex by 113 runs.

Robertson can only be described as a late developer as this was his debut for Middlesex at the age of 27. Despite being a strong and athletic Scot, Robertson failed to secure his blue at Oxford, but these six wickets were a sign of what was to come as he took almost 300 in a career stretching as far as 1891. His wicket-taking exploits were accompanied by aggressive hitting as a right-handed batter and his great hands meant he gave invaluable service at slip.

Edward Salmon was another of the fresh faces for Middlesex in this match, making an eye-catching debut courtesy of three catches and a stumping. He would be a regular the following season, but his first-class career comprised just 11 matches.

The Australian tourists arrived in mid-summer bringing glorious hot weather with them, not previously seen that season.

The hosts held their own initially, with Henderson's four wickets bowling out the tourists for 165 before Alexander Webbe's 50 led Middlesex to 107-2 in reply.

However, Thomas Garrett, from Wollongong in New South Wales, who had played in the inaugural Australia versus England Test match a year earlier, induced a collapse, taking 7-38 as Middlesex lost their last eight wickets for 15 runs.

Henderson claimed five more Aussie scalps second time around, but even so, Middlesex faced a daunting chase of 284, one they began on the second evening of the three-day encounter.

They were quickly in disarray at 13-5 and they came up well short, but not before Edward Lyttleton had played the innings of his lifetime. The right-handed batter was one of seven brothers, five of whom played first-class cricket. Indeed, one of his younger siblings, Alfred, also played in this very match.

Not out on 37 overnight, Lyttleton resumed on a Saturday where the *Wisden Cricketers' Almanack* for 1879 recorded that the temperature was a stifling 105 degrees at wicket level.

Nevertheless, the then 22-year-old blazed away, making his additional 76 runs that morning at more than a run a minute. *Wisden* reported, 'When he was out for 113, all present applauded him most lustily, the Australians joining heartily in complimenting him on the, unquestionably, finest hitting display in 1878.'

When his playing days were done, Lyttleton became both a teacher and an outspoken cleric, one sermon in 1916 where he called for reparations on Germany at the end of the Great War not to be over burdensome causing plenty of consternation. He resigned the post shortly afterwards amid something of a crisis of faith, but returned to curacy at a later date.

The boiling hot weather continued on to the next game against one of the powerhouses of the era, Nottinghamshire, with *Wisden* noting, 'The quicksilver on the second day bubbled up to 130.'

Yet, while Lyttleton's effort against the Australians was an impossibly hard act to follow, one of the club's stalwarts, Walter Henry Hadow, gave it his best shot. He played several in fact, unfurling an array of strokes on a fast and true pitch where the ball came on to the bat well. He cut and drove to good effect, picking up an all-ran five and 11 fours. There were two heartstopping moments, one when he was dropped by wicketkeeper Fred Wyld seven short of his hundred and another when he was struck by a ball from Fred Morley soon afterwards.

Hadow didn't manage to eclipse his highest ever score of 217 made against MCC seven years previously, but his innings was certainly the highlight of an encounter which finished in a draw.

He played one more season at Lord's, going on to be Her Majesty Queen Victoria's Commissioner of Prisons for Scotland, a position he held at the time of his death in 1898.

No sooner had Nottinghamshire returned north when Yorkshire, possibly the strongest team of the era, came to town and in keeping with the season to that point, it was a different member of the home side who caught the eye as 12 June marked the most successful day of Thomas Pearson's career.

A week shy of his 27th birthday, Pearson, educated at Rugby School before becoming a graduate of Christ Church, Oxford, repelled the opening-day fire of former England quick George Freeman, after the hosts had slipped to 16-4 in the first 18 balls of the match. In an innings of close to three hours, the right-hander plundered 11 fours in a score of 84.

The 1879 *Wisden Almanack* hailed the innings, comfortably the highest individual score of the match, 'A plucky good bit of all-round hitting that won the applause of the Yorkshire eleven and all the other men on the ground.'

Pearson, though, wasn't finished there. After Hadow reduced the White Rose to 0-2, Pearson weaved magic with his right-arm off-breaks to winkle out the middle order on his way to 5-36. It would prove a career best as he didn't surpass such figures in seven more seasons with the men of Lord's.

Half-centuries from brothers Herbert and A.J. Webbe and 79 from Edward Lyttleton allowed Middlesex to pile up 346 on the second day, setting Yorkshire 400 to win.

The visitors made a decent fist of the chase, reaching 213-3 thanks to half-centuries for Edward Roper (68) and George Ulyett (57), but three more wickets for Pearson and three for Alfred Stratford, more of whom shortly, restricted them to 310, giving Middlesex victory by 90 runs.

The run chase is remembered in Lord's folklore for a particularly thunderous blow by Ulyett, who launched a delivery from Hadow over the players' seats and on to the gravel path behind the pavilion. The drive was subsequently measured at 109 yards from hit to pitch. Of course in those days any shot which didn't clear the confines of the ground, even if it went over the boundary rope, only counted as four. Scant reward for a shot which would compare favourably with many sixes struck in the modern white-ball game. For the metric among us, 109 yards equates to a smidgeon under 100 metres.

After four matches at home it was time for Middlesex to go on the road and their first port of call took them across the river to The Oval to face Surrey. It was a game they would have almost certainly lost had not rain curtailed the final day with them struggling on 120-5 in pursuit of 341 to win.

Nevertheless, the match marked a high point in the career of Alfred Stratford. The slow right-arm bowler, in his second of four seasons with Middlesex, took six wickets in each innings, his 6-41 in the first of those marking his career best. The 24-year-old was indebted to wicketkeeper Salmon for his part in six of those dismissals, five caught and one stumped.

In the case of Stratford, however, his exploits on the cricket field were not his greatest claim to sporting fame. He was in fact the proud owner of three FA Cup winners' medals at football for Wanderers, having been part of a hat-trick of successive wins in the famous old trophy between 1876 and 1878.

The first of those triumphs saw Stratford, who played as a full-back, pitted against two of his Middlesex team-mates, Edward and Alfred Lyttleton, who were part of the Old Etonians line-up, the former at half-back and Alfred as a forward.

The games were played at the Kennington Oval, the first ending in a draw, and while both Lyttletons were commended for their performances in the replay a week later, it was Stratford who got his hands on the trophy.

It was now time to head north for the return fixture with Yorkshire, a game which would see Middlesex's most emphatic win of the season. Robertson claimed six wickets in the hosts' first innings, skittling them for 94, while Stratford took his third six-wicket haul in two games in the second as the visitors won by an innings and plenty.

They did so in no small part because of 94 from Alexander Josiah Webbe, the largest contribution in a Middlesex innings of 298.

Webbe deserves to be hailed a Middlesex man through and through. Born in Bethnal Green, he played 26 seasons for Middlesex, right up until 1900, scoring over 14,000 runs and taking 109 wickets with his right-arm pace bowling.

He captained the side for five years in the mid-to-late 1880s, during which time he was team-mates with a young C.T. Studd.

Studd introduced Webbe to D.L. Moody and in 1884 Webbe was converted to the Christian faith at one of the evangelist's rallies. However, while Studd ended his cricket career soon afterwards to become one of the so-called 'Cambridge Seven', Webbe clearly saw Middlesex as his mission. On retirement as a player he took up the task of secretary, a role he held for 22 years, and not content with that he then served as president until 1936. The history of Middlesex CCC may contain greater sporting legends, but not many greater servants.

From the high of administering a drubbing to Yorkshire came the low of a season finale with Nottinghamshire at Trent Bridge, where again, but for the rain, the team ably skippered by Isaac Walker would have been well beaten, in all probability by an innings.

The fact they remained unbeaten by another domestic side left them as the leading county that year, having played fewer games than several of their rivals, and perhaps Nottinghamshire in particular would have been more worthy winners.

And of course, they were never adorned with the title 'county champions' for their feat as the competition was not officially instigated until 1890. It would be another quarter of a century before Middlesex could claim that accolade, but this author felt it only right to honour the class of 1878 before embarking on the story of 1903 – one very much concerned with another stalwart of the county and one whose influence on the game was felt well beyond the boundaries of Lord's, a certain Pelham 'Plum' Warner.

Warner was born in Trinidad, the youngest of 21 children, and his father served as attorney general of the Caribbean island for 25 years. Initially schooled in Trinidad, he moved to England aged 13, a few months after the death of his father and continued his education at Rugby, having failed to pass the entry exam for Winchester.

After four years at Rugby he moved on to Oriel College, Oxford, where bouts of influenza prevented him from getting his blue for two years until the then first XI captain of Oxford, Gerald Mordaunt, became the first to nickname him 'Plum', which stuck, quipping that he would 'look good in a navy coat'.

Warner's debut for Middlesex in 1894 was far from spectacular, making six and four against Somerset at Taunton, and his first Championship hundred didn't arrive until three years later, 176 against Nottinghamshire in a drawn game at Lord's.

Warner's first Test cap came in 1899 against South Africa and 1900 marked a step forward as he passed 1,000 runs for the season for the first time, with plenty to spare at that, helped by five centuries and five more scores over 50.

During this era, Yorkshire all but ruled in Championship terms, though Middlesex could and perhaps should have won their first title in 1898 when they finished runners-up.

We should say by way of background that by this stage 16 counties were part of the County Championship, but the competition was still not at a point where each team played the same number of games. Yorkshire and Lancashire remained the busiest counties in 1903, playing 26 times, while Derbyshire played only 16. Middlesex as eventual champions played 18.

It operated on a very different scoring system than the ones seen today with simply one point added for a win and one taken away for a defeat. The team with the highest percentage of possible points to games played were declared champions.

We should note two other points of interest prior to a ball being bowled in the 1903 season. The Middlesex minute book shows that in a February committee meeting that year, the club voted in favour of a proposal by the governing body to widen the wicket from eight inches to nine. Furthermore, it was agreed to support a proposal to also heighten the wicket by an inch as in the view of those in the room too many Championship games were being drawn. At the MCC AGM that May, there was more support than expected for the change, but it didn't receive the two-thirds majority required to necessitate altering the existing playing law.

The other discussion at the February Middlesex committee meeting involved changing the length of a Championship game from three days to four. This proposal met with much dissension in the room. It is amazing to think it was another 85 years before the powers that be began this process of transition and 90 before four-day cricket became the norm.

At a time when cricket is experiencing turbulence amid Andrew Strauss's High-Performance Review with its threatened restructure of the county game, it is interesting to reflect that proposals for change were ever thus.

Warner or no Warner, 1903 didn't dawn with much optimism. Middlesex had endured a terrible season 12 months earlier, winning only three games, and with little or no change in personnel there was no reason to suspect that a first County Championship title was on the way.

Yet when the season began in earnest Middlesex were, to the surprise of most and maybe even themselves, something of a revelation with the tone set on the opening day of the campaign.

Winning the toss and electing to bat against Gloucestershire, Warner, performing captain's duties in the absence of regular skipper Gregor MacGregor, and Leonard Moon plundered 248 for the first wicket, the latter making 122.

It was the start of a solid season for the west London-born opener as part of a batting line-up in which, more often than not, one or more stuck their hand up. Moon spent a decade in Middlesex colours and his form in 1905 was good enough to earn him a spot on England's boat for the tour to South Africa, where he paid the penalty for failing to convert several promising starts and was not selected again. He became one of many former cricketers to die in the Great War, falling while advancing against Bulgarian forces in November 1916.

Warner went on to make 149 and there was a third centurion on that memorable opening day – one Albert Trott. As a journalist who is lucky enough to call the spaceship-like media centre at Lord's his summer office, I know you rarely get through a session these days, never mind a day's play, without hearing a tour guide regaling the story of Albert Trott, the only man to hit a ball from the square over the pavilion as it is today.

He had paid his own passage to England in 1896, having been overlooked for the Ashes tour for which his brother Harry was named captain. He even travelled on the same ship by which the Australians made passage – more than a little awkward, you might imagine.

Trott quickly established a spot in the MCC team, began playing for Middlesex two years later and toured South Africa with an England side led by Lord Hawke in the winter of 1898/99, so becoming the last man to be capped by both England and Australia.

He had the last laugh on his fellow countrymen too as his famous over-the-pavilion blow came against the touring Australian side of 1899. The mighty blow with his 3lb bat, considerably heavier than the norm, ended up in the garden of the then groundsman.

Trott's typically belligerent 103 that spring day against Gloucestershire in 1903 meant Middlesex were bowled out on the stroke of stumps for 502. Maybe 'Bazball' isn't such a new innovation after all. The imposing score would prove far too many for Gloucestershire as a collective effort from the Middlesex bowlers secured an innings victory.

Warner's sparkling start to the campaign continued with 135 of his side's first innings of 441 against Somerset, a total which was the foundation for another comfortable win by 112 runs. So there was momentum going into their early June clash with reigning champions Yorkshire.

Both meetings with the White Rose county the season before had been lost, one of them by an innings, but a year on this one played out very differently. Despite losing the toss the hosts responded magnificently, bowling Yorkshire out for 157, mainly thanks to another giant in the pantheon of Middlesex legends, J.T. Hearne, who returned 6-36.

Born in Chalfont St Giles, Hearne took 3,061 wickets in a career spanning more than 30 years. That figure remains the most for any bowler of medium pace or above. Of those scalps, 2,093 were taken in Middlesex colours – only the great Fred Titmus has more following his illustrious career of a similar longevity. More of him later.

Hearne had the ability to swing the ball, a rare talent at that time, and he could also produce an appreciably quicker delivery which caught out many a batter.

Bernard Bosanquet's 52 led the Middlesex reply and with seven of his team-mates hitting 29 or more the hosts built a huge lead of 192, whereupon Hearne claimed four more victims to make it ten in the match. Middlesex knocked off the 49 needed to win for the loss of only Warner to make it three wins out of three.

The electrifying start would be checked in mid-June as the rain arrived with a vengeance. Only 31 overs were possible against Nottinghamshire and the last two days of the Sussex game were washed out, while in between those two the match with Essex was abandoned without a ball being bowled.

However, when the rain relented with MacGregor back at the helm, Middlesex picked up as if there had never been an interruption. Surrey were the team on the receiving end, running into a man who had become their nemesis as far as Middlesex were concerned, George Beldam.

A right-handed batter and medium-pace bowler, Beldam spent eight seasons at Lord's, finishing up with batting and bowling averages which were all but identical.

Beldam had a particular penchant for the Surrey bowlers, having plundered his career-best 155 not out against them 12 months earlier. Here he made hay again, top scoring with 89 to take Middlesex to 300, Trott's 6-66 then helping the hosts to a first-innings lead of 80.

Still hungry for runs, Beldam went bigger second time around with a season's best 118, sharing a fourth-wicket stand of 134 with fellow all-rounder Bosanquet, whose 97 was also his best of the campaign.

The 1904 *Wisden* wrote of Beldam's efforts with willow in hand, 'Beldam showed a marked partiality for Surrey's bowling, batting equally well on a fast track at Lord's and a slow one at The Oval. He had some failures, but whenever he did well his batting was a model of watchful, patient, defence. Few batsmen at the present time impress one as being so difficult to bowl out.'

Beldam turned to art and photography post his playing days, achieving notoriety in both fields and collaborating with C.B. Fry on two cricketing books.

Faced with a mammoth 457 to win, Surrey were undone by the leg-breaks and googlies of Bosanquet, who completed an impressive match with 6-46.

If the name sounds familiar to readers of a certain age, then so it might as Bernard was the father of former newsreader Reginald Bosanquet. His cricketing claim to fame is to have been the first man to conceive of the googly, having previously been a quicker bowler. He perfected the delivery while studying at Oxford and famously bowled the great Australian Victor Trumper with it in Sydney in 1902/03. The delivery, now much more commonplace in the modern game, was on occasion referred to as a 'Bosey' in honour of its inventor.

Bosanquet claimed another six-wicket haul in the draw with Kent at Tunbridge Wells which followed the Surrey game. His exploits took him to Australia with MCC in 1903/04 where he made his England debut and the following English summer he claimed over 100 wickets.

Wisden would name him one of its five Cricketers of the Year in 1905, observing, 'The command of length is still to seek and will perhaps never be acquired but though he sends down more bad balls than any other front-rank bowler, Bosanquet is now a distinct power in any XI he plays for. On his good days he is more likely than any other bowler we have to get a strong side out cheaply on a perfect wicket.'

The aforementioned draw with Kent was spoiled by rain, which robbed the match of a good finish, arriving on the third morning with Middlesex on 151-3 chasing 329 to win, and Warner and Bosanquet both going well. And the weather had a big say too at Old Trafford in another draw where most of the second day was lost to rain.

When the first day of their fixture against Essex also succumbed to the elements another draw looked likely, but the visitors quickly made up for lost time by routing their hosts for 89 when the clouds rolled away for day two.

Moon's 62 secured a lead of 47 in the low-scoring encounter before Cyril Wells's mix of leg- and off-breaks led to figures of 5-14 as Middlesex won by seven wickets to gain impetus once more. Despite his efforts in a Middlesex shirt, Wells was probably more renowned for his rugby prowess, winning six caps for England.

The thrilling and vital win against Somerset which followed saw Wells again feature prominently, but mention must be made here of John Hunt.

He was a man who played for a decade for Middlesex, offering something with both bat and ball without ever cementing a place in the side. These days, without wanting to be uncharitable he might be termed a bits and pieces cricketer. Yet on a cricket field his exploits over those three days in early August surely marked his finest hour and were a crucial part of securing Middlesex's first County Championship. His 5-60 in the first innings turned out to be a career best, but despite his efforts the hosts rallied from the perils of 59-6 to post 253.

Wells and Beldam led the reply with 65 not out and 51 respectively to gain a lead of 59, but despite four more wickets for Hunt to make it nine in the match, Middlesex were left a daunting 313 to win.

This looked unlikely when the visitors lost Warner and MacGregor a few deliveries apart to be left on 77-3.

Half-centuries from Beldam and Bosanquet revived the chase, but it needed Hunt to come out and keep Wells, who made 59 not out, company as Middlesex got home late in the day by two wickets.

The end of Hunt's story is an unhappy, yet heroic one. The Winchester schoolboy and Cambridge graduate was another of cricket's war fallen. He died at the Battle of the Somme in the struggle to capture High Wood. His burial place is unknown.

His obituary in *Wisden's* 1917 edition read, 'He was a very good all-round cricketer, and so keen and enthusiastic that he was more valuable on a side than many players of greater natural gifts. He was a very plucky punishing bat, a useful bowler, right-hand fast, and a brilliant fieldsman wherever he was placed.'

The momentum was maintained in Bristol where Gloucestershire were ultimately beaten comfortably. However, the Seaxes had to battle back from a first innings deficit of 81 and did so largely thanks to a first and only double century for middle-order batter James Douglas. Bosanquet, MacGregor and Wells gave staunch support, propelling the visitors to 454 in their second innings.

Spinners Bosanquet and Wells then got to work, skittling the hosts for 101, the former claiming six wickets as Middlesex won by 272 runs.

However, their serene progress thus far would be checked in no uncertain terms in the return fixture with Yorkshire at Headingley where for once the batting failed and they never recovered from being shot out for 79 in their first innings. Eventually set 408, they crumbled a second time with only Warner and Beldam offering any prolonged resistance.

The humbling begged the question of whether the tide of the championship race had turned in favour of the reigning champions. Such ponderings became hollow rhetoric, however, as the weather gods intervened once more.

Games with Nottinghamshire and Lancashire were badly rain affected, while the meeting with another of the title challengers, Sussex, witnessed no play at all until the final day and the fixture with Kent was abandoned altogether.

Such precipitation meant Middlesex weren't beaten again and any lingering doubts about whether they would be champions for the first time were settled in emphatic fashion in their final match with Surrey at The Oval.

Beldam's century helped Middlesex put runs on the board and Wells's five-wicket haul ultimately sealed an innings victory, but this match will be remembered for Trott's six wickets in Surrey's first innings.

In truth, his bowling had been on the wane for some time, but here he gave a glimpse of his former glory, *Wisden* calling his display a 'flash of greatness'. There would be another such glimpse at Trott's benefit match in 1907 where he took four wickets in as many balls and then another hat-trick later in the same innings, a feat – two hat-tricks in the same innings – achieved on only one other occasion in the history of the first-class game.

Sadly, Trott died by his own hand in Harlesden, north-west London, in 1914 after suffering with a heart condition. He wrote his will on the back of a laundry ticket, leaving his landlady the sum of £4 and the contents of his wardrobe. Middlesex paid for a headstone to be erected on his grave in New Willesden Cemetery in 1994.

The title win clearly rankled with some, suggestions being made that MacGregor and his team were somehow lucky. A strong showing in the traditional end of season encounter between the newly crowned champions and The Rest – the cream of the county game from around the country – did much to dispel that theory.

The match saw Beldam pass 50 twice while Warner was back to his elegant best, stroking a classy second-innings century.

MCC would soon confer on Warner the honour of leading the Ashes tour to Australia that winter, their original preference Francis Jackson having not been able to commit to the time needed for the trip.

No doubt it was as much for this as his championship-winning exploits with Middlesex that Warner was named one of *Wisden*'s five Cricketers of the Year in 1904.

Part of the citation read, 'A more enthusiastic player it would be impossible to find anywhere. Cricket, if one may be permitted the expression, is the very breath of his nostrils. When our season is over, his greatest delight is to travel to some region in which the game is practicable during the winter months and few men have travelled so far or played in so many different parts of the world. From the time of his school days at Rugby, Mr Warner was a batsman of great promise, but he made no sudden jump into fame, his position having been gradually won by strenuous and persistent effort.'

Before we move on from this tale of Middlesex's inaugural championship we should note the minutes of the committee meeting of November that year recorded that professionals should be granted £10 each by way of bonus for winning the County Championship that summer.

It was also proposed that the 15 players who had played in five or more matches during the triumph be given gold medallions to mark the feat on the proviso they didn't cost more than £2 each.

1903 champions.

CHAPTER 2
1920 AND 1921

'Never in the history of the County Championship has there been anything so dramatic as the triumph of Middlesex last summer.'

So reads the opening stanza of the *Wisden Cricketers' Almanack* on Middlesex's second 'official' County Championship victory, in 1920.

Writers, myself included, and perhaps especially – though as those who know me well, including my co-author, will tell you my proneness to exaggeration is usually expressed in negative terms – are often accused of hyperbole. In hindsight, the history of the County Championship and indeed Middlesex's triumphs may lead us to argue this was such a case.

As we'll see later, two of Middlesex's championship titles were shared, one amid tense final-day drama, and they were two of three title races to be concluded so late on.

And those who witnessed the Seaxes' thrilling triumph over Yorkshire in 2016, again much more of which later, will no doubt argue that for compelling drama it would take some beating. I should mention as an aside that I missed the 13th championship clinching triumph. I had been working for Trinity Mirror Southern as a freelancer on cricket for all their regional titles, but lost my commission amid the savage budget cuts which took place around that time. Therefore, having no paper or digital site to write for, I missed the match in its entirety.

Despite having been Middlesex's most regular reporter for ten seasons at that point I missed the biggest triumph of their recent history.

I did so because I can't endorse the tendency of a minority in our industry who report what I consider to be 'God's game', to use their accreditation to 'freeload' when it's palpably obvious they are not 'working', bagging themselves a free lunch in the process. However, rant over as I digress.

On the basis the writer of the 1921 *Wisden* article was, as the expression goes 'walking in the light that he had', he made a compelling case for Middlesex's triumph of 1920 being extraordinary.

He continued, 'When on 27 July they lost their return game with Essex by four runs, nothing seemed more unlikely than that they would finish at the head of the list. From that time forward, however, they met with nothing but success, actually winning their last nine matches.'

The nine wins culminated in victory over their greatest rivals, Surrey, at Lord's, giving Pelham 'Plum' Warner the 'schoolboys' own' send-off of send-offs in his final match before retirement.

Mention of Warner of course means, despite 17 years, not to mention the Great War, having passed, we must in some ways pick up where we left off in the last chapter.

We left Warner basking in the triumph of 1903 where he'd been one of the batting stalwarts and vice-captain to MacGregor. Then 30, his best days with willow in hand still stretched out ahead of him. His first double hundred in first-class cricket in England – he'd made one on the tour of New Zealand in 1902/03 – came in 1905, but his most consistent years were 1906 to 1911, a period in which he made 23 centuries and 63 other scores of 50 or more.

By 1911, whether it was pressures induced by cricket or other aspects of life, he was far from well and his career-best 244 for England against Warwickshire was only possible with the encouragement of a little brandy and then a little more, something for which these days he would more than likely have failed drugs protocol.

Matters came to a head on that winter's tour of Australia where he suffered a breakdown on the ship to Sydney and had to be nursed back to health upon arrival, missing the rest of the tour.

He was never quite the same force with the bat again, even before the outbreak of war, during which he suffered another serious bout of ill health.

When cricket returned in 1919, he struggled and it was perhaps this which made him resolve to make 1920 his swansong, much to the dismay of the Middlesex committee, who by all accounts did their utmost to talk him out of it.

The presence of Warner notwithstanding, there were other similarities between the triumph of 1903 and this of 1920, most notably that as with 17 years earlier they went into the season with low expectations, regarded by most as likely also-rans.

Their performance in the 1919 Championship, where games were played over two days rather than three as cricket returned after the hostilities, had been woeful. They had finished 13th of the 15 counties, winning only twice with their bowlers misfiring badly.

Wisden recorded as the 1920 season opened, 'The prospects as regards bowling seemed rather hopeless.' Yet as in 1903 Middlesex defied expectations with ball in hand, with J.W. Hearne, only a distant relative of J.T. Hearne who we met in the earlier chapter, experiencing something of a renaissance. Both he and Frederick Durston took in excess of 100 wickets to spearhead the Championship charge. Unless you are something of a Middlesex devotee, these names will mean little to you, yet they stand proudly within the top ten of all-time wicket-takers for Middlesex and while we can debate such things as quality of pitches, uncovered wickets and the like their achievements are nevertheless considerable.

Batting-wise, this triumph will introduce us to Elias Henry Hendren, much better known simply as 'Patsy'. The word legend is thrown around far too glibly in sport and by writers in particular, but Hendren as we'll see is more than entitled to have that honour bestowed upon him. All-rounders Hearne and Henry Lee were the other principal run-getters in a golden summer with the bat for the north London side. In ten games at Lord's the batters passed 300 on nine occasions, setting up several victories in the process.

The season opener pitted Warner's men against the wooden spoon county of 1919, Warwickshire, at Lord's where the hosts recorded an emphatic innings win thanks in no small part to two of their lesser bowling lights.

The visitors were soon made to rue their decision to bat first, collapsing from 112-3 to 184 all out. The chief architect of their demise was one Churchill Hector Gunasekara, a man with quite a back story.

The first Ceylon-born cricketer to play the first-class game on these shores, he moved to England to study medicine at Cambridge, the outbreak of war denying him the chance to win his blue.

His career best had come in his debut season 12 months earlier when the right-arm medium-pacer tore through the Lancashire top order to record figures of 5-15.

His 5-51 here proved to be his last five-wicket haul in Middlesex colours as his medical duties increasingly took precedence over his cricket. A very athletic man, he was regarded as one of the best fielders in the game at that time.

He captained the first tour by Ceylon to India and even led his country in a non-first-class fixture against a team featuring the great Don Bradman. His athleticism lent itself to other sports too as he played tennis for his country against New Zealand.

By the end of the first day, Middlesex had sped past Warwickshire's total for the loss of only one wicket, thanks to a century by Lee, though Warner had been forced to retire hurt on 76 after suffering a severe bout of cramp.

The following day the hosts pressed home their advantage thanks to the first of five centuries in a golden summer for Hendren, his 158 scored at more than a run a minute. His dismissal signalled the hosts' declaration having piled up 543-7.

Victory from that position was all but a formality, but that shouldn't detract from a career best for Leslie Prentice in the second innings of his Championship debut.

The Australian-born off-spinner had made his debut for Middlesex a week previously against Oxford University and here he removed five of Warwickshire's top six on his way to figures of 6-95.

He would vanish from the first-class game almost as quickly as he'd appeared, playing only three more games for Middlesex that season and six in the title-winning side the following year without ever approaching such heights of performance again. Nevertheless, his efforts helped secure an innings win and got the title bid well and truly launched.

The early season feelgood factor was only increased by despatching Sussex in similarly dismissive fashion at HQ in a game which followed hot on the heels of the Warwickshire success.

Lee's 5-21 made sure Sussex got no further than 232 after choosing to bat, before he and Warner raced to 156-0 when stumps were drawn on day one.

The second day produced a memorable scorecard stat as the top four in the Middlesex order all recorded hundreds.

Warner's 139 would be the last of his 60 first-class hundreds, while Nigel Haig, at this stage more a batter than a bowler, though he would go on to achieve all-rounder status, made a career-best 131 batting at four.

As a consequence, over 500 had been made for the second game in a row, before Lee completed a remarkable individual performance with 6-47 as another innings win was sealed early on the third morning.

Rain affected the first day against Lancashire at Old Trafford where Warner's side were perhaps lucky to avoid defeat, but there would be no such escape against Nottinghamshire, where despite ten wickets in the match for Hearne, Middlesex crashed to a heavy 151-run loss.

Hendren led the response to this wobble with a big hundred (183) against Hampshire as Middlesex passed 400 for the third time in as many matches on home turf at Lord's, before first Durston and then Hearne worked their magic with the ball to return the side to winning ways ahead of the visit of reigning champions Yorkshire. The batting then creaked once more, forcing Middlesex to follow on, but a fine century by Hearne saved them from defeat.

The rest of June saw the championship challenge gather pace, the Seaxes stringing together three consecutive emphatic wins. Lee's unbeaten double hundred, a career best at that time, meant Hampshire were beaten for the second time in a matter of a few weeks, while another monster hundred from Hendren was key to thrashing Lancashire by an innings. Durston's fiery bowling saw him take six-wicket hauls in both matches.

The game with Somerset at Taunton initially proved a much tougher affair, an eighth-wicket stand of 121 between Haig and Gunasekara rescuing Middlesex from 81-7 in their first innings, leaving Hearne's latest five-wicket haul to set up an ultimately comfortable win.

Then came what appeared to be two season-defining games with Essex, the first of which saw the visitors hold out for a draw on the final day.

Later that same week Middlesex headed to Leyton for the return which proved a thriller. The hosts were bundled out for 133 after electing to bat, Middlesex responding with 57-2 by the close. The pivotal moment was in all probability the need for Warner to retire out for 22 in his first innings in order to head back to Lord's to attend the selection meeting for the upcoming Test with Australia.

In his absence, a first-innings lead of 79 was secured thanks to Lee's 80 and Middlesex still looked favourites after Hearne's employment of the googly earned him the first of two eight-wicket returns that summer, leaving the visitors needing only 118 to win.

Warner was back at the ground for the chase, but Essex skipper and medium-fast bowler Johnny Douglas reduced Middlesex to 67-8.

Warner found an ally in wicketkeeper Murrell, the pair adding 35 before the latter fell with 16 still needed.

Warner got the visitors within sight of victory, but Douglas, a gold-medal winning boxer at middleweight in the London Olympics of 1908, bowled him for 46 to have the last word, sealing victory by four runs.

The loss was a huge setback which in all likelihood meant Warner and his men needed to win all nine of their remaining fixtures to stand a chance of carrying off the championship laurels. What followed will forever be enshrined in Middlesex cricketing folklore.

The first of the nine games was against Sussex who were summarily despatched by an innings thanks largely to a young Greville Stevens taking 13 wickets in the match.

Stevens had been something of a schoolboy sensation and was honoured by *Wisden* when named one of five Schoolboy Cricketers of the Year in 1918.

The Hampstead-born youngster had caught Middlesex's attention while making an astounding 466 for his house in an interschool game at University College London in 1919, but when he made his Middlesex debut later that summer it was with ball in hand that he starred, claiming ten wickets.

An Oxford blue in all four years of his studies, Stevens mesmerised the Sussex batters with his leg-breaks and googlies, returning 7-17 in the first innings and 6-43 in the second. It is generally considered his cricket career never reached the heights it might have done as, after leaving university, his need to earn a wage restricted his opportunities with the men of Lord's.

The first major test of Middlesex's ability to stay the course came in the meeting with Kent at the St Lawrence Ground in Canterbury, a match they looked destined to lose on more than one occasion.

After winning the toss and batting, much of their top order collapsed to leave them 58-5 and it needed half-centuries from Hendren (77) and Haig (57) to carry them to 212.

The hosts were cruising in reply at 163-1 before Haig got ball in hand and induced a collapse with a season's best 7-33, an astonishing effort given his bowling had shown little sign of form prior to that. His heroics restricted Middlesex's first-innings deficit to a mere five.

Another batting collapse followed, however, and the visitors looked beaten at 47-6 with Warner, batting in the middle order, falling for a duck. Hendren and Stevens shared a half-century stand for the seventh wicket, but even so Kent's victory target was a seemingly paltry 123.

At 70-1 the chase looked a formality, but Hearne chose this moment to cap his bowling renaissance. In a period where you could opt to play for the county of your birth or current place of residence, Hearne was a Middlesex boy through and through. Born in Hillingdon in 1891, he signed for Middlesex soon after turning 18 and his leg-spin bowling was an immediate success.

The batting too soon came together and as early as 1911 he scored over 1,600 runs and among 102 wickets were nine in nine overs against Somerset. That return would remain his best for 22 years until, aged 42, a dusty Chesterfield wicket helped him yield 9-61 against Derbyshire.

At Canterbury in 1920 it was his 8-26 which turned the match on its head, Hearne completing a dramatic win by five runs when bowling last man and fellow leg-spinner 'Titch' Freeman for nought.

The schedule allowed no time to bask in the victory as they headed straight from Canterbury to The Oval where fortunately Surrey were rolled over by an innings, another dominant Hendren hundred and six more second-innings wickets for Hearne making it three wins on the spin.

Hendren's golden summer reached another peak back inside the Grace Gates against Nottinghamshire as the winning streak continued, his 232 making sure the batters didn't waste Durston's seven-wicket first-innings haul.

This double century seems as appropriate a moment as any to pay tribute to Middlesex's greatest ever run-scorer.

While others like Denis Compton and Bill Edrich – much more of whom later – may roll of the tongues of supporters more readily when discussing Middlesex batters of legendary status, Hendren's record compares favourably with them all.

His total of 40,302 runs for Middlesex will never be surpassed and was a part of 57,000 plus runs in all. His Middlesex tally is 15,000 more than Edrich and almost twice as many as Compton. Yes he played for longer, over 30 years in fact, less those lost to the Great War of 1914 to 1918. However, he played 300 more games than Compton or Edrich, averaging over 50, fractionally less than the former and considerably more than the latter. His stats are all the more remarkable when you consider he didn't once average 40 in the eight years prior to the First World War, scoring only six centuries in that period.

One of his brothers, John, died at the Battle of Delville Wood (part of the Battle of the Somme) in 1916 and it's not known whether this acted as an extra spur to Hendren, who also served with the Royal Fusiliers, as a survivor of the conflict, to make the most of his sporting talents.

Whatever the cause, his transformation from 1919 onwards was a dramatic one. The previous season to the one which concerns us, he'd averaged over 60, earning him a place among *Wisden*'s five Cricketers of the Year for its 1920 edition.

Part of the citation read, 'Hendren has abundant gifts, combining with his fine hitting great patience and self-control.'

His 232 here was the largest of his five centuries of 1920 which helped him earn a place on the boat for the Ashes series to Australia that winter. He would play 51 Tests in all, averaging almost 48.

On four occasions he would score over ten centuries in a season, part of 170 tons in all, a figure surpassed by only the great Jack Hobbs. Indeed, only Hobbs and Frank Woolley sit above Hendren in the all-time first-class run-scoring charts.

Regarded as something of a practical joker, he nevertheless took sport seriously and was perhaps the inventor of the first helmet when in 1933 he appeared to face West Indies quicks Manny Martindale and Learie Constantine at Lord's wearing a rubber hat or cap with three peaks, two of which came down over his ears.

He wasn't only a fine cricketer but a skilled footballer too, making 432 appearances for Brentford, mainly at outside left.

Hendren's runs and five second-innings wickets for Hearne saw off Nottinghamshire by nine wickets, after which it was straight off to Bradford for the reverse fixture with Yorkshire, who were still in with a chance of defending their title.

This was another epic encounter in which, as at Canterbury, Middlesex were on the back foot for most of the match. Bowled out for 105 batting first, Warner's men fought back to reduce the White Rose county to 69-7 in reply, but the hosts had secured a lead of 64 by early on the second day. Hendren's half-century gave the visitors hope, but the fact they had runs to bowl at was really down to a heroic innings of 86 from Haig in the lower middle order.

Yorkshire needed 198 to derail Middlesex's title hopes. Durston removed three of the top four cheaply as Yorkshire slumped to 112-7, but resistance from the tail carried them to within five runs of victory when the ninth wicket fell.

It was then that the cricketing gods smiled on Middlesex as Yorkshire all-rounder Roy Kilner, who'd been injured during the match, was unfit to come to the wicket, leaving the visitors winners by four runs.

Nine wickets for Hearne secured a seven-wicket win over Somerset, before Hendren's second double century of the campaign against Warwickshire kept the victory roll going.

Now only two more obstacles remained in Middlesex's path and Hendren's 170 made sure the return with Kent at Lord's didn't contain the nailbiting drama seen at Canterbury.

Everything now hinged on the season finale at Lord's against Surrey. Win and they'd be champions; anything less and Lancashire would, under the complicated points system, snatch the honours by mere fractions.

Despite 79 from Warner in his final match, Middlesex trailed by 73 on first innings and it was left to Lee and the lesser-known Challen Skeet to get the bid for glory back on course in a double-century opening stand at the second time of asking.

Middlesex v Surrey scorecard, 1920.

Cricket Match. Played at *Lords* Date *Aug 28 30 31* 19—

Middlesex VERSUS *Surrey*

First INNINGS OF *Middlesex*

ORDER OF GOING IN	BATSMAN'S NAME	RUNS AS SCORED	HOW OUT	BOWLER'S NAME	TOTAL
1	C. H. L. Skeet		c' Ducat	Rushby	2
2	Lee		c' Hitch	Fender	10
3	Hendren		Bowled	Reay	41
4	Hearne		c & Bowled	Hitch	15
5	P. F. Warner		Bowled	Rushby	79
6	F. J. Mann		c & Bowled	Fender	12
7	H. Hay		Bowled	Reay	18
8	G. T. S. Stevens		Bowled	Fender	63
9	H. K. Longman		Bowled	Fender	0
10	Murrell		c' Ducat	Hitch	9
11	Durston		Not out		0
	BYES 4	LEG BYES 13	WIDE BALLS	NO BALLS 3	27

RUNS AT THE FALL OF EACH WICKET: 1 FOR 4 · 2 FOR 23 · 3 FOR 35 · 4 FOR 88 · 5 FOR 109 · 6 FOR 149 · 7 FOR 239 · 8 FOR 245 · 9 FOR 268 · 10 FOR 268 **TOTAL** 268

Second INNINGS OF *Middlesex*

ORDER OF GOING IN	BATSMAN'S NAME	RUNS AS SCORED	HOW OUT	BOWLER'S NAME	TOTAL
1	C. H. L. Skeet		c' Fender	Hitch	106
2	Lee		Bowled	Hitch	108
3	Hearne		L B W	Rushby	26
4	Hendren		c' Sandham	Rushby	5
5	F. J. Mann		c' Peach	Fender	22
6	H. Hay		Bowled	Rushby	1
7	G. T. S. Stevens		Not Out		21
8	Murrell		Bowled	Reay	0
9	P. F. Warner		Not Out		14
10	H. K. Longman	Did not Bat Innings Declared			
11	Durston				
	BYES 14	LEG BYES 12	WIDE BALLS 1	NO BALLS	13

RUNS AT THE FALL OF EACH WICKET: 1 FOR 208 · 2 FOR 249 · 3 FOR 254 · 4 FOR 261 · 5 FOR 265 · 6 FOR 290 · 7 FOR 291 · 8 FOR · 9 FOR · 10 FOR **TOTAL** 316

PUBLISHED BY JOHN WISDEN & Co Ld ATHLETIC OUTFITTERS TO H.M. THE KING, 23, CRANBOURN St. LEICESTER SQUARE, LONDON, W.C.

BOWLING ANALYSIS *First* INNINGS *Surrey*

BOWLERS NAMES	WIDES	NO BALLS	NUMBER OF OVERS AND RUNS MADE FROM EACH BOWLER	OVERS	MAIDENS	RUNS	WIDES	NO BALLS	WICKETS
Hitch				32.1	10	66			2
Rushby				23	9	48			2
Fender		III		28	4	76		3	4
Remy				36	17	51			2
Ducat				3	1	10			
Shepherd				6	3	16			
				Extras		27			
						268			

BOWLING ANALYSIS *Second* INNINGS *Surrey*

BOWLERS NAMES	WIDES	NO BALLS	NUMBER OF OVERS AND RUNS MADE FROM EACH BOWLER	OVERS	MAIDENS	RUNS	WIDES	NO BALLS	WICKETS
Hitch				20	5	71			2
Rushby				22	7	73			3
Fender				16.5	1	70			1
Remy				18	4	61			1
Ducat				3	–	12	1		
Shepherd				4	–	16			
				Extras		13			
						316			

PUBLISHED BY JOHN WISDEN & Co Ltd ATHLETIC OUTFITTERS TO H.M. THE KING, 23. CRANBOURN ST. LEICESTER SQUARE, LONDON, W.C.   Entered Stationers' Hall.

Middlesex v Surrey scorecard, 1920.

Cricket Match. **Played at** Lords **Date** Aug 28. 30 31 192_

Middlesex VERSUS Surrey

First **INNINGS OF** Surrey

ORDER OF GOING IN	BATSMAN'S NAME	RUNS AS SCORED	HOW OUT	BOWLER'S NAME	TOTAL RUNS
1	Hobbs		c' Mann	Hearne	24
2	Sandham		Not Out		167
3	M. Howell	33	c' Murrell	Durston	7
4	Shepherd		c' Murrell	Durston	0
5	Peach		Hit. Wk. Bowled	Stevens	18
6	Ducat		Bowled	Lee	44
7	P. G. H. Fender		c' Hay	Durston	30
8	Hitch		Bowled	Durston	1
9	G. M. Reay		c' Hay	Lee	6
10	Strudwick		Bowled	Hearne	4
11	Rushby	Innings Declared	Not out		6
BYES	LEG BYES	WIDE BALLS		NO BALLS	24
RUNS AT THE FALL OF EACH WICKET.	1 FOR 59 2 FOR 78 3 FOR 62 4 FOR 128 5 FOR 227 6 FOR 275 7 FOR 277 8 FOR 312 9 FOR 333 10 FOR			**TOTAL**	341

Second **INNINGS OF** Surrey

ORDER OF GOING IN	BATSMAN'S NAME	RUNS AS SCORED	HOW OUT	BOWLER'S NAME	TOTAL RUNS
1	Hobbs		c' Lee	Hay	10
2	Sandham		c' & Bowled	Hearne	68
3	M. Howell		St Murrell	Stevens	26
4	Shepherd		c' Hendren	Stevens	26
5	P. G. H. Fender		Bowled	Durston	1
6	Peach		Bowled	Stevens	11
7	Ducat		L. B. W.	Hearne	7
8	Hitch		Bowled	Stevens	6
9	G. M. Reay	23	Bowled	Hearne	6
10	Strudwick		Bowled	Stevens	10
11	Rushby		Not Out		7
BYES 434	LEG BYES /	WIDE BALLS		NO BALLS	12
RUNS AT THE FALL OF EACH WICKET	1 FOR 22 2 FOR 62 3 FOR 120 4 FOR 122 5 FOR 143 6 FOR 155 7 FOR 166 8 FOR 168 9 FOR 176 10 FOR 185			**TOTAL**	185

PUBLISHED BY JOHN WISDEN & Co L.TD. ATHLETIC OUTFITTERS TO H.M. THE KING. 23, CRANBOURN ST. LEICESTER SQUARE LONDON W C

BOWLING ANALYSIS *First* **INNINGS** *Middlesex*

BOWLERS NAMES	WIDES	NO BALLS	NUMBER OF OVERS AND RUNS MADE FROM EACH BOWLER	TOTALS					
				OVERS	MAIDENS	RUNS	WIDES	NO BALLS	WICKETS
Durston				30	9	97			4
Haig				10	4	45			
Stevens		a		16	–	72	2		1
Hearne				24	8	57			2
Lee				15	2	66			2
				Extras		24			
						341			

BOWLING ANALYSIS *Second* **INNINGS** *Middlesex*

BOWLERS NAMES	WIDES	NO BALLS	NUMBER OF OVERS AND RUNS MADE FROM EACH BOWLER	TOTALS					
				OVERS	MAIDENS	RUNS	WIDES	NO BALLS	WICKETS
Durston				14	1	43			1
Haig				8		19			1
Lee				4	–	17			–
Hearne				11	–	37			3
Stevens				13.4	–	61			5
				Extras		12			
						188			

PUBLISHED BY JOHN WISDEN & Cº LTD ATHLETIC OUTFITTERS TO H.M. THE KING, 23, CRANBOURN ST. LEICESTER SQUARE, LONDON. W.C. Entered Stationers Hall.

Skeet can be seen as another man who picked the right time for his moment in the spotlight. Born in New Zealand but brought up in England, he had been a German prisoner of war having been taken captive at the Battle of Loos in 1915.

The opener played only three seasons at Middlesex and this was his solitary first-class hundred but what a time to play it.

The efforts of the two openers put Warner in a position to declare, setting Surrey 244 to win in three hours and ten minutes, or more pertinently from his perspective, three hours and ten minutes to bowl their London rivals out and claim glory.

At 120-2 it looked as if Warner's farewell would end in disappointment, but Hearne's caught and bowled to get rid of Surrey's first-innings centurion Andy Sandham turned the tide and thereafter he and Stevens (5-61) winkled out the visitors until the latter bowled Herbert Strudwick to clinch victory and trigger the celebrations.

Warner was chaired off the field and through the Long Room by his team-mates in the immediate aftermath of the triumph. He would be *Wisden*'s solitary Cricketer of the Year in 1921, making him one of only two players, Jack Hobbs being the other, to win the accolade twice – the normal rule was you could only win once, hence Messrs Compton and Edrich weren't put forward in 1948 for their prolific exploits of the previous summer which we will explore in the next chapter.

Part of the *Wisden* citation read, 'It was not his batting but his skill as a captain that made his final season memorable. His great asset as a captain in that month of strenuous matches, counting for even more than his judgement in changing the bowling and placing the field, was his sanguine spirit. He was full of encouragement and got the very best out of his men by making them believe in themselves.'

The reluctance of the Middlesex committee to allow Warner to terminate his tenure as captain, along with their appreciation of his leadership and service, can be found in the Middlesex minute book entry for 1920 which read as follows,

'The committee regret P.F. Warner feels the time has come for him to give up the captaincy of the eleven which he has held for nine years with conspicuous success. They congratulate him most heartily on the most glorious termination of his long and brilliant career, both for the county and in first-class cricket. They feel the triumph in the final match and the reception it received, by the huge crowd present, will never be forgotten. It was a wonderful tribute to the captain's unique personality and a recognition of his great services to the game. The committee tender the warmest thanks of the club to him for his long services and especially for his leadership this year which was the main cause of the success attained.'

Retirement as a player didn't dampen Warner's enthusiasm for cricket. He fulfilled committee posts at Middlesex and MCC, was chairman of England's selectors, and later tour manager of the Ashes 'Bodyline' series. He wrote widely on the game and founded *The*

1920 team. Inset: Wicketkeeper Murrell's winner's medal.

Cricketer as well as becoming a published author. He was knighted for his services to cricket in 1937.

While Warner's were big shoes to fill it seems Middlesex did have an obvious successor within their ranks in Frank Mann.

A solid middle-order batter, Mann had played for Middlesex since 1909, serving in the Scots Guards during the First World War, where he was mentioned in despatches on three occasions, seemingly underlining he possessed qualities of leadership.

It is remarkable to reflect that Warner's reign ended with nine wins, while Mann's tenure began with eight more, making 17 successive County Championship victories in total – all of which suggests the transition of power was a smooth one.

That's not to deny the winning run contained moments of adversity, one coming as early as the 1921 season curtain-raiser with Hampshire at Lord's where despite six wickets for Durston, who was to enjoy another fine season, Middlesex trailed by 55 runs on first innings.

They eventually needed the highest score of the match, 246, to win, but after losing two wickets cheaply, Hendren's first century of the season led them home with Hugh Dales and Mann playing excellent supporting roles.

Hendren produced a second hundred and Lee a first as Sussex were seen off more comfortably at Lord's. Hendren would make five of his seven centuries in 1921 before the end of June. His failure to master the bowling of the Australian tourists meant he could not command a place in the Ashes series of that year beyond the second Test, which was no doubt to Middlesex's advantage, but the scars suffered in England colours meant to many observers his batting wasn't at the level of the previous campaign.

The *Wisden Almanack* of 1922 observed, 'He was not quite the batsman he had been in 1920. He had lost much of his audacity and he was rather sparing of the astonishing pulls and hooks with which he had demoralised bowlers in the previous year. No doubt his ill success against the Australians impaired his confidence.'

Mid-May's trip to Trent Bridge to face Nottinghamshire underlined the all-round value of Nigel Haig to Middlesex's cause. For much of the game Haig kept the visitors in the contest, taking five Notts wickets in their first innings, before making what would prove a season's best 108 with the bat after Middlesex had slipped to 105-5.

A multi-talented athlete, Haig played rugby, lawn tennis and ice hockey among other sports when not occupied at cricket. He could swing the ball and was perhaps a shade quicker than he looked, with a stamina which meant he could bowl for long periods, so a captain's dream.

With willow in hand he could bat up in the top three or four, or aggressively in the lower-middle order as the situation demanded, and 1921 would be the first of three occasions in which he did the coveted double of 100 first-class wickets and 1,000 runs.

Awarded the Military Cross in King George V's 1917 birthday honours list for service in the Royal Field Artillery, Haig would later captain Middlesex from 1929 to 1934.

Haig's efforts ensured Middlesex kept their first-innings deficit to 59, but after being set 245 to win they were indebted to Mann for a splendid hundred, having promoted himself up the order to number three after the fall of an early wicket.

Another wicket soon followed, but with the support of first Hendren and then Haig, Mann's 112 proved match-winning, the captain leaving the stage just before victory was confirmed.

In any championship-winning team, there are always moments when what we might respectfully call a lesser light puts their hand up to impress themselves on a game and the meeting with Warwickshire at Lord's in late May proved one such occasion.

Clarence Napier Bruce was more renowned for rackets at which he was both a singles and doubles champion in many countries. He'd represented Middlesex to varying degrees since 1908, making his career best of 149 two years prior to this encounter.

He would nearly match that against Warwickshire, 19 fours contributing to his 144 to help propel what had looked at one stage likely to be an ordinary first-innings total to one of 366. *Wisden* observed of Bruce, 'If his defence were in any way comparable to his superb off-side hitting, he would be one of the best batsmen in the world.'

From there, the hosts were always able to control the game, which was wrapped up on the third day.

Somerset were beaten in routine fashion to take the winning sequence to five after which it was the turn of Nottinghamshire to feel the full force of Middlesex's dominant start to the campaign.

Haig's latest seven-wicket haul justified Mann's decision to put the visitors in as they were rolled over for 132. It was a score comfortably overhauled by Middlesex's opening pair of Harry Lee and Gerald Crutchley.

Now 30, Lee had been a stalwart of the Middlesex team for some years and this game would mark his greatest day as a Seaxe with bat in hand. He and Crutchley would add 231 for the first wicket, before Lee forged on into the second day to surpass his career-best 221 not out of 12 months previously and finish undefeated on 243 when the declaration came at 612-8, the highest score ever made in a first-class match at Lord's at that time.

Lee's story is a remarkable one which warrants our attention because, as we will discover, it is a something of a miracle that he ever played an innings of this nature after the First World War.

Lee had been taken on to the MCC ground staff in 1906 despite describing his first six balls in his trial as 'six of the worst balls that anyone could ever have pitched'. He received some coaching advice from Albert Trott among others, but didn't really get opportunities with Middlesex until 1912.

When war broke out Lee enlisted with the 13th London Battalion and was posted with them to France in early March 1915 where later that month he fought in the Battle of Aubers Ridge. He was shot in the leg by a bullet which fractured his femur and he lay in no man's land for three days, presumed dead, so much so his death was announced and a memorial service held.

It was the Germans who eventually found him, badly wounded but very much alive. He spent six weeks in a hospital in France before continuing on to Hannover where he became a prisoner of war.

He began to heal but was advised to exaggerate his injuries in order to be sent home to England and this was achieved, but it was subsequently discovered the injuries he sustained in battle would mean he was permanently left with one leg shorter than the other.

Lee spent much of the rest of the war in India before returning to Middlesex in 1919 and, despite his physical challenges and his dislike of two-day cricket played that summer, he established himself as a regular in the County Championship XI.

Wisden's assessment of Lee's contributions in 1921 was complimentary, while at the same time pointing out what it considered to be flaws in his technique, 'Lee was a good third in batting and though his average dropped from 46 to 39 there was no real falling off. One could wish that he would not crouch so much, and that he was less obsessed by on-side play, but no doubt he knows the game that suits him best.'

What of Crutchley, Lee's cohort in that mammoth opening stand? The right-hand bat managed 120 matches for Middlesex over a 20-year period in between his day job as a stockbroker in the city. The 145 here was one of five first-class hundreds he made.

Crutchley is someone with his own hard-luck story. As an Oxford blue he was selected for the 1912 Varsity match with Cambridge where he reached 99 not out at stumps, only to be struck down by a bout of measles overnight which ruled him out of the rest of the fixture. Crutchley was father to the late Shakespearean actress Rosalie Crutchley.

Hendren made hundreds against first Yorkshire and then Essex, Bruce making 94 against the latter as both games were won comfortably, before Lancashire brought the sequence of 17 wins in all to a stop by forcing a draw in June at Lord's.

Indeed, the Red Rose county dominated the match for the most part and looked likely to win after setting the hosts to chase 445. Middlesex looked beaten at 96-3, but Hendren, who made a century for the third game in a row, and Bruce added 184 for the fourth wicket to comfortably save a draw.

The roles became reversed in the return fixture at Old Trafford a week later, Hearne's first-innings hundred giving the visitors an early advantage. Hearne was restricted as a bowler by illness in 1921, but underlined his all-round value by averaging 52 with the bat.

Lancashire were routed for 111 in their first dig before another Hendren ton put the game out of their reach and while they resisted bravely second time around Middlesex won with time to spare.

Little has been mentioned to this point of fast bowler Frederick Durston and it would be remiss not to salute one of the key players behind these successive championship triumphs.

Born in the Bedfordshire village of Clophill, Durston had played very little first-class cricket prior to 1920, yet would take over 100 wickets in both seasons of Middlesex's back-to-back triumphs. He was a tall bowler who possessed the considerable weapon of being able to bring the ball back into the batter off the pitch. He certainly proved too much for Hampshire's batters down in Southampton in early July, claiming six wickets in each innings as the visitors won comfortably to make it ten wins in 11.

Wisden noted that Durston bowled even better in 1921 than his figures suggested, though it said that given his talents he could have targeted the stumps a little more, adding, 'He had spells of real brilliancy, and fully maintained the reputation he had gained in the previous year.'

Durston went on to take 1,178 wickets in a Middlesex shirt, seventh in the all-time list – only J.T. Hearne among quicker bowlers stands above him – so he more than merits his spot in the county's hall of fame.

At this point in his career it would not be unfair to class Durston as a 'ferret' when it came to batting – they go in after the rabbits – but while his bowling got slower, his batting improved with age and in company with Hendren, he set a new Middlesex record for the ninth wicket of 160 against Essex at Leyton in the summer of 1927. It would stand for 84 years until finally surpassed by Gareth Berg and Tim Murtagh in Middlesex's Division Two title-clinching match with Leicestershire at Grace Road.

Standing at 6ft 5in, Durston was also a more than useful goalkeeper, playing 44 games for Brentford in the Southern League between 1919 and 1921.

Middlesex had now been unbeaten for almost an entire calendar year but wouldn't quite reach that landmark, rivals Surrey ending their streak with a 19-run victory at The Oval. Even this was defeat with honour as, thanks to half-centuries from Lee, Stevens and a stockbroker called Leonard Burtt, who only appeared in one other match for Middlesex, they came close to chasing down 370 on the final day.

Hundreds for Hearne and Hendren ensured winning ways returned until the batters suffered a rare loss of wheels in a thrashing at the hands of Kent at Canterbury in early August. The wobble continued against Yorkshire up in Sheffield where they were hustled out for 82 on the opening day before rain came to their rescue, preventing any further play in the match.

The form dip proved temporary, however, and after something of a bore draw with Somerset, Hearne's unbeaten double hundred and six-wicket haul ensured that Warwickshire were demolished by an innings.

With two games remaining, standing between Middlesex and the title were the only sides to beat them all season, Kent and Surrey.

The defeat to Kent would be avenged by a five-wicket win, though that outcome was in doubt for much of the match. Trailing by 23 on first innings, the hosts found themselves facing the daunting prospect of making 314 to win on the final day.

Lee hit a half-century up the top of the innings, but at 165-4 hopes were fading. Mann then joined Hendren in a match-winning stand of 136 and though as earlier in the season at Nottinghamshire, Mann fell just short of the winning line, he had again as *Wisden* put it shown 'a happy knack of getting runs when they were needed'. The significance of this win was that it meant, unlike 12 months earlier, Middlesex only required a draw as opposed to a victory in the finale with Surrey to take the title, whereas for their rivals from south of the river only a win would see them snatch the crown away. For much of the contest it looked as if they would get their wish.

Thanks to Thomas Shepherd's century and a first-innings batting collapse Middlesex trailed by 137 at the halfway mark and were eventually set 322 to win.

With memories of the previous Friday's successful chase against Kent fresh in their memory, the hosts inched steadily towards their target on the final day thanks to Hearne and opener Richard Twining, making only his third appearance of the season.

Middlesex v Surrey scorebook, 1921.

Cricket Match. Played at Lords Date Aug 27. 29. 30 192.

Middlesex VERSUS Surrey

First INNINGS OF Middlesex

ORDER OF GOING IN	BATSMANS NAME	RUNS AS SCORED	HOW OUT	BOWLER'S NAME	TOTAL
1	R. H. Twining		Bowled	Hitch	10
2	Lee		L.B.W.	Reay	7
3	H. L. Dales		L.B.W.	Hitch	15
4	Hearne		C Shudwick	Peach	
5	Hendren		C Shudwick	Reay	
6	Hon C. H. Bruce		Bowled	Reay	
7	F. J. Mann		Bowled	Reay	29
8	N. Haig		L.B.W.	Peach	
9	Murrell		Bowled	Fender	16
10	A. R. Tanner		Bowled	Fender	0
11	Durston				

BYES 4   LEG BYES /   WIDE BALLS   NO BALLS /   6

RUNS AT THE FALL OF EACH WICKET: 1 FOR 9 2 FOR 29 3 FOR 54 4 FOR 74 5 FOR 77 6 FOR 86 7 FOR 91 8 FOR 126 9 FOR 132 10 FOR 132 **TOTAL** 132

Second INNINGS OF Middlesex

ORDER OF GOING IN	BATSMANS NAME	RUNS AS SCORED	HOW OUT	BOWLER'S NAME	TOTAL
1	R. H. Twining		Bowled	Peach	135
2	Lee		L.B.W.	Reay	20
3	Hearne		C Jardine	Reay	106
4	Hendren		Not out		17
5	Hon C. N. Bruce		Bowled	Peach	0
6	F. J. Mann		Not out		22
7					
8					
9					
10					
11					

BYES 4   LEG BYES 11   WIDE BALLS   NO BALLS   22

RUNS AT THE FALL OF EACH WICKET: 1 FOR 49 2 FOR 277 3 FOR 281 4 FOR 281 5 FOR 6 FOR 7 FOR 8 FOR 9 FOR 10 FOR **TOTAL** 322

PUBLISHED BY JOHN WISDEN & Co. LTD. ATHLETIC OUTFITTERS TO H.M. THE KING. 21, CRANBOURN St. LEICESTER SQUARE LONDON, W.C. Entered Stationers

BOWLING ANALYSIS *First* INNINGS *Middlesex*

BOWLERS NAMES	WIDES	NO BALLS	NUMBER OF OVERS AND RUNS MADE FROM EACH BOWLER	TOTALS					
				OVERS	MAIDENS	RUNS	WIDES	NO BALLS	WICKETS
Hay				26	8	93			2
Durston				26	7	117			4
Turner				8	1	14			—
Nevare		11		16	3	117	2		1
Lee				15.2	3	49			3
				Extras		19			
						269			

BOWLING ANALYSIS *Second* INNINGS *Middlesex*

BOWLERS NAMES	WIDES	NO BALLS	NUMBER OF OVERS AND RUNS MADE FROM EACH BOWLER	TOTALS					
				OVERS	MAIDENS	RUNS	WIDES	NO BALLS	WICKETS
Durston				17	2	56			3
Craig				23.2	4	62			5
Lee				14	3	60			1
Nevare				3	1	2			1
						4			
						184			

PUBLISHED BY JOHN WISDEN & Co Ltd ATHLETIC OUTFITTERS TO H.M. THE KING, 23. CRANBOURN St. LEICESTER SQUARE, LONDON, W.C.   Entered Stationers' Hall.

Middlesex v Surrey scorebook, 1921.

Cricket Match.   **Played at** Lords   **Date** Aug 27. 29. 30   1921

Middlesex VERSUS Surrey

First **INNINGS OF** Surrey

ORDER OF GOING IN	BATSMANS NAME	RUNS AS SCORED	HOW OUT	BOWLER'S NAME	TOTAL RUNS
1	D. J. Knight		Bowled	Durston	1
2	Sandham		Bowled	Durston	0
3	Ducat		c Hearne	Lee	2
4	Shepherd		Not out		128
5	D. R. Jardine		Bowled	Durston	25
6	M. Howell		Bowled	Haig	0
7	Hitch		c Murrell	Durston	0
8	P. G. H. Fender		c Tanner	Haig	10
9	Peach		c Murrell	Lee	1
10	G. M. Reay		Bowled	Hearne	21
11	Strudwick		Bowled	Lee	0

BYES 434   LEG BYES(1)(1)   WIDE BALLS   NO BALLS | 19

| RUNS AT THE FALL OF EACH WICKET | 1 FOR 3 | 2 FOR 18 | 3 FOR 56 | 4 FOR 200 | 5 FOR 201 | 6 FOR 202 | 7 FOR 233 | 8 FOR 236 | 9 FOR 268 | 10 FOR 269 | TOTAL | 269 |

Second **INNINGS OF** Surrey

ORDER OF GOING IN	BATSMANS NAME	RUNS AS SCORED	HOW OUT	BOWLER'S NAME	TOTAL RUNS
1	D. J. Knight		Bowled	Durston	70
2	Sandham		Bowled	Durston	17
3	Ducat		Bowled	Durston	7
4	Shepherd		c & Bowled	Haig	14
5	D. R. Jardine		c Tanner	Lee	3
6	M. Howell		c Henderson	Haig	0
7	Hitch		Bowled	Haig	26
8	P. G. H. Fender		c Murrell	Hearne	2
9	Peach		Not out		2
10	G. M. Reay		Bowled	Haig	0
11	Strudwick		L. B. W.	Haig	0

BYES   LEG BYES(1)   WIDE BALLS   NO BALLS | 4

| RUNS AT THE FALL OF EACH WICKET | 1 FOR 18 | 2 FOR 32 | 3 FOR 115 | 4 FOR 133 | 5 FOR 149 | 6 FOR 165 | 7 FOR 180 | 8 FOR 182 | 9 FOR 182 | 10 FOR 184 | TOTAL | 184 |

PUBLISHED BY JOHN WISDEN & CO LTD ATHLETIC OUTFITTERS TO H.M. THE KING, 23, CRANBOURN St. LEICESTER SQUARE LONDON W.C. Entered Stationers'

BOWLING ANALYSIS *First* INNINGS *Surrey*

BOWLERS NAMES	WIDES	NO BALLS	NUMBER OF OVERS AND RUNS MADE FROM EACH BOWLER	TOTALS				
				OVERS	MAIDENS	RUNS	WIDES	NO BALLS/WICKETS
Hitch		/		14	6	17	/	2
Remy				18.4	3	44		4
Sanders				12	2	41		2
Peach				14	4	24		2
					Extras	6		
						132		

BOWLING ANALYSIS *Second* INNINGS *Surrey*

BOWLERS NAMES	WIDES	NO BALLS	NUMBER OF OVERS AND RUNS MADE FROM EACH BOWLER	TOTALS				
				OVERS	MAIDENS	RUNS	WIDES	NO BALLS/WICKETS
Hitch		////		26	4	69	/	–
Remy				27	6	77		2
Sanders		///		33	10	73		4
Peach				27	14	44		
Jardine				4	–	16		
Shepherd				3	–	7		
Ducat				11	3	14		
					Extras	22		
					Total	322		

Both would make centuries in a second-wicket stand of 229 which all but secured the title. *Wisden* commented of Hearne's 106, 'It seemed from the first over and hour after hour the ball was in the middle of his bat.'

If Hearne's was a stoic effort then Twining's was little short of remarkable. He had only recently been able to resume playing cricket following a knee injury sustained in battle at Gallipoli in 1915. He had been despatched there six days after his wedding and in the wake of hearing of the death of his brother in action.

He returned to active duty later in the war despite the damage to his knee and was twice mentioned in despatches.

Before leaving the scene of 1921 we should note that this year witnessed the first two appearances of one George 'Gubby' Allen, the infancy of what would be an illustrious career for both the county and England for the fast bowler and hard-hitting lower-order bat. It's a sobering thought that there would be a second global war and his career would be in its twilight years before Middlesex tasted County Championship victory again.

And one final footnote. The Middlesex committee meeting in December 1921 opposed a proposal put forward by the board of control subcommittee that 'the selection committee should be given power to rest any player three days previous to a Test match'. An early nod towards central contracts here perhaps?

CHAPTER 3
1947 AND 1949

Middlesex's triumph in what has often been termed 'The Glorious Summer of '47' had parallels with their successes of 1920 and 1921 and will introduce us to some of the greatest legends of the club and others who, despite their heroics in that summer and beyond, live in the shadow of those same greats.

As with 1920, this win came in the aftermath of global conflict. The Second World War had broken into the midst of the 1939 season with cricket not resuming domestically for seven years. And again, as with 1920, the members of this triumphant Middlesex team had been scattered abroad during the conflict and re-emerged sporting its scars, be they physical, mental, emotional or all three.

The nation physically, emotionally and economically, was also trying to recover from its wounds. Rationing was still in force, industry was looking to rebuild, but anxieties were still high given the onset of the Cold War. Speaking of cold, the public mood hadn't been helped by the coldest winter in living memory in which power cuts were commonplace. The eventual thaw saw flooding of parts of the Thames and elsewhere.

It would be a big year in public life too, with the future Queen Elizabeth announcing her engagement to Philip Mountbatten, the future Duke of Edinburgh, and three future music legends in David Robert Jones, Reginald Kenneth Dwight and Marvin Lee Aday – better known as David Bowie, Elton John and Meat Loaf – were all born.

On the cricket field Middlesex were desperate to rid themselves of the bridesmaid's tag with which they had become synonymous since their 1921 victory. In the quarter of a century since Frank Mann's team had retained the trophy, they had been runners-up no fewer than six times, first in 1924 and then for five years in a row either side of the outbreak of war. On five of those six occasions they had lost out to the dominant force of that era, and indeed most eras for that matter, Yorkshire. The White Rose have lifted the title a record 32 times to date, dwarfing Middlesex's 13 successes. The other near miss had come at the hands of Derbyshire, the only triumph for the county founded in 1870.

In other nods to their history, Middlesex's winning captain of 1921, Mann, had just begun his term as club president, having taken the baton from the now Sir Pelham Warner, leader of the 1920 success.

Mercifully, the harsh winter and subsequent floods gave way to long warm summer days with two effects. Firstly, in an era where television was not yet established and with memories of hiding away from the bombings of the war fresh in their memories, crowds emerged seeking entertainment, and secondly it produced hard, true batting pitches up and down the country which made for a feast of runs to satisfy that thirst for something to lift the spirits.

Middlesex's batters more than any others were happy to feed and indulge that thirst for fun, to lift onlookers out of the mundane everyday struggles of that postwar period.

Denis Compton, Bill Edrich, John 'Jack' Robertson and Sydney Brown were cricket's answer to the Four Musketeers with their flamboyant, devil may care brand of batting which set up so many wins, the first two making over 3,000 runs in an English summer, statistics which will surely never be erased from the history books.

The 1948 *Wisden Almanack*, reflecting on the triumph, wrote of Middlesex's 'dynamic attitude' before going on to state, 'From the first ball in every match they pursued only one object – victory … Their batting possessed a sense of urgency, their bowling full of purpose and their fielding rarely fell from a high standard. By their remarkable rapid scoring the batsmen usually gave the bowlers maximum time to dismiss a side twice, and frequently Middlesex finished the first day with 400 runs made and three or four wickets taken cheaply.'

The spotlight when talking about Middlesex in 1947 inevitably falls on Compton and Edrich and their batting exploits, without parallel in other English summers. Edrich had brothers who played the game, while Compton's sibling Leslie was part of the 1947 legends, yet it was these two batting doyens who were referred to as twins, so intertwined were their stories.

Writing in tribute to the pair in the 1948 *Wisden*, R.C. Robertson-Glasgow joyously penned, 'Compton and Edrich are of that happy philosophy which keeps failure in its place by laughter, like boys who fall on an ice slide and rush back to try it again. They give the impression whether batting, bowling or fielding that they are glad enough merely to be cricketing for Middlesex or England – "Fate cannot harm me I have played today." And they seem to be playing not only in front of us and for us, but almost literally with us. Their cricket is communicative.'

Both had established their cricketing credentials before the war, Compton being named one of *Wisden's* five Cricketers of the Year back in 1939, having made his first Test hundred against Don Bradman's mighty Australians the previous summer. Edrich joined him in winning the accolade the following year after his 219 in England colours in what turned out not to be a timeless Test after all against South Africa in Durban, proceedings having to be called to a halt with England in sight of victory for fear of missing the boat home!

They were two young men of huge talent who, like so many others, would lose some of the best years of their playing career to armed conflict. The experience may have broken lesser

Denis Compton.

men, yet it seems in the case of these two sporting Goliaths that their experiences over those six years may have been a catalyst for their exploits with ball and especially bat once the fighting stopped.

Compton served with the Royal Artillery, ultimately being posted to India in a bid to quell the Japanese, but at least managed to squeeze in some Ranji Trophy fixtures around the task.

Edrich, meanwhile, rose to the ranks of squadron leader in the RAF, earning the Distinguished Flying Cross for his part in the air raids on Cologne in 1941 when piloting a low flying Blenheim Bomber in which 12 of the 54 planes and many of Edrich's comrades were lost.

Bill Edrich.

Little wonder then as survivors of such a conflict, two young men who had already exhibited a zest for adventure came home determined to squeeze every ounce out of a life they had been lucky enough to keep.

Speaking in 2020 after his grandfather had been voted Middlesex's greatest ever player in a fan poll, batter Nick Compton reflected,

'The war was a tough time, but he enjoyed some of the camaraderie and there was a good sporting ethos behind it.

Those years in the army gave him some perspective and developed that insatiable attitude to go back, really dominate and score a lot of runs. That's what he enjoyed doing.'

However, it would be remiss to place all the credit for Middlesex putting an end to 25 years of domination by the northern counties and Yorkshire in particular, on the shoulders of simply Edrich and Compton.

Robertson, who was actually named a *Wisden* Cricketer of the Year in 1948, and Brown were hugely influential as were spinning duo James Sims and John Young – more of this quartet presently. And, even when Compton, Edrich, skipper Robins, Robertson and Sims were away on Test duty, the men of Lord's showed their resilience, winning seven of those games and losing only two.

All of that said, the season opened in unpromising fashion with defeat to Somerset. Edrich made the first of his eight County Championship centuries and followed up with four wickets to give the hosts a lead of 97, but the worst batting display of the season followed as they were shot for 78 second time around. Even then they seemed favourites to win when Somerset's ninth wicket fell at 151, with 25 still needed. However, Maurice Tremlett, father of Tim and grandfather of Chris, and number 11 Horace Hazell scrambled the west countrymen over the line. It would be Middlesex's last reverse for almost six weeks as they responded to adversity with a run of seven wins in a row.

Gloucestershire were the first side on the receiving end of the backlash, thrashed by an innings, Edrich's 6-28 bowling them out for 88 in their second knock. Though it didn't surpass his career best of 7-48 taken 12 months earlier, the return helped Edrich to 67 wickets by August, raising hopes he would achieve the double of 3,000 runs and 100 wickets in a season, only previously achieved by J.H. Parks in 1937 – a record which still stands today. However, a shoulder injury then ended his hopes of adding to the tally for the rest of the season.

The match was notable for Robertson's first hundred of the summer and 88 from George Mann, son of president Frank Mann. Like his father he would later go on to captain England in 1948/49 and was the chairman of the Test & County Cricket Board at the time of the first rebel tour to South Africa in 1982 – a trip which changed the course of Middlesex history as we shall see later on. George Mann's son Simon was jailed on charges related to an attempted coup in Equatorial Guinea in 2004, but later pardoned.

Of the 'Twins' it was Edrich at this stage who was making the running, and he excelled in Compton's absence against Warwickshire, his 225 made in a shade under six hours. Young took six second-innings wickets for the second game in a row as another innings victory was secured.

Compton, though, would give a glimpse of what was to come back at Lord's against Worcestershire, his masterful 88 not out more than twice as many as any other batter from either side managed in their respective first innings. Cricket's answer to Errol Flynn then made 112 second time around, but Edrich was hardly upstaged, taking five wickets in each innings for ten in the match.

Robertson-Glasgow wrote in *Wisden* of Edrich's art with ball in hand, 'Edrich began as a muscular slinger, as but a moderate advance on village heroics; then he grew into knowledge of swerve and variety.'

Both Edrich and Compton made centuries as Sussex were swept aside, before Robertson unfurled the highest score of his prolific summer, 229 in the crushing of Hampshire.

Robertson's early development came from a cricket-playing father who promised him half a crown for every 50 runs he made. This was raised to half a crown for every hundred once he made it into first-class cricket via former fast bowler Frederick Durston's indoor school in Acton. The 12 half-crowns he earned in the 1947 season from a father true to his word were among Robertson's greatest treasures.

Wisden, commenting on his batting in its 1948 citation, observed, 'When the numerical details of his play are forgotten the classical style and elegant stroke-play remain a pleasurable memory.'

Robertson's run-scoring in the years immediately after the war was all the more remarkable given his service limited him to a couple of victory Tests and an odd few balls from fellow officers on the lawns in Norfolk where he was stationed with the Duke of Wellington Regiment.

Test duty called for Compton and Edrich at the start of June and on a sporty Lord's pitch, Young's 7-46 bowled out visitors Glamorgan for 99. *Wisden* remarked that the slow left-arm bowler 'mixed his deliveries cleverly, kept immaculate length and imparted quick spin'.

Middlesex replied with only 102, a score which would have been far worse but for Robertson's 43. Laurence Gray, the workhorse bowler of the Middlesex attack, whose stamina allowed him to plug away for long spells without complaint, then returned 7-69 to leave the hosts needing 201 to win. The chase appeared in jeopardy at 102-5, but Alexander Thompson, who'd scored his maiden first-class hundred 12 months earlier, played the key hand of 81 not out to see his side home.

A 'Magnificent Seven' wins was rounded off with the defeat of Nottinghamshire by seven wickets at Lord's. Key to the success was a record stand of 310 for the first wicket between Robertson and Brown, erasing that set by Pelham Warner and James Douglas against the same opposition in 1904. The first-wicket partnership record has been eclipsed a few times since, most recently by Sam Robson and Mark Stoneman, who raised it to 376 against Sussex at Hove in 2021. However, Robertson and Brown's effort remains the highest opening partnership made against the men of Trent Bridge.

The good batting wickets that season played to the strengths of Brown who was a back-foot player, strong on the pull, hook and cut. His strong immediate postwar form may have been down to his being stationed with the British Army at Aldershot during the conflict, a posting which allowed him to contest several matches, many of them played at Lord's.

Rain wiped out almost the entire first day and ruined the draw with Yorkshire, which broke the winning sequence, but not before Robertson and Brown had posted another double-century stand, both scoring hundreds in the process.

However, some doubts were raised about Middlesex's championship-winning credentials when shorn of their England stars, including skipper Robins, they were thrashed by Essex despite Robertson's second-innings ton. And those murmurings got a little louder when, even with England stars back in harness, they were rapidly bowled out for 124 up at Headingley by reigning champions Yorkshire, Edrich making 70 of those.

Compton though hit back with the ball, taking four wickets as Yorkshire were bundled out for 85, after which a second-innings century from Edrich set up a comfortable win.

July opened with a win over Hampshire in a low-scoring affair, before Edrich and Compton shared a stand of 277 for the second wicket as Middlesex racked up over 600 against Leicestershire at Grace Road with Edrich, now in sublime form, making 257 to Compton's 151. Compton then produced magic with the ball to complete a ten-wicket win.

That game wouldn't be the last time Edrich and Compton dominated in partnership together. Following a narrow defeat to Somerset at Taunton and a win over Essex secured by a Compton century, the two maestros were at it again at the County Ground against Northamptonshire. Edrich was again the mainstay with a superb unbeaten 267, his highest score in this summer of all summers, while Compton played the supporting role with 110.

Robertson-Glasgow summed up Edrich thus, 'Compton is poetry; Edrich is prose robust and clear. Far more than Compton, Edrich uses the practical and old-fashioned methods and areas of attack. He likes the straight hit and the pull drive, but also he is a hooker nearly as vicious as his great forerunner Patsy Hendren.'

The victory over Nottinghamshire which followed was notable for a second-innings hundred by Alan Fairbairn. It meant the Winchmore Hill left-hander had made hundreds in his first two first-class games, but sadly it appears he was troubled by a knee injury and these were his only two three-figure scores in a first-class career of just 21 appearances.

Centuries for Robertson and Compton and a six-wicket haul for Sims meant Sussex were brushed aside at Hove before the former's next century helped save a draw with Kent at Canterbury after the London side had been asked to follow on.

Middlesex's top four came within a whisker of a very rare feat across the Thames against Surrey next time out. Robertson, Compton and Edrich all made three figures, the latter pair sharing an unbroken stand of 287 for the third wicket in a massive score of 537-2. Brown proved the odd one out, but only just, bowled by Stuart Surridge for 98. Such batting heroics were the foundation of an innings victory with Compton claiming 12 wickets with the ball, six in each innings. Despite this haul and others like it in 1947, his brand of left-arm googlies and 'Chinamen', unlike his batting, was at the experimental stage, but somehow no less joyous to witness.

Middlesex first innings			4s	6s
SM Brown	b Surridge	98		
JDB Robertson	c and b EA Bedser	127		
WJ Edrich	not out	157	18	-
DCS Compton	not out	137	9	-
FG Mann	did not bat			
*RWV Robins	did not bat			
AW Thompson	did not bat			
+LH Compton	did not bat			
JM Sims	did not bat			
LH Gray	did not bat			
JA Young	did not bat			
Extras	(8 b, 4 lb, 6 nb)	18		
Total	(2 wickets, declared, 118 overs)	537		

Fall of wickets:

1-211, 2-250

Surrey bowling	Over	Mdn	Runs	Wkts	Wide	No-Balls
Gover	17	0	84	0	-	1
AV Bedser	20	3	67	0	-	4
Surridge	18	2	77	1	-	1
Parker	21	3	83	0	-	-
Squires	17	0	95	0	-	-
EA Bedser	19	0	82	1	-	-
Holmes	3	0	13	0	-	-
McIntyre	3	0	18	0	-	-

Middx's 1st innings scorecard v Surrey at The Oval – the Four Musketeers at the top of the order doing fab things.

'Compton's left-arm bowling has about it a certain casual humour,' said Robertson-Glasgow. 'He brings unrehearsed jokes on to the legitimate stage. He can bowl in a Test as if he were trying things out on a friend in the nets. He is still among the joys and errors of experiment. Anything may yet happen.'

The pivotal game of the season was without question the return against Gloucestershire in mid-August, which began with the hosts four points to the good at the top of the standings. To make things even more challenging for Middlesex, they were without Compton and Robertson, the latter newly called up to the South Africa Test series, and although Edrich was in harness having lost his Test place, his shoulder injury ruled him out of the bowling arsenal.

His absence from the attack mattered less than it might have however, as this was a game dominated by spinners on a pitch with plenty of turn.

Edrich's half-century and a last-wicket stand of 37 between Sims and Young took Middlesex to 180. The two spinners then combined with the ball to take all ten Gloucestershire wickets, Sims claiming six to Young's four as Middlesex secured a lead of 27 – not huge, but precious nonetheless. A young Harry Sharpe, who'd served as an able seaman during the war, was then promoted up the order, the punt paying off as he made 46 and shared a third-wicket stand of 70 with skipper Robins. Another collapse followed, but the partnership meant Gloucestershire needed 169 on a pitch now turning sharply and Young's 5-27 proved decisive. The win took Middlesex eight points clear, an advantage they were never again to surrender.

There was a maiden first-class century for Leslie Compton in the win over Derbyshire which consolidated the triumph against Gloucestershire, but much of the back end of the victorious campaign was again about his younger sibling. When he wasn't terrorising South Africa's bowlers, Denis was piling up County Championship runs for fun. There were five centuries in successive games which lit up August, culminating in his highest Championship score of the campaign, 178 against Surrey at Lord's in a win which put Middlesex on the brink of the title.

According to grandson Nick, it wasn't just the volume of runs, but the mode of acquiring them which endeared Denis not only to Middlesex fans but other devotees of the game.

'Being [a] *Wisden* Cricketer of the Year at 20, 21, having scored 2,500 runs in a season isn't likely to happen very often,' said Nick. 'He burst on to the scene when he was a young player and did pretty well when he first came in. He brought a new energy and played in a certain way that captivated people. He made an impression on people very early on.

'My grandfather obviously had a flair and a way of playing that was quite dashing and I think that tied in with the time in which he played in a sense it was postwar Britain. He brought a particular sort of vibrance to the game that perhaps people were looking for and perhaps needed.

'He always looked to score runs, and played with a sort of charisma that lightened people's day. I think people wanted to come and watch that.

'I don't think anyone will ever amass the amount of runs he did in 1947.

'Maybe those years in the army perhaps gave him some perspective and when he came back his run-scoring ability was ridiculous, the amount of runs he scored. I don't think it will ever be beaten. I don't think it can be really because there were more games played then.'

Nick admitted that it is hard to compare eras and that his grandfather played in a very different cricket world to that of the modern years. Some aspects of cricket in the 1930s, '40s and '50s were tougher for batters, such as uncovered pitches, while the type of bowlers faced may in the main have been less fearsome than the speed merchants of the modern era.

'You read things and you hear things and it is hard to know. I think a lot of the bowlers were a bit like Neil Dexter – a lot of wily foxes like that who could use conditions. They were able to swing it and uncovered pitches would have made it very difficult. So if you look at all the old footage and stuff a different technique was employed.

'Now you play on much truer surfaces, so there is a much more stable kind of hitting through the line of the ball and batsmen dominating hitting the ball on the up.

'Back then it was more about touch. Sure, you hit the bad ball, but I think there was a way of manoeuvring the ball around and playing it very late. The challenge was different.'

Nick also pointed out that Denis played at a time when there was little camera footage as well as a lack of the wealth of statistical information available in the modern era. He believes his grandfather used that to his advantage to develop a truly unique style of play, rather than one learned from a manual or the copying of others,

'If you look at the footage it was much less about brawn and power back then. The bats were smaller, the wickets weren't as good, so the sweep and the late cut and shots like that were examples of that touch and the ability to manoeuvre the ball. You saw more of the natural techniques.

'Now, you see a lot of players brought up on coaching manuals and bowling machines, so you get a lot of visual clues in the sense that we can watch hours and hours of players batting on TV. So, as a kid growing up now you formulate a technique based around your heroes.

'Back then TV was not a prominent form of media, so you just batted and found your own unique way that worked for you. That is why you see all these strange and wonderful techniques back then don't you. That is kind of the art of batting – finding your own way – and I love looking at and reading about how different people went about things. He was one of those who found his own way.

'He played with a couple of unique shots. The sweep shot was something that got associated with him and became the "Compton sweep". And when you get a particular shot that gets associated with you, there is obviously a defining sort of quality there or a unique selling point.'

As with any sporting genius, Denis Compton had his foibles. His judgement of a single once led England legend Trevor Bailey to quip, 'A call for a run from Compton should be treated as no more than a basis for negotiation.' Or as former Middlesex team-mate John Warr once so eloquently put it, 'He [Compton] was the only player to call his partner for a run and wish him luck at the same time.'

And Compton also acquired a reputation for being rebellious, with stories abounding of him turning up for play dressed up in the tuxedo he'd been out to dinner in the night before and with his kit nowhere to be seen – stories Nick believes are almost certainly accurate,

'Turning up without any kit is quite bizarre. I can only say regarding that, I suppose it was part of his charm and a way of taking pressure off himself even. It was almost as if he had the attitude he was playing another club match, knowing he had the talent to just go out there and make it work. That was part of his freedom and a way of taking away intensity.

'I don't think it was something that he put on. You get the feeling it was a pretty natural part of who he was and the character he was. It is certainly something that wouldn't happen today, would it?

'I don't think Grandad and authority went together particularly well. I think people let him off because they just thought, "Oh God, there goes Compo again." They just all got on with it where if you had taken it seriously you might have got quite angry with him at times.'

The combination of Compton's batting form and three wins in a row meant by the time Middlesex welcomed Northamptonshire to Lord's for the season's penultimate game they knew victory would clinch a long-awaited title. For their part the men from the County Ground were heading for the wooden spoon.

The trusty opening pair of Brown and Robertson laid the platform after Middlesex won the toss with an opening stand of 147 and though wickets tumbled regularly thereafter, Compton's 60 made sure the hosts got to 273.

Young's six-wicket haul then all but settled matters by securing a lead of 126, which Middlesex increased to 429 led by 85 for that man Compton and 73 for Brown. Young took his tally to 11 in the match as Northamptonshire were despatched for 74 and the title was back at Lord's.

The season ended in defeat to Lancashire, but even there Middlesex deserved credit for making a valiant attempt to chase down a mammoth 372 in the fourth innings rather than blocking out for a draw. Compton still managed to sign off in style with his 11th Championship hundred, carrying him to over 2,000 Championship runs for the season made at an incredible average of 96.80.

Robertson-Glasgow summed up the legend that was Compton in this fashion, 'Compton cannot help it. He has the habit of batting, as the sun has the habit of journeying from east to west … Compton has genius, and, if he knows it, he doesn't care.'

So it was in the last of his six summers as captain that Robins won Middlesex's fourth official County Championship crown, and the dynamic way in which it was secured befitted a man described by *Wisden* in its obituary of him as being 'impatient of dull cricket'.

After his playing days, Robins became a selector, but his calls for the England side, of whom he was captain for three Tests in 1937, to implement his vision for 'brighter cricket' fell on deaf ears, seen as outdated for postwar Tests.

This quest for a more attacking brand of cricket led him to unsuccessfully bid to unseat Len Hutton as England captain in 1954, and as tour manager to the West Indies in 1959/60 there was friction between himself and the then captain Peter May.

Middlesex v Northamptonshire scorecard, 1947.

MATCH BETWEEN	Middlesex	+	Northamptonshire		
PLAYED AT	Lords	ON	August 27 28 29	19 47	
UMPIRES	Holmes + Heston	SIDE WINNING TOSS		Middlesex	
W Neville		1st INNINGS	Middlesex		

Order	TIME IN OUT	BATSMEN'S NAMES	RUNS AS SCORED	HOW OUT	BOWLER	Totals
1		Robertson J.D	12 1 113 4 3 1 1 1 1 4 1 4 4 1 4 1 4 1 2 1 3 4 4 1 3 1 1 4 1 1 1 2 1 1 4 4 1 1	B	Broderick	85
2		Brown S.M	2 2 3 1 2 1 4 2 1 1 3 1 1 1 1 1 2 2 1 1 2 1 1 1 1 1 3 1 2 1 4 1 2 1 1 2 3	B	Broderick	62
3		W.J Edrich	1 2 1	L B W	Clarke C.B	4
4		Compton D	1 2 1 1 1 1 4 2 1 1 2 4 1 4 2 1 2 1 4 1 1 1 2 1 2 1 2 1 3 1 2 1 1 2 1	C + B	Clarke C.B	60
5		A. Fairbairn	4 2 1 2 2 4 3	B	Clarke C.B	18
6	Capt	F.G Mann	1 1 3	B	Clarke C.B	5
7		Compton L	2	L B W	Broderick	2
8		Sharp H	1 1 4 1 1 1 1 2	B	Broderick	13
9		Sims J	1 4 1 1	B	Broderick	4
10		Young J	2 1 1	B	Clarke C.B	4
11		Gray L		not	out	0
BYES	4	22	LEG BYES 1 2 1 WIDES	NO BALLS	TOTAL EXTRAS	13
					TOTAL	243

RUNS AT THE FALL OF EACH WICKET	1 FOR 147	2 FOR 156	3 FOR 158	4 FOR 236	5 FOR 243	6 FOR 246	7 FOR 250	8 FOR 266	9 FOR 273	10 FOR 273
OUTGOING BATSMAN'S No.	1	2	3	5	4	6	7	9	8	10

Hrs of play. 12-7 NB 176 at 60"   D Compton reached 3000 runs. with 55 here
12-7
11-30-6

ANALYSIS OF BOWLING

BOWLERS	1	2	3	4	5	6	7	8	9	10	Wides	No Balls
Partridge												
Clarke R												
Broderick												
Clarke C.B												
Timms												

BOWLERS' NAMES	Overs	Maidens	Runs	Wickets	Wides	No Balls	BOWLERS' NAMES	Overs	Maidens	Runs	Wickets	Wides	No Balls
Partridge	17	6	36	—									
Clarke R	15	2	47	—									
Broderick	25	9	46	5									
Clarke C.B	27.3	1	123	5									
Timms	5	—	8	—									
			13 243										

MATCH BETWEEN	Middlesex	+	Northamptonshire		
PLAYED AT	Lords	ON	August 27th 28th 29th	19 47	
UMPIRES		SIDE WINNING TOSS			
		1st INNINGS	Northants		

Order / Time In Out	BATSMEN'S NAMES	RUNS AS SCORED	HOW OUT	BOWLER	Totals
1	Brookes D	2 2 1 4 1 1 1 4 2 4 2 /	L B W	Young	26
2	Davis P	1 2 1 1 1 /	c Compton D	Young	4
3	A.C.L. Bennett	1 1 1 3 4 4 /	c Edrich	Young	14
4	Timms J.E	1 1 4 /	L B W	Sims	6
5	Barron W	1 1 2 /	L B W	Sims	4
6	Broderick VM	4 4 1 1 2 3 3 4 4 1 1 2 2 /	B	Sims	32
7	C B Clarke	1 2 1 1 3 1 4 1 4 /	c Mann	Young	18
8	A W Childs-Clarke Capt	4 4 1 1 3 1 1 4 /	c Edrich	Sims	19
9	Partridge R.J	1 1 1 1 /	c Mann	Young	4
10	Clarke R	1 1 4 2	not	out	8
11	Fiddling K	1 /	c Compton D	Young	1
BYES		LEG BYES 4 2 1 WIDES	NO BALLS 1	TOTAL EXTRAS	8
				TOTAL	147

	1	2	3 FOR 48	4 FOR 58	5 FOR 71	6 FOR 114	7 FOR 118	8 FOR 132	9 FOR 146	10 FOR
OF EACH WICKET										
OUTGOING BATSMAN'S No.	2	3	1	3	4	5	7			

ANALYSIS OF BOWLING

BOWLERS	1	2	3	4	5	6	7	8	9	10	Wides	No Balls
Gray												
Young												
Sims												
Compton D												

BOWLERS' NAMES	Overs	Maidens	Runs	Wickets	Wides	No Balls	BOWLERS' NAMES	Overs	Maidens	Runs	Wickets	Wides	No Balls
Gray	8	—	14	—									
Young	25.5	10	44	6									
Sims	23	3	63	4		1							
Compton D	5	—	21	—									
			147										

Middlesex v Northamptonshire scorecard, 1947.

MATCH BETWEEN	Middlesex + Northamptonshire			
PLAYED AT Lords		ON August 27, 28, 29		19 47
UMPIRES		SIDE WINNING TOSS		Middlesex
	2nd INNINGS	Middlesex		

Order	TIME IN OUT	BATSMEN'S NAMES	RUNS AS SCORED	HOW OUT	BOWLER	Totals
1	15 15	Robertson		c Childs-Clarke	Partridge	0
2	15 49	Brown	1441 21212124 333 144 11141 121111121 311+2 2	B	Timms	43
3	17 36	Edrich	112 1124 2 1114 4 312 2133 144	B	Broderick	50
4	38 42	Compton D	51321 42213 414 144 11114 3 14112 14224 2111321	B	Broderick	85
5	48 49	Fairbairn	3	L B W	Broderick	3
6	49 17	Mann	11111112 4 1114 424 211222 3	not	out	43
7	54 56	Compton L	2 12 144 244 44	L B W	Clarke R	28
8	56 13	Sharp	121	not	out	4
9			Innings closed 303 for 6 wkts 2nd day 6.30			
10						
11						

BYES 444	LEG BYES 14	WIDES	NO BALLS	TOTAL EXTRAS	14
				TOTAL	303

RUNS AT THE FALL OF EACH WICKET	1 FOR 0	2 FOR 84	3 FOR 209	4 FOR 219	5 FOR 220	6 FOR 268	7 FOR	8 FOR	9 FOR	10 FOR
OUTGOING BATSMAN'S No.	1	3	2	4	5	7				

NB 262 in 16th   W. J. Edrich reaches 3000 runs with 39th run

ANALYSIS OF BOWLING

BOWLERS	1	2	3	4	5	6	7	8	9	10	Wides	No Balls
Partridge												
Clarke R												
Broderick												
Clarke CB												
Childs-Clarke												
Timms												

BOWLERS' NAMES	Overs	Maidens	Runs	Wickets	Wides	No Balls
Partridge	9	1	33	1		
Clarke-R	7	-	37	1		
Broderick	29	7	68	3		
Clarke CB	16	1	95	-		
Childs-Clarke	3	-	21	-		
Timms	9	3	32	1		
			303			

MATCH BETWEEN	Middlesex	+	Northamptonshire			
PLAYED AT *Lords*		ON August 27ᵗ 28ᵗ 29ᵗ			19 47	
UMPIRES		SIDE WINNING TOSS	*Northants*			
		2ⁿᵈ INNINGS				

Order	TIME IN OUT	BATSMEN'S NAMES	RUNS AS SCORED	HOW OUT	BOWLER	Totals
1	5.41 / 5.50	Brookes	114	B	Young	6
2	5.41 / 5.16	Davis	1421	c Robertson	Gray	8
3	5.26 / 6.19	Bennett	121	B	Sims	4
4	5.27 / 6.27	Timms	14124 111111	LBW	Young	18
5	6.30 / 6.39	Barron	1121	c Compton L	Young	5
6	6.30 / 6.47	Broderick	31	c Compton D	Young	4
7	6.40	Childs-Clarke	2114 11 421	not	out	14
8	6.48 / 6.50	Clarke C B	/	B	Young	0
9	6.55 / 6.59	Partridge	1	c Compton L	Sims	1
10	7.0 / 7.5	Clarke R	13	st Compton L	Sims	4
11		Tiddling		absent		

Won by 355 runs 4ᵗ innings defeat. 6ᵗᵖ time repeat

BYES 3	LEG BYES 22	WIDES	NO BALLS	TOTAL EXTRAS	
				TOTAL	74

RUNS AT THE FALL	1 FOR 116	2 FOR 14	3 FOR 35	4 FOR 39	5 FOR 46	6 FOR 57	7 FOR 59	8 FOR 64	9 FOR 74	10 FOR
OUTGOING BATSMAN'S No.	1	2	3	4	5	6	7	8	9	10

ANALYSIS OF BOWLING

BOWLERS	1	2	3	4	5	6	7	8	9	10	Wides	No Balls
Gray												
Young												
Sims												

BOWLERS' NAMES	Overs	Maidens	Runs	Wickets	Wides	No Balls	BOWLERS' NAMES	Overs	Maidens	Runs	Wickets	Wides	No Balls
Gray	5	-	13	1									
Young	13	2	36	5									
Sims	6.2	1	18	3									
			7/74										

For all that, he was hailed elsewhere in *Wisden's* obituary as 'one of the most dynamic cricketers of our time' – something to which those lucky enough to witness his champions of 47 would say a resounding Amen.

* * *

The title defence of 1948 was one to be filed under the category of near miss as Middlesex finished a close third behind Yorkshire and Glamorgan, the latter taking the honours to Wales for the first of their three title wins to date. A late-season defeat to Warwickshire at Coventry effectively ended the London side's hopes. The highlight of the season from a Middlesex perspective came in mid-May as Compton and Edrich rewrote the record books with a third-wicket stand of 424 against Somerset at Lord's, a total which stands to this day and in all likelihood will never be beaten. The season saw Francis Mann now as skipper and he was still at the helm when the 1949 campaign got under way.

Understandably given the heights to which they had risen, neither Compton or Edrich could match their feats of the summer of 1947, or for that matter 1948 – although Compton still topped the batting averages at a smidgeon over 50.

Yet it wasn't the batting but the bowling which lacked depth with spinners Young and Sims, the latter now 45 years old, shouldering most of the burden. For all that it would only be two late-season defeats to Surrey which would deny Middlesex the title outright.

Middlesex made almost the worst possible start to the 1949 against Nottinghamshire at Lord's, where, despite a polished first-innings century by Robertson, they were left hanging on for a draw after collapsing from 139-1 to 195-9 in pursuit of 222 to win. Leslie Compton, who had gone to hospital after suffering an ankle injury while keeping wicket, returned to the ground on crutches and came out with a runner to play out the final over and avert defeat.

The first win came against Northamptonshire courtesy of centuries for Brown, Denis Compton and Edrich, before Compton then shone with ball in hand, taking eight wickets in the match as Essex too were comfortably seen off. And a third win in a row ensued as Leicestershire were summarily despatched by an innings in a low-scoring affair at Lord's.

The visit of champions Glamorgan to London was ruined when the whole of the second day was lost to rain and the following game with Lancashire at Old Trafford was destined to be a draw for similar reasons. Nevertheless, two England stalwarts lit up the gloom when play was possible, Cyril Washbrook's 141 for the Red Rose county trumped by Compton's masterful 179 for the visitors.

The bad weather continued through to the return with Glamorgan where Middlesex were on the back foot for most of the first two days, before their pursuit of 310 on the last day was ended by the return of the rain at 139-2 with Compton seemingly warming to the task.

This match marked the fourth appearance of Horace Brearley in first-class cricket, 12 years after his last one. That had been for his native Yorkshire back in 1937, where he'd studied for a BSc at the University of Leeds.

He would make only one more appearance later that season having moved to the capital to accept a post at City of London School. Unremarkable as his very short first-class cricket career was, Middlesex fans will be forever grateful for his educational summons south. Without it, son Mike may have been born and raised a Yorkshireman and much of the London county's exploits of the 1970s may not have been written.

Compton would save his best score of the season, a masterful 182 for his benefit match at Lord's, but John Langridge's second-innings century for visitors Sussex meant Middlesex's run of draws continued.

There would be two more in the sequence as first Warwickshire's last pair of Bert Wolton and Eric Hollies managed to bat out time after their fourth-innings pursuit of 321 came up just short. And the game with Yorkshire petered out on the last day after centuries by Robertson and the great Len Hutton for their respective sides.

At this stage Worcestershire were the Championship's pace-setters, but the last week of June and the opening one of July, during which Middlesex played four games – and they say there's too much cricket now – saw the Lord's tenants pile up points to close the gap.

It was a short tour of the west country which restored winning ways, Gloucestershire being swept aside by nine wickets. In many ways Harry Sharpe's century was the difference in a game where the ball was generally on top against the bat, but James Sims took ten in the match – five in each innings – to clinch the 12 points awarded in those days for a win.

Sims's career best had come 14 years earlier, so for him to still be bowling to this standard into his 40s was a feat in itself. He bowled his leg-break and googly appreciably quicker than most, terming the latter 'The Old Wozzler'. He was a man of wry humour, Denis Compton recalling in a tribute after his death of him laying a trap for Gloucestershire batter Charlie Barnett, who hit a long hop towards the square leg boundary, only for the fielder to come in too far and allow it over his head and away for four. Sims, who had lost the flight of the ball, turned and asked what had happened whereupon Compton broke the bad news.

'Should have hit him on the head,' retorted Sims out of the side of his mouth as was his wont, before breaking into a huge smile to demonstrate no malice was really intended.

His tally of 1257 puts him fourth on Middlesex's list of all-time wicket-takers. Only Fred Titmus, J.T. Hearne and J.W. Hearne have more. He is just ahead of John Emburey, who to this author's surprise played over 50 more first-class games than Sims. Little doubt then this dual County Championship-winner deserves his place in the Middlesex CCC hall of fame.

Commenting on his feats in 1949, *Wisden* recorded, 'Special praise must be given to Sims. At the age of 45 he bowled his leg-spinners and googlies almost as well as ever.'

The two heroes of the win in Bristol both went on to serve stints as Middlesex scorer, Sharpe succeeding Sims after the latter's sudden death from a heart attack in 1973. Sharpe would occupy the role for much of the golden era of the 1970s and '80s.

From there Middlesex headed to Bath and a wicket where runs proved hard to come by. It is this match which will give us a chance to salute a man who has so far been a mere footnote in our story – one George Oswald Browning Allen, better known to everyone simply as 'Gubby'.

Cast your minds back to the previous chapter and you'll remember that Allen played one match for Middlesex in their triumph of 1921 while still at Cambridge University, and he would again have been a footnote in 1947.

A quick bowler and fierce lower middle-order hitter, Allen had almost always had to fit cricket around his need to make a living, first at the Debenhams department store and then as a stockbroker in the City. It meant periods where his participation was sporadic and he sometimes struggled to achieve the fitness levels and rhythm of bowlers who could devote themselves to the game on a more regular basis.

Despite his periods away from the game he still took over 400 wickets for Middlesex, including all ten in an innings against Lancashire at Lord's in 1929, a feat achieved only three times previously at the home of cricket and never since. It remains the only instance of the feat in a County Championship fixture at the stadium.

He played 25 Tests for England, a figure which would have been higher but for the presence of the great Harold Larwood, though both were on the boat for the 'Bodyline' Ashes series where Allen refused to adopt the tactic. He was the second-oldest man to captain England, after W.G. Grace, when he led the tour to the West Indies in 1947/48.

At Bath in 1949 it wasn't his bowling but his batting which came into focus as, coming in at five, he made 91 out of a score of 193, in a game where only one other batter scored 50. Middlesex won by 36 runs.

Allen made another batting contribution of 98 later in the campaign, but these runs at Bath were probably of greater consequence and meant he had at least in his twilight years played a small part in this County Championship win. With or without the contribution, however, his legacy at Middlesex was already secure – as the presence of the Allen Stand testifies.

Before leaving the Bath match we should record that other absences meant there was a debut for a 16-year-old called Fred Titmus. Whatever happened to him? Worry not, we will find out shortly.

Lancashire were seen off at Old Trafford before a brilliant comeback against Leicestershire took their winning streak to four. Trailing on first innings by 142, Edrich's hundred allowed the visitors to set a target of 192, something Sims's seven wickets meant was never a possibility.

Dull draws with title contenders Yorkshire and then Warwickshire, the latter ruined by rain, broke the winning run ahead of the trip to New Road at the back end of July to face Worcestershire, who were still at the head of the Championship standings..

By this time Robertson had chalked up his second Test hundred in the second rubber of the summer against New Zealand, only to then be left out again for the returning Cyril Washbrook. His response at the beautiful New Road was little short of astonishing. No thought of sulking from Robertson, who instead produced the highest score of his career, an unbeaten 331 made in six and a half hours. It remains to this day the highest individual score by a Middlesex player and the highest made at New Road.

Robertson's efforts secured an innings win to send Middlesex top yet there was no Test recall that summer, or indeed the year after. He played five more Tests in 1951, making 11 in all in which he made two centuries and six 50s. It says much about the calibre of cricketer England had to call on at that time that a man with such figures could play so few Tests and be so frequently overlooked.

Robertson followed up with another century in the win over Hampshire, where Edrich, despite not being the force of the previous two years, made 182, his highest score of the summer.

Like his 'twin' Compton, Edrich wasn't adverse to mixing business with pleasure when it came to his cricket. His Test-best score of 219 referred to earlier came under threat of the axe from England colours and by all accounts he'd taken being in the last chance saloon somewhat literally by partying hard for most of the night before.

Such antics would catch up with him again in 1950 when he was supposedly heard sneaking back to his room three sheets to the wind during the first Test against the West Indies. The resulting disciplinary proceedings earned him a Test ban later in that series and he wasn't recalled again until the Ashes of 1953.

When Edrich died suddenly in 1985, he was one of very few players to be awarded the honour of having his ashes scattered at Lord's.

His two worlds of decorated war hero and cricket doyen came together again at a memorial service some months later where Denis Compton gave the eulogy and Anne Shelton, a renowned singer of the war years, sang a rendition of one of Edrich's favourite songs, 'A Nightingale Sang in Berkeley Square'.

Just as everything looked to be heading towards another title, Middlesex incurred a bump in the road against Sussex where the batting failed first time around and despite a valiant effort following on and reducing the hosts to 27-4 in their quest for 148, they couldn't complete the turnaround.

Good sides though respond well to adversity and Brown, dropped for the Sussex encounter, responded with a double hundred as Middlesex posted 362-7 in the first innings against Kent at Canterbury. The rest of the match entered around the brilliance of Young, who returned 7-47 in the first innings before winkling out six more second time around.

The son of a music hall performer, Young made the cricket field his stage, reserving some of his best feats for these title-winning years of 1947 and 1949, though he was also prolific in 1951 and 1952. He was probably unfortunate to make his Test debut against Bradman's all-conquering Australians in 1948 and never quite transferred his county success to the biggest stage of all. Nevertheless, his 1,182 wickets put him sixth on Middlesex's all-time list.

Back on top of the table, Middlesex's failure to win the title outright hinged on their two matches with Surrey, the first of which took place at Lord's in mid-August. Losing a crucial toss meant the hosts were kept in the field for more than 150 overs, by which time Surrey had piled up almost 450. Stuart Surridge's six wickets then gave Surrey a massive lead and though they chose not to enforce the follow-on, they went on to win comfortably.

Again, Middlesex responded well to the setback, seeing off both Kent and Worcestershire, the latter victory all but ending the New Road club's own fading title hopes.

Derbyshire were also crushed in a match which provided Leslie Compton a rare chance to step out of his brother's shadow by top-scoring with 88 in the hosts' only innings.

Cricketing success didn't come as easily to Leslie as it did to Denis and he never played for England as his younger brother did, despite being a tidy wicketkeeper and useful lower middle-order batter.

However, it could be argued he outshone Denis at football where they both played for Arsenal. Even here reward was hard-earned as Leslie wasn't a regular through much of the 1930s and didn't play enough matches to qualify for a medal when the Gunners won the old First Division championship in 1937/38,

War then intervened where he served in the army before returning to Arsenal and finally winning a league title medal in 1947/48, a season in which Denis played enough games to win one too. And before all these exploits on the cricket field in 1949, the brothers won the FA Cup, beating Liverpool in the final. They remain the only brothers to win national titles at both cricket and football. Leslie finally achieved something his brother never did in 1950 when becoming the England football team's oldest ever outfield player to win a first cap in the game against Wales aged 38 years and 64 days. He remains the oldest England debutant of the postwar era.

The win over Derbyshire meant with two games to go it was Middlesex's title to lose, but another coin toss proved crucial in the return fixture with Surrey at The Oval.

On a wicket certain to deteriorate, Mann again called incorrectly, giving the hosts first use. Compton's five wickets restricted Surrey to 259 and despite seven wickets for Alec Bedser, 40s from Robins, Leslie Compton and Young gave the visitors a 100-run lead.

Sadly for Middlesex, it wouldn't prove enough as despite only needing 146 to win, they were undone by Bedser once more, the England seamer trumping his first-innings effort to claim eight wickets, making it 15 in the match as the visitors crumbled to 94 all out.

This second reversal at the hands of Surrey in a matter of weeks meant Middlesex could ill afford another slip-up in their final fixture with Derbyshire if they were to have any hope of returning the County Championship trophy to Lord's. Derbyshire, though, despite their lowly position in the standings, would make life very difficult for the would-be champions.

Young's final five-wicket haul of the campaign allowed the hosts to restrict Derbyshire to 228, but as it had done a few days earlier the batting collapsed in reply, only a resolute 45 from Robins taking Middlesex as far as 139.

Help arrived from an unexpected quarter as 22-year-old medium-pacer John Warr, in only the eighth game of his first season of Championship cricket with the county, produced what was then a career-best 5-36 to skittle the visitors for 103 at the second time of asking.

An Ealing County Grammar schoolboy, Warr was still studying History at Cambridge at the time of these heroics, having served four years of national service in the Fleet Air Arm. He would go on to play 12 seasons of first-class cricket for Middlesex, taking more than 700 wickets as well as captaining them for three difficult seasons between 1958 and 1960. After retiring he became a correspondent for the *Sunday Telegraph* and served a four-year stint as chairman of the Jockey Club.

Despite Warr's bowling stint, Middlesex looked destined to lose after collapsing again to 36-5 chasing 193 to win. Denis Compton, though, stood firm when it mattered most, finding a staunch ally in Robins, with the pair adding 90 for the sixth wicket.

After Robins fell to the spin of Albert 'Dusty' Rhodes, Leslie joined his brother to take up the chase and though he too departed before the end, Sims ensured the winning line was crossed with Denis on 97 not out.

Middlesex were 12 points ahead again, but Yorkshire still had to visit Newport for a clash with the soon-to-be-deposed champions Glamorgan and Norman Yardley's men won comfortably enough helped by five-second innings wickets apiece for Alec Coxon and slow left-arm bowler John Wardle.

It meant the County Championship title was shared for the first time since its inception in 1890. Amazingly, having waited 59 years for such an occurrence it happened again 12 months later with Lancashire and Surrey sharing the honours. Nor would that be the last time Middlesex would be involved in such a finish to the domestic season as we shall see later.

There would though be no more Championship wins in the Compton/Edrich era, several generations of cricketers passing through the Grace Gates before success returned, the one constant of these barren years being a youngster we met earlier in this chapter – Fred Titmus.

Middlesex v Derbyshire scorebook, 1949.

	TIME IN OUT	BATSMEN'S NAMES	RUNS AS SCORED	HOW OUT	BOWLER	Totals
1		Elliott C		c Compton D	Young	14
2		Smith D		c Compton D	Young	44
3		M. Fredericks		c Robertson	Compton D	12
4		L Johnson		c Warr	Young	0
5		Revill a		not	out	73
6		Rhodes A.E		L B W	Young	36
7		D C Brooke-Taylor		c Brown	Young	3
8		Gladwin C		c Robins	Compton D	5
9		Dawkes G.		c Compton D	Warr	28
10		Copson W.H		c Compton L	Warr	0
11		Jackson L		B	Edrich	4

MATCH BETWEEN Middlesex + Derbyshire
PLAYED AT Lords ON Aug 24 25 26 1949
UMPIRES H. Parks + F. Chester
H.R. Murrell + C Baker
SIDE WINNING TOSS Middlesex
1st INNINGS Derbyshire (put in)

BYES 2|2 LEG BYES 1|2| WIDES NO BALLS
TOTAL EXTRAS 9
TOTAL 228

RUNS AT THE FALL OF EACH WICKET
1 FOR 57 2 FOR 60 3 FOR 64 4 FOR 84 5 FOR 129 6 FOR 133 7 FOR 140 8 FOR 215 9 FOR 215 10 FOR 228
OUTGOING BATSMAN'S No. 2 1 4 3 6 7 8 9 10 11

HB 197 after 91st

ANALYSIS OF BOWLING

BOWLERS	1	2	3	4	5	6	7	8	9	10	Wides	No Balls
Edrich												
Warr												
Young												
Compton D												

BOWLERS' NAMES	Overs	Maidens	Runs	Wickets	Wides	No Balls	BOWLERS' NAMES	Overs	Maidens	Runs	Wickets	Wides	No Balls
Edrich	11.4	2	38	1									
Warr	24	6	44	2									
Young	39	12	80	5									
Compton D	26	10	57	2									

68

MATCH BETWEEN	Middlesex	+	Derbyshire			
PLAYED AT Lords		ON Aug 24", 25", 26"			19 49	
UMPIRES H. Parks + F Chester		SIDE WINNING TOSS	Middlesex			
H.R. Murrell + C Baker		1st INNINGS	Middlesex			

Order in/out	TIME	BATSMEN'S NAMES	RUNS AS SCORED	HOW OUT	BOWLER	Totals
1		Robertson J.D	24111 /	c Dawkes	Gladwin	9
2		Brown S.M	/	c Revill	Copson	0
3		J.G. Dewes	211114 41111 131113 11411 /	c Fredericks	Jackson	39
4		W.J. Edrich	11311112 11 /	c + B	Gladwin	13
5		Compton D	12114 11112 11 /	c Dawkes	Copson	18
6		F.G. Mann	/	c Smith	Jackson	0
7		R.W.V Robins	11211122 4 1114 146 44 4 /	B	Copson	45
8		Compton L	/	Run	out	0
9		Sims J	11 /	B	Copson	2
10		Young J	1413 /	Run	out	9
11		J. Warr		Not	out	0
BYES			LEG BYES 4 WIDES	NO BALLS	TOTAL EXTRAS	4
					TOTAL	139

RUNS AT THE FALL OF EACH WICKET	1 FOR 0	2 FOR 26	3 FOR 50	4 FOR 71	5 FOR 71	6 FOR 85	7 FOR 85	8 FOR 102	9 FOR 135	10 FOR 139
OUTGOING BATSMAN'S No	2	1	4	3	6	5	8	9	7	10

Badlight 12.14
12.35

ANALYSIS OF BOWLING

BOWLERS' NAMES	Overs	Maidens	Runs	Wickets	Wides	No Balls	BOWLERS' NAMES	Overs	Maidens	Runs	Wickets	Wides	No Balls
Copson	12.2	1	50	4									
Gladwin	23	11	28	2									
Jackson	26	7	57	2									
			139										

69

Middlesex v Derbyshire scorebook, 1949.

MATCH BETWEEN	Middlesex	+	Derbyshire			
PLAYED AT Lord's		ON Aug 24, 25, 26.				19 49
UMPIRES H Parks + J Clester		SIDE WINNING TOSS Middlesex				
H.R. Murrell + C Baker		2nd INNINGS Derbyshire				

Order	TIME IN OUT	BATSMEN'S NAMES	RUNS AS SCORED	HOW OUT	BOWLER	Totals
1	2/25 3/30	Elliott	112111 /	L B W	Warr	4
2	2/15 3/5	Smith	1 /	B	Warr	1
3	3/9 3/24	Fredericks	1 /	L B W	Sims	2
4	3/37 4/5	Johnson	321 /	L B W	Young	6
5	3/31 1/5	Revill	12111111 21111114 1112114 11224 124 11144 1 /	c Compton R	Edrich	62
6	4/6 4/49	Rhodes	1211 /	c Robertson	Warr	5
7	4/6 5/7	Brooke-Taylor	31 /	c Compton R	Warr	4
8	5/6 5/67	Gladwin	221111 11 /	Run	out	12
9	5/68 5/68	Dawkes	/	c Edrich	Young	0
10	5/6 5/24	Copson	/	c Mann	Warr	0
11	6/2	Jackson	1	not	out	1

BYES 1	LEG BYES 11	WIDES	NO BALLS	TOTAL EXTRAS	3
				TOTAL	103

RUNS AT THE FALL OF EACH WICKET	1 FOR 2	2 FOR 11	3 FOR 11	4 FOR 26	5 FOR 36	6 FOR 50	7 FOR 79	8 FOR 83	9 FOR 91	10 FOR 103
OUTGOING BATSMAN'S No.	2	3	1	4	6	7	8	9	10	5

2nd Day Bad light 5.57 / 6.12

ANALYSIS OF BOWLING

BOWLERS	1	2	3	4	5	6	7	8	9	10	Wides	No Balls
Edrich									W			
Warr												
Sims												
Young												

BOWLERS' NAMES	Overs	Maidens	Runs	Wickets	Wides	No Balls	BOWLERS' NAMES	Overs	Maidens	Runs	Wickets	Wides	No Balls
Edrich	8.4	3	15	1									
Warr	22	5	36	5									
Sims	23	6	43	1									
Young	9	6	6	2									
			103										

MATCH BETWEEN *Middlesex* + *Derbyshire*
PLAYED AT *Lords* ON *Aug.* 24th 25th 26th 1949
UMPIRES *H. Parks* + *F. Chester* SIDE WINNING TOSS *Middlesex*
H R Murrell + *C Baker* 2nd INNINGS *Middlesex*

Order	TIME IN OUT	BATSMEN'S NAMES	RUNS AS SCORED	HOW OUT	BOWLER	Totals
1		Robertson		B	Copson	0
2		Brown		c R will	Gladwin	1
3		Edrich		c Smith	Gladwin	1
4		Compton D		not	out	97
5		Dewes		B	Jackson	12
6		Mann		c Dawkes	Jackson	0
7		Robins		c Smith	Rhodes	50
8		Compton. L		B	Gladwin	18
9		Sims		not	out	10
10			Won by 3 wkts 4.49 pm 3rd Day			
11						

BYES 4 LEG BYES 11 WIDES NO BALLS 1 TOTAL EXTRAS 7
TOTAL 196

RUNS AT THE FALL OF EACH WICKET:
| 1 FOR 1 | 2 FOR 1 | 3 FOR 11 | 4 FOR 34 | 5 FOR 36 | 6 FOR 126 | 7 FOR 179 | 8 FOR | 9 FOR | 10 FOR |

Hrs of play 3rd day 11-0 5-0 NB 185 after 65th

ANALYSIS OF BOWLING

BOWLERS	1	2	3	4	5	6	7	8	9	10	Wides	No Balls
Copson												
Gladwin												
Jackson												1
Rhodes												

BOWLERS' NAMES	Overs	Maidens	Runs	Wickets	Wides	No Balls	BOWLERS' NAMES	Overs	Maidens	Runs	Wickets	Wides	No Balls
Copson	12	4	31	1									
Gladwin	21	7	54	3									
Jackson	23	3	69	2		1							
Rhodes	12	2	37	1									
			192										

CHAPTER 4
1976

'Fred's bowling wasn't just about Fred. It was a triumvirate, which was Fred, J.T. Murray and Peter Parfitt. J.T. would tell Fred when he was bowling the right pace and Fred would pick up from that.

'Parfitt reckoned he could read Fred really well, so he said it always seemed to be the fourth ball of an over that I knew to stand up a bit taller because he would be bowling it a little bit shorter and a bit wider, so the batter would be looking to cut rather than push forward. Most catches off spinners come down very low. That's the kind of info they engaged in.

'He was a very pragmatic bowler. He got so many people out with the arm ball. But you could bowl a straighter line back in those days because leg-side fields could be more packed. So he would bowl straight and occasionally bowl the drifter which is where Parfitt came into play. He would then bowl swing which he bowled off the index finger and would start outside leg stump.

'Graham Gooch told me the first piece of advice he got from Keith Fletcher was not to sweep Fred because people would see this ball coming down and they'd all go to sweep and almost before they got into the position J.T. would be appealing for lbw. He was a masterful bowler, absolutely masterful. It was an education watching him.'

The words above are from Mike Selvey, former Middlesex seamer and now club president, recalling a podcast done with Parfitt about the late Fred Titmus in 2017.

The eloquent sentiments illustrate perfectly how the boy who'd bowled those 12 balls almost unnoticed in the shadows of the 1949 triumph transformed into a legend. Barely a footnote among the greats of that postwar success, he'd risen to sit in the pantheon alongside Denis Compton, Bill Edrich and Robertson, not to mention Gubby Allen and those who had gone before, Patsy Hendren and Pelham 'Plum' Warner to name but a few.

Not only had Somers Town-born Titmus eclipsed the feats of 1949 spin twins James Sims and John Young, but he was on the way to supplanting the legendary J.T. Hearne and making himself Middlesex's all-time leading wicket-taker.

The signs were encouraging from the get-go as in the summer of 1950, still only 17 and bowling a mix of medium pace and the off-breaks which made him famous, Titmus played almost every County Championship match, gleaning 45 wickets in the process.

With the country only five years on from the Second World War, his cricketing journey with the tenants of Lord's would be interrupted by an obligatory two years of national service, but Titmus kept his hand in by turning his arm over for the Combined Services team.

The two faces of Fred Titmus – the fresh faced 16-year-old of 1949 and the Championship winner of 76, now 43.

Consequently, he picked up pretty much where he'd left off when the 1953 season rolled around, snaffling over 100 first-class wickets for the first time. It was a sign of things to come as he would achieve this feat on no fewer than 16 occasions.

If 1953 was good then 1955 was spectacular with Titmus claiming 191 victims, including 18 five-wicket hauls and ten or more victims in the match on six occasions. His batting was on the rise by now, too, with his maiden first-class century, 104 in a losing cause against Hampshire, helping him on his way to 1,000 runs for the first time. Titmus's sparkling form led to a call from the England selectors as the first of his eventual 53 Test caps came that summer against the touring South Africans. That tally would surely have been higher were it not for greats like Jim Laker and Derek Underwood blocking his route.

The all-rounder's double of 1,000 runs and 100 wickets became a habit for Titmus as he married flight, changes of pace and deadly accuracy with the ball to resilient batting in the lower middle order. He clocked up the feat every year but one between 1956 and 1962, 1958 the one anomaly.

1962 was also the year of his career-best figures as he claimed 9-62 against Cambridge University at Fenner's, an occasion which saw future cricket committee chairman and club president Bob Gale take the tenth wicket of the innings with a caught and bowled. Oh to have been a fly on the wall in that dressing room afterwards. Such feats allied with 21 Test wickets and a career-best 137 not out on the tour to Australia that winter, where he opened in the Ashes on one occasion alongside the great Geoffrey Boycott, saw him named one of *Wisden's* five Cricketers of the Year in 1963.

His Championship best of 9-57 fittingly came at Lord's against Lancashire in 1964 and he captained the Seaxes from 1965 through to the end of 1968. The fact he was still playing in the 1970s was a tribute to his resilience, having fought back from losing four toes in a boating accident on England's tour of the West Indies in 1967/68.

Clive Radley knew Titmus as well as most at that time and believes it typified the spirit of a man who knew how to survive and who passed on the secrets of the art to him, albeit often the hard way,

'Fred was hard as nails. He got over 10,000 runs and he did the double a number of times. It was just the way he went about his business. I learned more from him than anyone else throughout my playing career, not through him voluntarily giving me advice particularly, but just by watching him. I didn't learn much about technique or things like that, but the art of survival.

'In my first ever game against Yorkshire [in 1966 at Scarborough] some years before, Fred Trueman was still almost in his pomp. He was certainly still pretty quick. I got in to face him and he was whizzing them around my head. I'd been trying to fend him off for two or three overs and I'd taken a few bruises. After the second or third over of this Fred came down the wicket between overs and I thought he was going to say, "If you want to take one I'll take him for a bit."

'He didn't. He said, "Illingworth is turning it square down my end so I'll look after him and you stay down Fred's end." I learned something from that which was to look after yourself. He gave me all sorts of bits of advice, not necessarily about cricket or technique, but just about life.'

Radley recalled another occasion at Lord's where Middlesex were taking to the field again following the lunch interval. Radley was making his way to his customary position at slip when he felt a hand on his shoulder. It was of course Titmus, ready to dish out some more sage advice on the art of survival. As always, Fred couldn't remember Radley's name, so resorted to his usual default position of 'Thingy'. 'Thingy, you have got two things to do this afternoon,' he began. 'The first is to catch them off me because you will be stood at slip. And secondly, I'll be bowling from the Pavilion End, so can't see what's going on behind me, so you'll have to tell me when you see the bald and grey-haired men in suits sticking their heads out on the balcony from the dining room.'

'Why's that?' ventured Radley, a little bemused.

'That's when we start diving around again in the field because they hire and fire us,' came Titmus's retort.

Nor was Fred's advice solely about cricket – there were life lessons too. He and Radley were travel buddies for away games. Well. I say buddies, perhaps companions would be a better description in an era where senior players spoke and younger players listened respectfully.

Titmus would pick Radley up at the Grace Gates at Lord's. The two men would settle into Titmus's VW Beetle, whereupon Fred would wind the window down, light his pipe, take a few puffs and off they'd set. The silence on the journey would be punctuated only by Fred telling stories or passing on some pearl of wisdom or another.

This was the way of it for a few years until one day, as they were pootling down the A1 to play Yorkshire at Headingley, Radley plucked up the courage to venture a thought.

'Look Fred, we've been travelling up this A1 to Leeds for years,' he began with some trepidation. 'There's an M1 that's just been opened and that's much quicker. Why don't we go up there?'

Fred said, 'It might be much quicker, but the A1 is flatter and it'll save half a gallon of petrol.' That's the sort of thing you'd learn from Fred.

Yet for all Titmus's personal accolades, the 1949 County Championship win became an increasingly remote memory. Summers came and went, yet team success remained elusive and Middlesex's tally of titles remained stuck on five.

Not that there weren't great players at Lord's during that era. We've already referred to two, J.T Murray and Peter Parfitt.

Murray's original trial with Middlesex came aged 13 where he was accepted on to the MCC ground staff purely as a batsman, but then sporting fate took a hand as the school leaving age was raised to 15, delaying his arrival through the Grace Gates by 12 months.

The intervening year saw Rugby Boys' Club of Notting Hill, where Murray played his cricket, reach the final of the London Federation of Boys' Clubs tournament, and again the cricketing gods smiled on the teenager as the team's regular wicketkeeper broke a thumb leaving a vacancy behind the stumps ahead of the big day.

I had the honour of meeting J.T. back in 2014 where he recalled, 'I don't remember why I kept wicket, but I obviously did all right because Paul Pawson, who was the warden of the club, wrote to Lord's and said to Archie Fowler [to] have a look at John as a wicketkeeper. The trial obviously went OK because I was a wicketkeeper from then on – within two years I was playing for Middlesex.'

Such was the teenager's love for cricket and his newly discovered art in particular, not even England legend Tommy Lawton could persuade him to part with the gloves in exchange for a chance at professional football. Murray had proved a sporting all-rounder, representing England Boys' Clubs on several occasions and luckily for him the father of boys' club warden Pawson was friendly with the Brentford FC chairman. 'They played bowls together,' said Murray.

Whatever was said, word reached Lawton during his time as player-manager of the Bees, so one Sunday morning there was a knock at the family's door. Young Murray was still in bed – but not for long.

'My dad almost went berserk he was so excited,' said Murray. 'He came up the stairs shouting, "Get out of bed, I've got Tommy Lawton in my hallway and he wants to see you."'

Murray would play for Brentford's youth team with some distinction, being part of their run to the semi-finals of the inaugural FA Youth Cup in 1952/53, but when it came to making a choice there was no contest,

'Tommy offered me professional terms, but by then I was 17 and I knew cricket was what I wanted to do, not football. I loved my football, but it was only ever going to be cricket for me.'

History shows it was a shrewd choice and football's loss was definitely cricket's gain. One of *Wisden's* five Cricketers of the Year in 1967, his 1,223 dismissals effected behind the timbers for Middlesex is a record which is, with due respect to present incumbent John Simpson, a tally never likely to be surpassed, while his career total of 1,527 is only eclipsed by the man he termed the greatest practitioner of the art, the legendary Bob Taylor.

The elegant mover with great hands played 21 Tests for England too, yet it is a sobering thought his first-class average of a shade under 24 may have seen him shunned in the game as it is today.

Norfolk-born Parfitt's story also has a link to Middlesex's County Championship-winning side of the late 1940s.

He was spotted by Bill Edrich when playing for the county of his birth in the annual charity match against Edrich's XI in 1955.

Edrich spoke with the youngster in the aftermath, encouraging him towards a career in county cricket, only to be told by Parfitt, 'It's my intention to go to Loughborough Physical Training College.'

So Edrich was rebuffed, but fate took a hand as Parfitt failed the interview and having enquired of Edrich if his previous offer was still on the table, he hot-footed it to Lord's in 1956 to sign a three-year contract.

Following two years of national service he was capped in 1959 in the wake of a century against Sussex, before as resident of the number three spot in the order, his eight first-class centuries in 1961 resulted in him being named Young Cricketer of the Year by the Cricket Writers' Club.

England duty followed where a golden year in 1962 saw him make four centuries in five Tests. He played 37 in all for his country and his 21,000-plus runs – made at an average of 40 – puts him in the top ten of all-time where Middlesex is concerned.

Among others deserving of honourable mention from this era are seamer Alan Moss, who took over 100 wickets at an incredible average of just over 12 at the peak of his powers in 1961, and John Waugh, whose 703 scalps for the county were among 956 first-class wickets in all during a distinguished career.

So, a distinguished roll call of cricketing talent, but there were of course mitigating circumstances for the lack of silverware, two dynasties who dominated between them for close to 20 years.

Surrey, having shared the title with Lancashire in 1950, then made it their personal property, winning seven on the trot from 1952 onwards. The mantle then headed from south London to Yorkshire as the northern giants won seven times between 1959 and 1968.

In all that time Middlesex only really came close twice when finishing third in both 1960 and 1961.

According to Mike Selvey, given the two giants of the era, that was a feat in itself as any other participating counties had little or no scope to dream of glory,

'Teams pretty much for 20 years were playing for second place before they started. So the fact Middlesex didn't win the title didn't mean they weren't fine cricketers and a fine side. It just meant they were competing against truly great sides.'

However, 1970 marked a low as only their five County Championship match victories to Gloucestershire's three – the two counties having finished level on points – prevented Middlesex from picking up the wooden spoon. Change was needed and in the winter of 1970/71, the committee looked to Mike Brearley in their quest for a turnaround in fortunes.

Brearley had first played for Middlesex a decade earlier as an 18-year-old in the summer of 1961. However, most of his early cricket was played at Cambridge University where he studied for a degree in Classical and Moral Sciences. He captained the university side from 1964 through to 1968. A glimpse into Brearley's talent came in the winter of 1964/65 when, selected as captain of the MCC touring party to Pakistan, he made an unbeaten 312 against North Zone – it would remain his highest first-class score. He followed that up with 223 against Pakistan's youngsters. However, the array of talent in front of him meant it was too early for a call to the full Test side.

A full season with Middlesex followed, but he was absent altogether in 1966 and 1967 and only sporadic in the years immediately leading to his appointment.

As *Wisden* observed when naming him one of its Cricketers of the Year in 1977 for his exploits in the previous English summer, 'For the next five years books largely supplanted bats. He researched philosophy at his old college, St John's, and taught at the University of California and Newcastle University.'

At the time of his promotion to the top job at Middlesex he hadn't made a Championship hundred. In fact, one didn't materialise until 1973 so in that sense his elevation could be seen as something of a punt. Turns out it was a great call.

What he had noticed in his decade in and out of the dressing room was a hierarchical structure where senior players, especially those of international standing, formed an exclusive clique. It was an environment where those senior voices commanded respect and did the talking while youngsters listened and learned.

As a figure who bridged the gap between that era and the next, Radley admitted that he accepted the status quo, believing it to be commonplace across cricket,

'I'd probably been in the team for ten years and I hadn't really noticed until he came along that we had been two teams in the one dressing room, in as much as we had some high-quality players who were internationals and they tended to stick together a little bit.

'I hadn't given that another thought because I just assumed it was par for the course and all teams were probably like that anyway.' In those first years you'd go away to Colchester where there were two dressing rooms for the away team and you'd find all the established internationals would gravitate to one dressing room and the other lads to another.'

Brearley challenged the culture, normal or not, attempting instead to foster an environment where all voices could be heard and therefore bring about a more united team ethic. This was a brave and perhaps somewhat dangerous line to walk for a man who had hardly established himself as a certain starter in the XI.

However, another of the golden era breed, Roland Butcher, who came into the dressing room during that transition, saw its effects and saluted Brearley's forward thinking.

'Obviously, Mike Brearley would have come into that situation as a young player himself and it must have been quite tough because we were still in the era of the old pros,' he said.

'I can imagine the likes of Titmus, Murray, Parfitt, John Price and Eric Russell literally running the dressing room with the youngsters being in a corner and only speaking when they were spoken to.

'So, I think you have to look back to when Brearley first came into the Middlesex setup and how that influenced what he did later. He would have come into that old-fashioned old pros situation. I think that clearly influenced the way he went about things later on. Maybe he decided very early that if he became captain, he would take a different line. I would imagine that would have been his thinking. I certainly think he would have been influenced by what happened that he didn't want to repeat.

'Here he was, a Cambridge blue taking over a Middlesex team of old pros. I can imagine they didn't look too kindly on him. They may have regarded him as a privileged guy who hadn't done anything in the game, taking over at Middlesex where we have had all these legends, Compton, Robertson, Edrich and others. So it must have been really tough, but he showed his strength, character and vision because those guys disappeared pretty quickly and it changed to a different setup.

'He was more of a visionary. You have to give him credit for realising the old approach wouldn't work with the new breed of young cricketers he was inheriting.'

There was a new emphasis on being fitter too, hence regular running sessions around the Barclays Bank Sportsground in Ealing which some found more challenging than others.

Gradually the old guard dropped away. Previous captain Parfitt called time at the end of 1972 with Eric Russell following him out the door.

Price stayed for three more years, establishing himself in the pantheon of the county's best seam bowlers, and Murray too called it quits in 1975, ending a glittering career behind the timbers, one heavily influenced by his almost telepathic relationship with Titmus.

In the same interview referred to earlier, Murray, who collapsed and died after being taken ill while watching his beloved Middlesex in 2018, talked through his on-field relationship with the great off-spinner,

'I could say to Fred, "You're bowling like a prat, Titmus, now come on." It wasn't only if his arm was getting a bit low, but the pace as well. I could decide the pace he bowled at certain players depending on the pitch.

'I would say to him "off stump" and he would bowl there, or if I said "leg stump" he would bowl there or straight he would bowl straight – that was two people working in tandem.

'You're telling the bowler things because you know the batsman. How they move their feet, where they look to play their shots, so you've got to be a big part of what goes on.'

As the veterans left, younger players began to emerge, Butcher, John Emburey, Selvey, Mike Gatting and Ian Gould among them.

The on-field transition took longer, however. Surrey were champions in 1971 just to make Brearley's inaugural season in the hot-seat all the tougher, and there was little sign of an end to the title drought in the years which immediately followed.

Then came 1975 and a glimpse of what was to come as Brearley and his young charges reached the finals of both the Benson & Hedges (55-over) and the Gillette (60-over) cup competitions.

The former saw them beaten by five wickets by Leicestershire after being hustled out for 146 with only Mike Smith (83) putting up prolonged resistance.

The Gillette final brought more disappointment and an even heavier defeat at the hands of northern giants Lancashire.

Losing the toss in a September final didn't help and they were unable to post a competitive score, Clive Lloyd leading the Red Rose county to victory with an unbeaten 73 despite a frugal spell of 1-21 from a full 12 overs from Selvey.

While obviously disappointed to lose in two big Lord's finals, Selvey believed that simply being part of these occasions marked a turning point in his own and his team-mates' thinking,

'The two one-day finals we lost in 1975 were an indication, "We actually can do something here." Up to that point we were always competitive, but I never felt when I was going out to play a game of cricket that I was ever playing for very much. There never seemed to be very much on the line as it were. I can't tell you where we finished in the championship in those preceding years, but we wouldn't have been right up there anyway.

'Then in '75 we had this run through both those cup competitions. I bet Clive [Radley] didn't tell you he is the only man to score a hundred in all four competitions in the same year which he did that year. We lost both finals, one to Leicestershire and one to Lancashire, but for us to get to Lord's and to have the place packed out was a great experience for us. Maybe that gave us a new belief.'

Despite being born in Chiswick, Middlesex, Selvey had begun his career across the other side of the River Thames with Surrey in 1968. He'd been to university, first in Manchester and then Cambridge, before getting wind in 1971 of the fact that the Brown Caps were not keen to keep him.

The opportunity to join Middlesex loomed, with coach Don Bennett known to be a fan of the swing bowler. However, around this time Bob Willis's move from Surrey to Warwickshire might have scuppered Selvey's plans to come north of the river.

He managed to persuade the future England captain to delay the announcement of his departure for fear it would cause Surrey to hang on to him, despite his opportunities remaining limited.

Selvey revealed that a sparkling performance for Surrey's second XI against Middlesex at Edmonton in the summer of 1971 had helped clinch the move.

'I got a hat-trick including Brearley in the middle of it. He nicked one off to slip which helped,' he recalled with a wry smile.

By the winter of 1975 it was clear that Selvey needed a new-ball partner to increase the potency of the attack and give Middlesex a genuine chance of regularly taking the 20 wickets needed to win matches.

Bennett, acknowledged as a great identifier of talent, alighted on a supposed journeyman, Allan Jones, to fill the void.

Jones had begun his first-class career with Sussex before heading south-west to spend six seasons with Somerset.

His best year to that point had been 1974 when he took 67 first-class wickets at 22 apiece. His relationship with the Cidermen had not been an easy one, however, with many reported clashes between himself and then skipper Brian Close.

Again, you could argue that his recruitment was something of a gamble, but as the 1976 season would show it was in fact inspired and Selvey claimed they dovetailed together as a pair.

'The recruitment of Allan Jones was very far sighted,' he said. 'Jonah was a much-maligned cricketer because of his reputation. He had been around the block a bit from Sussex to Somerset. At Somerset he had bowled well, but was regarded as a very difficult character. Brian Close didn't get on with him at all. The stories of Closey are legendary and Allan had a lot of run-ins with him.

Mike Selvey delivering a trademark outswinger.

'We recruited him and he was a magnificent bowler for us in that season of '76, quick and very hostile.

'He was a curious animal, Jonah, in that you would never see a more uncoordinated cricketer until he started running in to bowl and then suddenly he was an athlete. It was a really strange transformation. He was a really fine sight in full flow, Jonah. He used to have the Jones grunt which people at the time used to think was him appealing. So Jonah was a real kingpin to that triumph because he gave me a high-quality bowling partner who operated from the other end. Particularly at Lord's, I always wanted to bowl from the Nursery End and Jonah was a Pavilion End bowler anyway, so the two of us complemented each other very well.'

The two men became close friends off the field, but had something of a love-hate relationship on it as the world that is competitive sport overtook Selvey at least, with him wanting to always be the bowler in the spotlight.

It was also an era where new-ball bowlers didn't compare notes as they do now, meaning it was less of a partnership than it might have been. Selvey clearly regretted this, wishing that back then things had been far more like they were by the time of our interview,

'Jonah became my friend, my bowling partner and my bowling adversary in many ways as I did compete against him.

'With Jonah, and maybe I was wrong about this, I never bought in to the idea it didn't matter who was taking the wickets as long as you are winning the game. I always wanted to be the one taking the wickets. If Jonah got a wicket I resented it because it was a wicket I wanted to get. That was kind of how it went really but I think it egged us both on.

'I travelled a lot with him to games so we were good friends. One thing we never did though which I deeply regret now, not just with Jonah but in general in those days, we never really collaborated very much.

'You would finish your over and wander off to third man or fine leg and then you'd come back and bowl the next over. I regret we weren't at mid-off or mid-on which would have been the right place because then you collaborate. The same thing happened with Wayne [Daniel], we never did that either. It happens all the time now with Stuart Broad and Jimmy Anderson, Ro-Jo [Toby Roland-Jones] and Murts [Tim Murtagh] and that's the way it should be as then you can bounce stuff off each other.'

The newly formed spearhead showed its value immediately with both Selvey and Jones claiming five-fors in the 1976 County Championship curtain-raiser as Kent were vanquished by 97 runs.

The Seaxes then avoided defeat against Northamptonshire having been nearly 200 behind on first innings, but next they were beaten by Warwickshire in an early stumble.

The latter game saw Titmus make the last of his six first-class hundreds and his first for over a decade, opportune with young John Emburey waiting in the wings for his chance. The great survivor had produced again and couldn't resist reinforcing the point with his mate 'Thingy' as soon as he got back to the dressing room. The gist of the message was, 'Little Emburey will have to wait a little bit longer now, won't he.'

Rain ruined the London derby with Surrey, but Middlesex's challenge gained early momentum with four wins on the trot in June, Selvey starting the charge with ten in the match as Essex were beaten by six wickets at Lord's. He felt the wickets at HQ that season played to Middlesex's strengths,

'Jim Fairbrother was still the groundsman at Lord's but he was starting to lose it a bit and a lot of his pitches in the mid-to-late '70s were not great in terms of holding together, so what he used to do was to leave them quite damp.

'That suited us because other teams didn't really know these pitches were damp, so other sides might want to bat on it, or we would put sides in, as we knew we could bowl teams out first innings with seamers and then second innings when they started drying out they would rag for our spinners. That's why the stats say I'd bowl a lot of overs first innings and not many second dig as Philippe [Edmonds] came on with Fred and then latterly Norman [Featherstone]. That's probably why I got 30-something wickets in June in four games.'

Jones picked up the baton with a five-for of his own as his inaugural county Sussex were brushed aside at Hove, before he and Selvey joined forces in an innings win over his previous port of call, Somerset. For Jones, having Close caught at slip by Radley for a duck in the first innings must have been especially sweet.

The winning run was then capped by Selvey's career best of 7-20 against Gloucestershire at the Wagon Works Ground where the hosts were hustled out for 55 in the first innings before Brearley even had a chance to make a bowling change. Selvey admitted the damp conditions played a big part and said his six in each innings – for 12 in the match – against Nottinghamshire 12 months earlier was his greatest feat ball in hand.

Not that this early season success was all about the bowlers. Brearley and Smith both had a big hundred to their name, but it was Graham Barlow who had really caught the eye.

Barlow had played the odd game for the Seaxes as far back as 1969, before playing more regularly in the 1974 and 1975 seasons. However, the two summers had yielded just seven half-centuries in total as promise failed to produce the wanted currency of runs.

The 1976 summer changed that. Two scores of 80-odd in the first two games set the tone and Barlow would pass 50 twice in the match in the win over Essex.

These innings proved foundational and a prelude to his first County Championship hundred, reaching 132 in the victory over Sussex at Hove. Fast forward to August where what proved his career best of 160 came in a vital win over Derbyshire and it was a score he might have topped next time out against Essex had Middlesex's first innings not been forced to close with him undefeated on 140 (the first innings of three-day matches back then were limited to 100 overs).

The latter two centuries were made at the perfect time, catching the eye of the England selectors, who promptly called Barlow up for the one-day series against the touring West Indians and he was subsequently named in the tour party for India that winter. Sadly for him, the flirtation with international cricket proved too fleeting, but he remained pivotal to Middlesex's top order for years to come.

'Graham had been a pretty average player in many respects,' said Selvey.

'He'd been a wonderful athlete, a fantastic fielder and a great runner between the wickets but never got the runs. Then, suddenly in '76, he got the best part of 1,500 runs as I recall which got him on the England tour that next winter and led to his Test caps. That made a big difference to us.'

First Test call-ups for Brearley and Selvey meant others like Butcher and Tim Lamb were required to step up and fill the breaches to sustain the title challenge. Notes from the county's minute book that year reveal the above two players, along with Martin Vernon, were issued with notices mid-season by the committee to the effect that they may not be retained for the following year. In the event, Butcher survived the cull to go on to achieve great things in subsequent years, while Lamb received a stay of execution for one more season before heading off to Northamptonshire. Vernon was not so fortunate, moving on to Gloucestershire for a year before leaving the first-class game.

The youngster who showed most promise was perhaps Mike Gatting. A local boy from Brent, Gatting had been on the books since 1973, making his first XI debut the previous year. He and his good friend Ian Gould had been 12th and 13th men respectively for the two one-day final losses in 1975, but a year later he played more than half of Middlesex's Championship games, getting close to 500 runs at an average of 26.

He was given first-hand experience of Brearley's new inclusive, every voice counts policy spilling over from the dressing room on to the field and admitted it caught him somewhat off guard, but in a good way,

'I do remember very early on in my years in the team, it might have been 1976 or 1977, I came out after lunch one day and obviously wasn't paying attention. I can look back on it now and have a chuckle.

'All of a sudden Mike [Brearley] came up to me and said, "Gatt, who do you think should be bowling? What do you think should be done?"

'I thought, "Bloody hell, I'm 19, 20, and the captain has come up and asked me what we should be doing."

'What he'd actually really done, rather than give me a bollocking, was to get me to watch the game a bit more, rather than letting my mind drift. I thought that was magnificent. That's the sort of person he was. He wasn't out to impose himself on people. He wanted everybody to feel a part of it all. He was in charge obviously, but he wanted to lead a collective. So, it was very, very interesting, yes.

'For me the most amazing of the Brearley title wins was probably 1976 because young guys got picked like myself and Gunner [Ian Gould].'

Ironically, Middlesex were pretty much back to full strength when they suffered a form slump from late June through much of July, losing four games out of six. The most agonising of those losses came at Bradford where Yorkshire beat them in a tense thriller. Fate didn't smile kindly on the visitors with Radley suffering a broken finger while fielding in the slips during Yorkshire's first innings, which left him unable to bat in the visitors' reply. Middlesex were eventually left chasing 237 to win and Radley came out as last man with his arm in a sling and five needed, only to be stumped for three, leaving Yorkshire the victors by one run.

The slump culminated in a catastrophe of a game with Kent at Dartford where Titmus was mysteriously left out on a pitch expected to turn. The omission appeared inconsequential when the visitors gained a first-innings lead of 154, but instead of batting again Middlesex enforced the follow-on and, with the wicket by now turning square, ended up being hustled out by Derek Underwood in the fourth innings to lose by 57 runs.

To complicate matters further, by this juncture they were in the midst of a wicketkeeping crisis which was about to get worse. With Murray retired, Nigel Ross had started the season with the gloves, only to suffer injury, leaving Ian Gould as the man in possession. The man known as Gunner played the next nine games, but was then called up for the England under-19s. Ross returned only to succumb to injury once more, meaning Roderick Kinkead-Weekes had made his debut in the Dartford debacle.

Middlesex immediately headed home to take on the touring West Indies side at Lord's where the injury curse struck again as Kinkead-Weekes broke a finger during the visitors' first innings. It would be the South African-born keeper's last appearance in Middlesex colours. Brearley, who had started life as a wicketkeeper/batter, donned the gloves only for his back to give out later in the match, meaning Butcher performed the honours for the rest of the draw.

With Derbyshire due at Lord's for a crucial Championship fixture in less than a week, the search was on for someone to fill the void behind the timbers and Brondesbury Cricket Club stalwart Mike Sturt was the man to answer the county's SOS call.

A Middlesex man by birth, Sturt had been an able deputy when J.T. Murray was on Test duty in the 1960s, but with his opportunities limited by the presence of the great man he'd left the first-class game to go into business and consequently hadn't played at this level for some eight years.

There was, however, very little sign of rustiness, as on a dry pitch of prodigious turn Sturt pulled off three catches and two stumpings in Derbyshire's second dig, helping the hosts to a precious 106-run win. He became a fixture as the wicketkeeper for the remainder of the season.

'Mike was a very fine keeper standing up,' remembered Selvey, 'and on the dry pitches the ball ragged in August. Mike was a very important factor in that as we did need a quality keeper. So, a few things aligned there really.'

Unsurprisingly, it was Titmus who was the main beneficiary of Sturt's glovework. No doubt smarting from his surprise Dartford omission and with that elusive first Championship medal within reach after nearly three decades in the game, Titmus became the chief tormentor of opposition batters over the final push.

On pitches scorched bare by the drought, the old maestro proved almost unplayable. A remarkable 30 batters fell under his spell in the last month of the campaign, including a seven-wicket haul against Glamorgan at Swansea and six men of the Red Rose, albeit in a draw with Lancashire at Lord's. He finished the season with 65 Championship scalps.

Selvey revealed that although Titmus bowled spin and he pace, it was the wily slow bowler he went to for advice,

'Fred was my mentor as a bowler. Everybody has a mentor, somebody who they would go to. You have so much advice coming at you, even more these days, but we didn't really have a coach. Don Bennett was nominally county coach, but we didn't have a first-team coach.

'I went through a difficult spell early on in my time at Middlesex where I got a little bit of a niggle, but you don't tell anyone about it because if you do someone else will be in the side and you might not get back in. They kept sending me to different people and they'd try and say there were things I was doing wrong, which are the exact same things I did when I was bowling well.

'Fred got very angry and said "if you need to know something ask me". So I listened to Fred.

'I asked him once how he did his variations and he said he didn't really have any.

He said, "You get enough variation trying to bowl the ball in the same place twice. Nobody bowls it in the exact same spot twice, so that is variation."'

Titmus, though, wasn't the only spinner to benefit from the arid, dry conditions. Philippe Edmonds, much more of whom later, took 16 wickets to finish with 64, just one behind Titmus, while Norman 'Smokey' Featherstone claimed 23 of his 32 wickets in all in this same period. The fact they came at a shade over 14 each propelled Featherstone to the top of the national averages in what proved his best season with the ball in a Middlesex shirt.

The wickets proved timely for Featherstone as a debate had been ensuing in the committee room concerning his future. Plans were afoot to recruit West Indian paceman Wayne Daniel for the 1977 season. With only two overseas stars allowed per county at that time it meant there wasn't going to be room for both Rhodesian Featherstone and a youthful Larry Gomes, who was enjoying his best English summer yet alongside Daniel as part of the all-conquering West Indies touring side.

Both men had their supporters and by all accounts discussions around the topic were rigorous, but in the end the lot fell to Featherstone by eight votes to two.

So, it was 23-year-old Trinidadian Gomes who had to bid farewell. He would never return to English county cricket, but went on to play 60 Tests for the West Indies, averaging 40 with the bat. Selvey admitted that it was easy to be retrospective about such things, but in his view the wrong decision was made for the wrong reason,

'I have mixed feelings about Smokey and I don't think this is being harsh. Featherstone had been there right throughout my time at Middlesex and there came a point in '76 where we had to make a decision about who we retained as overseas players because Wayne was going to come.

'In the end we retained Smokey and we let Larry go. You may say it's hindsight, but I think one of the reasons we did that was because Smokey was everybody's mate, so there wasn't a great deal of pragmatism involved in that decision.

'Larry was a kid who played 80-something games for Middlesex and it was only this year when Gus [Fraser] and I went through the list of Middlesex capped players we noticed he hadn't been capped. So, we retrospectively awarded him his county cap. Larry was very quiet, very young and a callow player, but he became one of the great players in the greatest West Indian team and we were wrong not to recognise that.

'Feathers was often what we call an August player, around contract times. Maybe that's unfair as he was a good all-round player and those wickets he got in '76 were a wonderful time for him. I still think we made an error of judgement in retaining him as I'm not sure how much he played subsequent to that, where Larry might have played for quite a while.'

Middlesex's upturn in form was stalled by their wet trip to Worcestershire in the penultimate fixture, where the last two days were lost completely to rain. Even so, by the time they faced Surrey in the finale, only bonus points stood between them and a first County Championship for 27 years.

They were made to wait a while as the hosts made 308-8 in their first innings, so denying the champions elect a bowling bonus point.

However, on the second afternoon, it was a typical Clive Radley nudged single which ended the wait for a trophy and sparked the victory celebrations. It wasn't long before the champagne was flowing and not content with that, Selvey and Jones hot-footed it to the bar in The Oval Long Room to, as the former put it, 'neck a few pints'. The pair's revelry would, however, be interrupted as three quick wickets fell in the final session, meaning both had to race – or should that be stagger – back to the dressing room to get padded up. Selvey admitted that he was really in no condition to bat, yet perhaps with inhibitions lost he more than surprised himself,

'I was pissed as a parrot and I'd never played as well in my life. I played shots I never thought I could play. That told me a bit about myself and my confidence levels. Some people have that innate ability to do that without getting pissed. That's what made them what they were and made me what I was I suppose.'

Edmonds and Featherstone both claimed five-fors as Surrey were bowled out for 172 second time around, but their rivals threatened to take the shine off the victory celebrations when reducing Middlesex to 36-5 in their quest for 173 to win. However, the two all-rounders joined forces in an unbroken sixth-wicket stand of 140 to see the champions home, Featherstone making 67 and Edmonds a belligerent 72.

For Radley, there was something all the sweeter about claiming the title in their arch rivals' backyard,

'London rivalry was strong in cricket – more so than football I reckon. If you wanted to beat any team as a Middlesex player it was Surrey. The Yorkies would be nice to beat, but in my particular case anyway, Surrey are the ones you have got to beat.

'The brown hatters south of the river. The working men's clubs south of the river. They were all a bunch of moaners. There would be Graham Roope and Robin Jackman having a moan about this and that. We just loved to stick it up Surrey.'

It's easy to picture Titmus, now 43, perhaps sitting in one corner of the dressing room, adorned in his championship medal, having a few puffs on his trusty pipe. By now it had been announced he was being allowed to leave a year earlier than originally planned, having been approached by Surrey to take up a coaching role.

It would lead to the emergence of John Emburey into the spotlight a year later, but as history tells us, it wouldn't be the last time that Titmus would turn his arm over in a Middlesex shirt.

Few would have imagined then that Brearley's men would go on to enjoy something of a dynasty of their own, becoming the dominant force in county cricket for almost two decades.

Brearley's personal elevation as a player and a leader was, though, perhaps easier to foretell. To again quote the *Wisden Almanack* of 1977, 'To play for England and captain the champions are the game's highest rewards and Brearley did both in 1976.

'To Fenner's spectators over his four years there [Cambridge] it would have seemed inconceivable that a dozen years would pass before such a talented batsman was capped.

'Brearley however decided cricket would be secondary to academic development and so has actually had three cricket careers: orthodox progress from school prodigy to the heights of the first-class game, a more or less fallow spell, then successful return to full-time play. It is a measure of his talents that, like an old-fashioned scholar-sportsman, he has climbed such peaks, despite the sterner, modern approach.'

The immediate question at hand as 1977 loomed was whether the Seaxes could, as they had done in 1921, follow up their success after winning the title. We were on the threshold of one of the more bizarre county seasons on record, where the destiny of the trophy would go down to the wire.

CHAPTER 5
1977

'Being champions brought different expectations and pressures with people looking at us thinking, "Can they do it again?"' said Mike Selvey.

Middlesex began 1977 in unfamiliar territory. The season past had seen them journey from also-rans over more than two decades to become unexpected champions. They were now the hunted with the prize everyone else coveted. They were the target.

As with all champions of any sport the challenge now was to evolve and improve, rather than stagnating and leaving themselves easy prey to the plethora of challengers, and there can be little doubt the first step in that process of evolution was the recruitment of Wayne Daniel.

The Barbadian quick had first journeyed to England with the West Indian schoolboys side of 1974, aged 18, and it was there that Middlesex's eagle-eyed coach Don Bennett had alighted upon him, hence he played in the county's second XI the following year. In all likelihood, he would have graduated to the first XI in 1976 had he not been called up to the West Indies party to tour England that summer. While in the shadow of Michael Holding and Andy Roberts, his 13 wickets played their part in rendering hollow England skipper Tony Greig's promise to make the West Indies 'grovel' as the visitors won the series 3-0. More importantly, it reinforced Bennett's view that Daniel should come to Middlesex. It would prove an inspired choice with several greats of Middlesex's golden era labelling Daniel the county's best ever overseas signing, something for which Clive Radley claimed Bennett deserves huge kudos.

'Wayne Daniel was another great signing by Don Bennett,' he said. 'He'd toured the previous year when he battered Gatt [Mike Gatting] a fair bit. Don, technically and encouragement-wise, wasn't a brilliant coach I didn't think, but he did know a good player when he saw one and he made some top signings; not only Wayne Daniel, but he got Wilf Slack on board and all sorts of people. He was a great judge of a cricketer and picked them up from all over the country and all over the world.

'Greatness is a difficult thing to analyse and he [Daniel] probably wasn't a great in the pantheon of fast bowlers, but he was one of Middlesex's greatest overseas signings.

'We didn't realise it at the time, but we would have him for around 13 years because he wasn't good enough, with the great fast bowlers the West Indies had, to get in their side. They had some bloody good bowlers to keep him out. He was a great trier, who gave 100 per cent for however long he was out there. He was a brilliant bloke to have around.

'It was great to have someone with the ability to roll over nine, ten and Jack which you always need and you could rely on Wayne doing that because he was fast and frightening.'

If anything, Mike Gatting pushed the envelope even further regarding Daniel, calling him one of the greatest overseas players to grace county cricket. He saluted Daniel's fitness and longevity and suggested that those claiming players in the early 2020s play too much cricket need to have a rethink,

'There are not too many overseas signings in county cricket that have been better than Wayne. Malcolm Marshall, Michael Holding or maybe Courtney Walsh to be fair.

'Wayne was just, as Mike Smith nicknamed him, "The Diamond". He never got injured, always wanted to play and he was another one who hated losing.

'When kids talk about we play too much cricket these days, guys like Wayne, Malcolm Marshall and all these other guys, they always played and they never got injured. So, what are these guys talking about?'

Smith's nickname for Daniel stuck with everyone and was indicative of the key role the veteran opener played in helping the 20-year-old to settle quickly into life at Lord's. As Roland Butcher succinctly put it, the two men had 'chemistry'. The pair lived quite close together in north London, so were travel buddies to and from games, but many of those journeys didn't happen in a hurry.

Being married to the finest Jamaican woman there is, I know that culturally time can be something of an elastic concept – half her family were somewhat late for our wedding, even though she herself, with my full knowledge, arrived half an hour later than advertised.

However, in the case of Smith and Daniel, it was the former's somewhat bizarre driving ritual which meant the two travelled in their own sweet time. John Emburey explained:

'Mike used to drive Wayne everywhere because Mike lived in Enfield and Wayne lodged with a family nearby. Smudge [Smith] had this saying where if we were travelling after a match on a Tuesday night or a Friday night and we were going long-distance, he would as he used to put it, "never travel in the heat of the day". So he and Wayne would be in the Tavern having a drink and only once it started to get dark would they leave. It might be a three-hour drive or something going north, but they wouldn't go until it started to get dark.'

The 1977 season was in stark contrast to the one which had gone before. Gone were the sun-drenched days with temperatures in the 90s, arid conditions, dry grass and bare, cracked pitches.

In their place came rain, lots of rain, meaning grass-covered pitches – well, grass-covered whenever the heavens shut up long enough for the ground staff to get the covers off them.

Stormy weather was matched by turbulent events off the field as far as English cricket was concerned. The Test captain Tony Greig was sacked from his post shortly before the start of the Ashes when the British media broke stories showing him to have been a major recruiter of players for billionaire businessman Kerry Packer's upcoming cricket circus.

The impact on Middlesex as a county was seismic with the England selectors turning to Mike Brearley to fill the void for the battle with the Aussies.

In a season where conditions were tough for batters, Brearley's runs at the top of the order were missed whenever his country called, the absences made longer when he earned his first one-day international caps later in the summer. Whenever he did play for Middlesex he excelled while others struggled, averaging almost 70 with the help of three centuries.

Even more so than his runs, the astute, tactical leadership which had ended the trophy drought 12 months earlier was also missed. The contrast was indeed stark. All five County Championship defeats came while he was on international duty, making the defence of the title so much more difficult.

Veteran Smith was the man to take up the captaincy in Brearley's absence, and while he lost more than he won, the extra responsibility didn't affect his batting form as he topped the run-scoring charts, his tally of 1,226 bolstered by three centuries.

According to Emburey, Smith was the dressing room comedian and while he wasn't the most aesthetically pleasing player to watch, he was very effective at county level,

'Mike Smith was a character. He had all the chat, all the little one-liners. He was dry, but funny. Something would happen in the dressing room and he would say something, just out of the blue and everyone would laugh or smirk.

'He was a good player – very much an onside player. He would walk across his stumps and flick everything to leg.

'I remember one game we played Northamptonshire and it was right at the bottom of the square on the Tavern side. It was a 48-, 49-yard boundary and it had to be 50. We agreed to play, so Northamptonshire put all nine fielders on the leg side to protect the Tavern, knowing Smudge was a leg-side player anyway.

'Smudge was batting at the Nursery End and Sarfraz bowled the perfect ball which pitched middle, moved up the slope and ended up bowling him with no one on the off-side at all. Of course, everyone was laughing, Smudge made a funny quip as he walked in. He was a very funny person without him actually realising it.'

Norman Featherstone was the only other batter to make three figures for the Seaxes, but two others joined Smith in reaching 1,000 runs without the aid of a century. Gatting came of age that season, passing 50 on ten occasions, while the more experienced Radley clocked up eight half-centuries of his own.

Radley admitted that it was a year to implement some of the survival mentality he'd learned all those years ago from Titmus,

'There were two or three of us and I'm not excluding myself from this in that team who would look after ourselves without making it too obvious.

'I'd be making sure if there was some big quick bowler at the other end, I was leaning on my bat handle at the other. There were one or two others who were a bit like that, but if you are looking after yourself and getting plenty of runs then ultimately the team is benefitting.'

Radley's admission speaks echoes of a different era, one in which players were largely allowed to focus on their specialty and expected to deliver on it.

And in the case of Middlesex, it was a time when the policy was very much one of encouraging batters to score only enough to give the bowlers something to bowl at as they were the ones who would ultimately win the game, especially in an era of three-day Championship cricket where things had to unfold that much more quickly. According to Selvey, Radley was the master of knowing just how many runs were actually enough.

'It was a damp year, so for Clive to average 38 was pretty decent,' he said. 'Middlesex have always taken the view the job of the batters is to get you enough runs to bowl at. You don't win games of cricket by getting 550 and not being able to bowl the opposition out. You win by getting 300 and bowling them out for 299. And I think largely that is what pragmatists like Clive would do. They would understand that is the name of the game.

'Somebody like Clive was very good at understanding what a good total was. He would be "this is a 300 pitch" or "this is a 250 pitch". It is a great skill to have and that is why you had experienced players like that. Clive's currency was getting runs; my currency wasn't to get lower-order runs, my currency was to get wickets and everything else was a bonus.'

The wet weather dogged the cricket from the outset. The second day of the opening game with Surrey at The Oval was completely washed out, all but ruining hopes of a result. The frustration for Middlesex was their fast-bowling triumvirate of Selvey, Jones and now Daniel had routed the hosts for 93 on the opening day, Jones returning what would be a season's best 4-27.

Worse followed when rain meant only 41 overs were possible in the Seaxes' first game at Lord's against Kent, but these were enough to hint at the value of Daniel, who returned 3-15, and it soon became clear that his arrival had been timely with Jones increasingly stricken due to a back problem which would seriously restrict his game time. Whenever he did play, he did so having squeezed into a corset in a bid to limit his discomfort.

The weather gods relented sufficiently to allow Middlesex to chalk up a first win of the campaign, an innings success against Glamorgan in which Selvey took five wickets in the first innings and Daniel four in the second. And the potency of the new-ball pair was underlined again at Trent Bridge where Daniel took five in both innings and Selvey four, the hosts brushed aside for just 57 in their second dig as Middlesex won by an imposing 254 runs.

Gatting believed that the two pacemen dovetailed beautifully with Daniel charging in from one end and Selvey craftily bowling his away swingers from the other.

'Wayne without doubt was a hugely important part of our success,' he said. 'He was that guy who because of his pace and aggression would get people out. Then you would have guys like

Selvey at the other end who is swinging it and batters think "I'll have a go at that" and whoosh they get caught in the gully.

'So, although Wayne a lot of the time didn't get as many wickets as he should have, he got a lot for other people.

'He was a lovely man too. I don't think he was that mean on the pitch. He didn't say very much – he just ran in and bowled quick. And you knew if he was going to bowl quick at you the old knees would start going and you knew things were going to happen.'

Defeat to Kent at Hesketh Park stalled the early season momentum, but the response from Daniel was an emphatic one, an 11-wicket haul against Sussex at Hove getting him and his team-mates back to winning ways. The rain returned to ruin the clash with Hampshire at the United Services Ground in Portsmouth before the Middlesex batters ran into an inspired Mike Hendrick against Derbyshire at Ilkeston where they were skittled for 54 first time around and went on to lose by an innings.

Again though, the response to adversity was a strong one. Brearley returned from Test duty for the trip to Worcester and promptly made a daddy hundred, while seven wickets each for Daniel and Jones sealed an innings victory. Reports at the time suggested that Worcestershire's dressing room was sporting several walking wounded at the end of the drubbing, such was the hostility of Daniel's bowling.

Until this stage of the season, with seam bowling being the mode of choice, Philippe Edmonds had borne the brunt of spin bowling duties, assisted when necessary by Norman Featherstone.

Zambian-born Edmonds was a top quality left-arm spinner, an imposing presence and temperamentally challenging. With Brearley having encouraged a more united and open dressing room in which all voices were heard, Edmonds was without question his greatest challenge as Selvey explained,

'You could never really get on top of Philippe. Philippe was very much his own man. Brearley didn't operate as a captain in the way people outside might think he did. Brearley understood what his resource was and he was able to use that resource, but if you look, he always successfully captained a very good bowling side. With Middlesex he'd got me, Jonah [Jones], Philippe, Fred [Titmus], Daniel and Embers [John Emburey]. You don't lose control when you have got that. With England he'd got Beefy [Ian Botham], Bob [Willis] Chris Old and Mike Hendrick, so you've always got control.

'Young captains like Joe [Root], when he was in charge of England, tried to be really autocratic, but Mike wasn't like that. He trusted his bowlers to know what they wanted. So it wasn't a case of, "We'll go out into the field and have this, this and this." It was what you wanted and you would do it until something didn't work and then you'd collaborate.

'He'd say, "Why don't we try this?" and you might say yes or you might say no. Ultimately the bowler did pretty much what the bowler wanted because you have to be happy with how you do it. So, Mike wasn't a magician who moved people around magically or did that sort of thing. That's where he was very good for me, but where he fell out a bit with Philippe because sometimes they disagreed about things. For example, if he said to Philippe let's have a silly point, and Philippe said he didn't want one, if one was put there Philippe would bowl short and wide deliberately so silly point had to move again.

'They would have dressing-room arguments about stuff. It was quite an abrasive dressing room at times, certainly in the early '70s it was.'

As for Featherstone, with runs tough to come by on seaming pitches, he was more in the side for his batting in the middle order, any wickets in the first half of the campaign being a bonus.

Meanwhile, the obvious heir apparent to Titmus, one John Ernest Emburey, had been restricted to just a couple of cameo appearances, his batting not yet at the levels it would reach later on and so make him one of county cricket's most respected all-rounders.

'Embers hardly knew what end of the bat to hold back then,' ventured Gatting.

However, the increasing need for a second specialist spinner meant it was time for Emburey's emergence from the shadows.

Emburey was born in Peckham, not much more than a long stone's throw from The Oval, and so started his county career as a member of Surrey Young Cricketers in 1969 and 1970. He toured Canada with them in 1970 and spent the entire winter of 1970/71 training with the first and second XI at Crystal Palace in the hope of landing a contract with the south London county.

Surrey's coach at the time, Arthur McIntyre, recommended him for one, but his pleas fell on deaf ears and the recommendation was not pursued as too many others were ahead of him in the pecking order.

'It was a time when there wasn't much money in the game and you can bet if Surrey were feeling the pinch everybody else was too,' said Emburey.

'Surrey already had Pat Pocock and Intikhab Alam, plus Chris Waller and Geoff Howarth could also bowl off-breaks if needed.'

McIntyre suggested to Emburey that he might have more joy over the river with Middlesex, but the youngster's Peckham roots meant despite the rejection, his affections still lay with Surrey and he initially didn't pursue the matter.

Unbeknown to Emburey, however, McIntyre, not wanting to see a young cricketing talent wasted, contacted Don Bennett to put in a good word for him and ask if the off-spinner had been in touch. When he was told no, McIntyre passed on Emburey's address – amazing to think that under data protection rules today such a transfer of information couldn't have happened and Emburey might have been lost to the game. As it was, however, Emburey got a letter through the post from Bennett, inviting him down for a trial. The rest, as they say, is history.

Emburey reported for the trial where he bowled alongside the first and second XI. That led to a second XI game at the Crabble Ground in Dover, where Bob Woolmer was one of two victims at very small cost. Next time out he returned 5-80 against Hampshire which was enough to earn him a three-month contract to the end of that season.

'I was working for the Amalgamated Engineering Union at their head offices in Peckham in the finance department,' explained Emburey.

'I had to say to them, I'm playing these couple of matches and whatever, so I had to take holidays for those games I played.'

Emburey was offered either a one- or two-year contract at the end of the 1971 season, but it took some time for his registration to be switched from Surrey to Middlesex, one of the reasons why moves between counties were a much rarer event back then.

There were also far fewer opportunities to play the game abroad in the off-season at that time, so with contracts only running for the summer Emburey needed to find alternative employment from October through to the end of March. It would ultimately lead to an interesting association with a British gold medallist from the 1956 Olympics in Melbourne.

'The more established players went overseas,' Emburey said. 'A lot went down to South Africa, Australia wasn't as popular in those days, neither was New Zealand. It wasn't really until the late '70s that people started to go down to Australia and not South Africa.

'But in those early years I was living at home, so I had to find work. I gave Mum half my salary. At first I worked for Southwark Council in the rates department for a couple of years before I went to Lonsdale Sports in their shop in Brixton. The guy who ran the shop was Terry Spinks, who was a boxer, a little flyweight.

'He was an East Ender, very Cockney and whatever, but he was only a tiny little bloke. I worked with him and his wife Valerie in the shop. He won a gold medal at the 1956 Olympics. Terry was good because Brixton was pretty rough in those days. There were a lot of racial issues in the early '70s.

'Lonsdale was very much boxing, so we used to do the gowns, the shorts, the tops for all the clubs. I used to go along when they had professional fights where Lonsdale had their posts in the corner. So I used to help them erecting some of the rings for some of the fights in hotels down Park Lane, the West End or whatever. I did that for a couple of years.'

The continuing presence of the legendary Titmus limited Emburey's opportunities at first, meaning he spent effectively five to six years serving a cricketing apprenticeship in the second XI or the under-25s as it was termed then.

A team which included the likes of Gatting, Roland Butcher, Ian Gould and others was very successful, but in any event Emburey doesn't resent his time in the shadows, learning tricks of the trade and preparing himself for what would be a tough first XI dressing room. It's a grounding he feels players miss out on today by their insistence on county hopping if they're not a regular by the age of 20 or 21.

'I had six years more or less in the second XI and it was very much an apprenticeship because Fred was still a crackerjack bowler,' he said. 'So, although I played the occasional game from 1973 onwards I probably played two or three in 1973, two or three in 1974, a couple in 1975, and in 1976 when we won the Championship I played four. And then 11 or something like that the following year.

'Young players have got no patience nowadays. They think at the age of 19, 20 they've done it and they want to play. If not, they look to go somewhere else. We served an apprenticeship in the second XI. You learned about bowling on wet wickets, drying wickets. You learned to bowl at different speeds because of that as well and you played on good pitches in good weather when it warmed up a little bit.'

There was, as Emburey has alluded to, the odd chance to shine in the first XI, with his Championship debut coming against Derbyshire at Buxton in 1973. A long tidy bowl in the first innings brought no tangible reward, but his maiden Championship wicket arrived second time around when he castled legendary wicketkeeper Bob Taylor, who'd been serving as nightwatchman. Two more victims, Fred Swarbrook and veteran Indian spinner Venkat, left him with tidy figures of 21-6-50-3 – a solid day's work.

He returned to the second XI only for another opportunity to present itself, suddenly and unexpectedly. A phone call from Bennett out of the blue in the middle of a second XI fixture told Emburey that Titmus was struggling with a knee problem and that he should get himself down to the Crabble Ground at Dover to face Kent.

Emburey advised that he would have to return to London to get some fresh kit and that he would catch the early train from London Bridge to Dover on the day of the game.

True to his word, Emburey picked up the required kit and was on the train from London Bridge as planned the next morning. All was well until it pulled in at Rochester. Emburey took up the sorry tale,

'We got to Rochester where I was in the back half of the train and in those days it split. We were sitting in the station for 20 minutes, so I put my head out and said to the guard, "When does the train go on to Dover?" He said, "The front half of this train went to Dover 20 minutes ago!"'

Now in a blind panic, Emburey leapt off the train, raced up and down the stairs out of the station and hailed a cab to cover the rest of the journey. He recalled that it cost him £12, a considerable sum for any cricketer at that time, never mind one trying to make his way in the game. However, if he thought his troubles were over, he would be wrong as his cab driver got lost on the way to the coastal ground.

'The games started at 11.30am in those days and by the time I got to the ground it was 11.05 and Mike Denness and Mike Brearley were walking off the field having done the toss,' recalled a rueful-sounding Emburey.

He knew that meant team sheets had been exchanged and that his name would not be on them as he'd arrived too late. His absence meant that Titmus had to play, injury or not.

'I got the biggest bollocking from all the senior players,' Emburey said, and the punishment didn't stop there.

'The dressing rooms were at ground level, but the dining area was three-quarters of the way up a huge slope, so the senior players had me running up and down that all day, getting this and getting that.

'That's what turned me off ever being 12th man again because it's a thankless task and in those days it wasn't even a big job like it is now, where whoever it is runs on with drinks every five minutes.'

Suitably chastened by his experience, Emburey tried to make the most of the few opportunities which presented themselves over the next two seasons, Titmus's longevity and survival skills largely keeping him at bay.

The two off-spinners only played together a few times and while Titmus was never strictly speaking a mentor, Emburey did glean a few lessons from the elder statesman, most of them learned the hard way.

'To be honest, Fred was very frugal with any advice,' he said. 'He didn't say much, you had to go to him, but even then he didn't really give too much away. When I played a couple of games with him in 1974 and 1975, then he would help me. If a batsman came in he would perhaps say this guy will look to hit you over the top straight away, so have a man back, but Mike Brearley as captain always wanted to attack and not be seen to be defensive.

'So, I'd end up having to go along with the captain and of course the guy would come down, hit me over the top and then we'd put a fielder back. I'd look at Fred and he'd just shrug his shoulders and say, "Told you."

'These were little things you'd pick up and they were part of your knowledge-building. From the first game where you face certain players you learn how they play.

'Then when you'd see them for years after you'd know what their strengths were, where they are looking to hit you and you would bowl accordingly. It takes a long time to build up that knowledge and gain the experience.

'It stood me in good stead and I never, ever forgot that advice from Fred. So he was good in some ways when we were on the field, but trying to get other information when we were off it wasn't so easy, possibly because he wasn't a great communicator to other people, particularly young players.'

There was one other gem Emburey managed to extract from Titmus, which perhaps explains the frugal bowler he would become over the next two decades in a Middlesex shirt,

'One thing Fred always said to me was, "What's a batsman's job?" I would reply, "To score runs."

Then he'd say, "What's a bowler's job?" and I'd reply, "To take wickets." He'd say, "No, it's to stop him scoring runs. If you stop him scoring runs, it's not going to hurt your figures, you'll put him under pressure and make him make a mistake.

'Good balls are always going to be good balls, but if you stop him scoring runs, he is going to give something away."'

A couple of wickets in a win over Nottinghamshire at Lord's were merely a prelude to a stint of 32-10-82-5 in the second innings of the following game against Yorkshire at Lord's. Emburey's victims included all of Yorkshire's much-vaunted top four, namely Geoffrey Boycott, Barrie Leadbeater, Jim Love and Jackie Hampshire – a pretty auspicious quartet. His efforts threatened to secure a final-day victory before the White Rose county clung on for a draw.

The five-wicket haul proved to be the first fruits of an incredible second half of the season for the 24-year-old. Seven more hauls of five or more followed and twice he took ten or more in the match as he raced to 68 wickets in what was really his first proper season of first XI cricket. Amazingly, Emburey confessed to having 'no memory' of the 12 wickets – six in each innings – against Essex at Lord's, or the 11 taken in a losing cause against Northamptonshire. His final tally was just four shy of the much more experienced Edmonds.

Selvey, like Edmonds, would finish with 72 Championship wickets, one more than Daniel, meaning Middlesex's four principal bowlers had in excess of 280 wickets between them. Bowler's season or not, that is some feat.

For all that, there is much discussion about whether Middlesex's success that year was a lucky one, certainly the luckiest of the 13 titles won to date. The debate is not without some basis.

The other two protagonists in the title race can justifiably claim that the weather gods were crueller to them than their London rivals. Gloucestershire lost two matches altogether to the weather and in a time where nothing was awarded for a draw that meant no points. Kent lost one in that fashion, and Middlesex none.

However, Middlesex's players from that era can themselves point to games where they fell agonisingly short of victory, others decimated by rain where points won were consequently thin on the ground and still more where human error or rules threatened to tell against them.

In the first category was a run chase against Essex at Southend which finished with them six short and eight wickets down. If that game had drama, the next against fellow title chasers Gloucestershire had all of that and controversy to add.

Middlesex dominated the early exchanges, Brearley hitting 145 and Gatting 79 as the hosts posted 343-6 before declaring with one ball of their innings still available.

Spin twins Edmonds and Emburey then got to work, the former dismissing Pakistani great Zaheer Abbas and heralded South African all-rounder Mike Procter, both for nought in figures of 6-18.

Only another Pakistani legend, Sadiq Mohammed, put up any prolonged resistance, but Emburey had him taken by Radley at slip for 32 as the west countrymen were hustled out for just 80 and forced to follow on.

Thanks to Mohammed (82) and redoubtable wicketkeeper and fellow opener Andy Stovold (81), Gloucestershire fared much better second time around, reaching 270-4 and seven in front with time running out.

However, Edmonds induced a collapse, returning career-best figures at that time of 8-132 as the visitors capitulated to 337 all out.

It was at this juncture a miscalculation would prove costly to Brearley's men, with the two umpires, Bill Alley and Jack van Geloven, the latter in his first year standing in county cricket at the heart of the drama.

The calculation was 75 off 12 overs – a task which would be routine these days even in a red-ball fixture, but back then it was quite an ask. Only later would it transpire that it should have been 75 from 13. Smith with 22 and Gatting's unbeaten 21 took up the challenge, but they reached 63-7 when the teams shook hands on a draw with one ball left.

'We were deprived of one over in a run chase where one more would have given us a chance of winning the game,' remembered Selvey, dolefully.

'It was to do with the regulations and when the last over should be started and Bill Alley got it wrong.'

Emburey's 12 wickets sealed the win against Essex at Lord's before another remarkable game with Yorkshire up at Abbeydale Park in Sheffield which in its turn played a key part in the destiny of the title.

They arrived at the ground on the first morning to find a pitch that Selvey termed as 'nasty', which translated meant quick and with variable bounce from the off.

Working on the theory that the pitch would deteriorate, stand-in skipper Smith chose to bat first and thanks to a typically pugnacious 57 from Gatting and 20s from Radley and Gould, the visitors clawed their way to 181.

'Wayne and to a certain degree myself then battered Yorkshire,' recalled Selvey.

'I broke Richard Lumb's fingers and Wayne struck Jackie Hampshire on the point of the elbow before breaking Arnie Sidebottom's arm.'

Hampshire and Sidebottom took no further part in the match and while Lumb returned to the crease at the tail end of the Yorkshire innings and batted in the middle order in the second, he was seriously restricted.

Despite these wounds Yorkshire, thanks to 50 from David Bairstow, were only 18 in arrears on first innings, leaving everything to play for.

In the event it was Smith who emerged to play a dazzling match-winning hand with an innings of 141, far beyond anything any other batter had achieved.

His Herculean effort lifted Middlesex to 310-9 declared, which proved well beyond the reach of the depleted Tykes.

'What Mike did in that game was stay leg-side of the ball and smack it through the off-side whereas the tough Yorkies got in line and got hit,' said Selvey.

Among the victory celebrations that night was a sting in the tail, one which had an impact on the title race as Selvey explained,

'The upshot was although Yorkshire were all out in their first innings, we didn't get full bowling points because "retired hurt" didn't count as a dismissal or a wicket. So, we were deprived of a bonus point there.'

Defeat to Leicestershire at Grace Road followed before, back in London, the weather intruded again, proving the catalyst to an extraordinary sequence of events in the clash with rivals Surrey at Lord's.

Rain washed out the opening day and continued to fall on the second morning too. Rules of the competition at the time stated if there was no play before 4pm on the second day, the game would revert to a one-innings affair with 12 points for the win and all bonus points scrapped. Therefore both sides began preparing themselves for the one-innings shoot-out.

However, matters took a turn when umpires Eddie Phillipson and Jack van Geloven deemed conditions fit for play to commence shortly before the 4pm cut-off point, thus rendering the contest a two-innings match once more.

Daniel quickly had Alan Butcher caught behind for one as Surrey got to the interval at 8-1, only for the heavens to open once more and wash out any further play.

It meant the title contenders seemingly faced the worst of both worlds, a two-innings match with time running out and a result looking beyond their reach.

Selvey, who commuted to and from his home in Milton Keynes every day, left the ground that second evening feeling disconsolate, but en route to Lord's the next day his mindset changed dramatically.

'I remember standing on the platform at Wolverton Station, which was where I travelled from as Milton Keynes itself didn't have a station in those days, on the third morning thinking, "I know how we can win this game,"' he recalled.

'I don't know if others were thinking the same as me, but I came in the dressing room and said, "I know how we can win this game. Wayne and I bowl them out, we declare, we bowl them out again and knock them off." That's genuinely what I said and it's pretty much what happened.'

The plan was adopted and part one executed to perfection as the brown hatters were routed for 49, Daniel taking 5-16, Selvey 3-29 and Gatting, who in those days often had to be cajoled to turn his arm over, returning 2-2.

Off the field, however, Middlesex's attempts to speed up the game met with resistance from those in authority. A hurriedly arranged phone call to the Test & County Cricket Board – as it was back then – was arranged between the innings to try and advance the game even more quickly, as John Emburey explained,

'We said we have lost all this time, we've bowled a side out cheaply, we want to move on quickly, can we forfeit our first innings?'

The right of a side to forfeit an innings didn't come into cricket's 'Bible' until a few years later, however, meaning Middlesex's plea to exercise ingenuity fell on deaf ears as they were told in no uncertain terms they had to 'go out and bat'.

Maybe it was Brearley's progressive thinking or something else, but, undeterred, Middlesex hatched another plot. Emburey was padded up and asked to go out and face the first ball of the innings with Brearley up at the non-striker's end. The still very much novice batter took an almighty swipe at the delivery from Robin Jackman and missed, the ball sailing through to the keeper. As it turned out it was a free hit as Brearley, having satisfied the wishes of the powers that be, promptly declared at 0-0 after that one ball, sending Surrey back out to bat.

Surrey were quickly in disarray once more, Daniel and Selvey tearing into the top order to reduce them to 59-8.

'It was Monte Lynch's second ever game for Surrey and his first ever at Lord's and he got a pair before lunch,' quipped Selvey.

Only a few blows from former England seamer Geoff Arnold got Surrey to 89 before Middlesex chased down the target of 139 with 11 balls to spare, thanks to a century opening stand between Brearley (66 not out) and Smith (51).

What had looked a disastrous turn of events 24 hours earlier had played out to Middlesex's advantage as they'd got 12 points for the win and four bowling points to boot.

Fearsome pace bowler Wayne Daniel in delivery stride.

Middlesex v Surrey scorecard – Daniel's nine wickets helped secure an unlikely win.

Defeat to Warwickshire where they just failed to chase down a target of 305 in two hours and 40 minutes, and a further stumble at Northamptonshire stalled progress once more, but in the meantime Brearley's men, having succumbed to Gloucestershire in the quarter-final of the Benson & Hedges Cup, were on the verge of another final in the Gillette 60-over competition. Somerset stood between them and a place at Lord's and once again events had ramifications for the County Championship race.

The wet weather had returned with a vengeance by mid-August and torrential rain fell throughout the three days allocated for the contest, so much so that it was abandoned without a coin toss having ever been made.

The Cidermen were due back in London for a County Championship fixture starting the following week, but with the question of who would face Glamorgan in the Gillette showpiece still unresolved, the Test & County Cricket Board decreed the one-day fixture should take precedence, hence the Championship game was deferred to a later date.

The rain continued to fall, however, threatening to scupper the newly devised plan. The first two days allocated for the match were again washed out and only late on the third day did umpires Alley and Ken Palmer consider conditions fit for play.

A 15-over game was declared and with no restriction on the number of overs any one bowler could bowl, Middlesex had the good fortune to win the toss, whereupon Daniel and Selvey promptly bowled out the west countrymen for only 59.

Despite four wickets for 'Big Bird' Joel Garner, Middlesex knocked off the runs to claim their date with Glamorgan at Lord's, but in the meanwhile their rivals for the County Championship, Gloucestershire and Kent, were quietly, or perhaps not so quietly, seething.

It's not hard to spot the cause of their ire. They realised along with everyone else that, had the Championship fixture gone ahead at its originally scheduled time, it would have been all but washed out, leaving the men from north of the river with no points.

The rearranged game became the penultimate three-day fixture of the season and because of preparations having to be made for the showpiece one-day final at Lord's, the clash took place in the unfamiliar setting of Chelmsford.

The rain had travelled eastwards to greet both sets of players and restricted play on the first day. Middlesex eventually bowled out their rivals on day two and by stumps, thanks to Radley's season's best of 85, they were 38 in front with two first-innings wickets standing.

Hopes of manufacturing a result via some creative declarations were thwarted, however, as the inclement weather prevented a ball being bowled on the final day. Nevertheless, Middlesex gleaned seven points from the encounter, much to the frustration of their title challengers.

'It rankled with some sides,' admitted Selvey.

From Chelmsford, Brearley and his team headed straight to Lord's for the Gillette final due to begin the following morning, a few prayers being offered that the weather gods wouldn't spoil the showpiece.

Unlike the finals of two years previously, the toss favoured Middlesex and they had no hesitation in fielding first.

For once Daniel was not at his best but Selvey, as in the 1975 final, was almost impossible to get away, picking up the wickets of opener Alan Jones and the dangerous Collis King for a measly 22 runs in his full 12 overs, six of which came in one big hit from Mike Llewellyn. He admitted that it got him a reputation no one would want in today's modern game.

'Gatt once wrote a book about one-day cricket where he described me as the master of the defensive new-ball spell which would be an anathema now,' said Selvey. 'I used to bowl eight overs straight through at the start of a John Player League game because you would put the opposition behind the game – that's how it was then.'

Llewellyn gave some substance to the Welsh county's effort with 62, but with Edmonds in frugal mood (2-23) and three late wickets for Featherstone, Middlesex restricted them to 177-9.

The target was modest even back then, but Middlesex made the worst possible start with Brearley caught behind to the first ball of their reply, bowled by Malcolm Nash. Legend has it the dismissal caused a commotion in the Middlesex dressing room as the next man in, Radley, had to be summoned from the toilets with trousers around his ankles, albeit padded up.

Having to literally gather himself together in somewhat of a hurry may go some way towards explaining why, at the start of Nash's next over, Radley felt for one outside the off stump, nicking it straight to King at second slip, but as fate would have it the chance went straight in the West Indian's hands and out again. Glamorgan's players and fans probably suspected then that they had witnessed the pivotal moment of the match – and so it proved. Radley, in his typically unflustered way, went on to take the player of the match honours with the decisive knock of 85 not out. It was the first, but by no means the last time he would take centre stage in a showpiece domestic occasion.

Celebrations were muted as John Player League commitments less than 24 hours later meant that Middlesex had to head straight off to Maidstone to face Kent, where they chased down 207 with ten balls to spare to take third in the league that year.

The biggest challenge still remained however as the last round of County Championship matches got under way with three sides still in the hunt.

Gloucestershire, despite their two games lost to rain, led the way with 216 points, five ahead of both Middlesex and Kent. The leaders were the only team with home advantage as they entertained Hampshire at Bristol. The chasers were on their travels, Kent to Edgbaston to meet Warwickshire, while Middlesex headed north-west to Blackpool to face Lancashire.

There was drama ahead of the game when initially no stumps could be located. It prompted Lancashire captain David Lloyd, latterly of Sky Sports commentary fame, to visit the away dressing room and quip something to the effect of, 'Don't worry boys, we'll just put a couple of jumpers down.' Wrong sport, surely?

Stumps were fortunately and eventually located it soon became clear that this was to be a match for spinners. Despite this the hosts opted to bowl first and only Gatting with 50, during which he passed 1,000 Championship runs for the season for the first time, held up the bowlers for too long.

At 127-9 the visitors were struggling for a precious batting point as last man Daniel joined Selvey. The former began swinging the willow to good effect and they were within two runs of said bonus point when the cricket gods turned against them.

'Flat' Jack Simmons bowled a roundhouse swinger to Selvey, who saw it as a chance to turn the ball down to fine leg for one, or even the two runs needed. He missed it and to his horror the next thing he saw was the umpire's raised finger, giving him out lbw to a ball down the leg-side. You could tell by his tone when we spoke that the intervening half a century had done little to cool his fury.

'There was no way on God's earth he should have given me out lbw but he did,' Selvey said exasperatedly. 'It was a weird, weird season.'

There weren't many to defend, but Edmonds showed all his craft to claim six wickets as the hosts were rolled over for 108 by early on the second morning.

Half-centuries for Radley and Gatting then meant Middlesex could declare early on the third day, setting Lancashire 278 to win, and with Emburey stepping forward to claim a six-wicket haul the victory was wrapped up with time to spare.

Strangely, with the other two games still in progress, the Middlesex boys set off for home with no idea whether they would be champions or not. Their route took them past Birmingham where they somehow gleaned that Kent had won, taking 16 points to finish level with the Seaxes.

News eventually came through that Gloucestershire had lost, a brilliant 94 from Gordon Greenidge helping Hampshire reach a victory target of 271.

They therefore missed out, leaving Middlesex and Kent to share the spoils, only the third time in the competition's history that there had been such an occurrence, two of course having involved Middlesex.

It seems incredible to think of a sporting team not celebrating such an achievement, but this – like almost all Middlesex's triumphs of that era – was won on the road, mainly due to the Gillette final being the season finale at Lord's.

These were different times. Winter beckoned and other jobs awaited.

'I can't even remember how I heard the Championship had finished in a tie,' concluded Selvey.

'We had homes to go to and it was a long way back from Blackpool, but it would be unheard of now not to celebrate together.'

There would be no hat-trick of wins in 1978 and in fact, there would be a few bumps in the road before Middlesex's golden era could resume.

CHAPTER 6
1980

Mike Gatting, 'It was a fantastic team. We did have a team to win all four competitions and at one stage I think we were very close to doing that, but we won two instead.' Mike Selvey, 'In 1980 we kind of felt we should have run away with everything because we had a great bowling attack.' The two quotes above both reflect a mixture of emotions on the part of speakers, Selvey and Gatting.

On the one hand they reflect on arguably the greatest year in Middlesex's history. A team, certainly a bowling attack in Wayne Daniel, Vintcent van der Bijl, Mike Selvey, John Emburey and Phil Edmonds to compare with the great Surrey and Yorkshire sides of yesteryear.

However, listen closely and you can definitely detect a sense that, never mind greatness, they had in fact glimpsed cricketing immortality only for it to in the end remain elusive.

Certainly there would be plenty to celebrate. A third County Championship in the space of five years and a Gillette Cup to go with it, both won as autumn began to draw her veil over another English summer.

However, it could indeed have been so much more. An unprecedented quadruple and a clean sweep of domestic silverware looked at one stage very much on, but the cricket gods would prove something of a divine tease as some prizes slipped away.

A Benson & Hedges Cup quarter-final that Middlesex looked to have control of was not so much wrestled from their grasp as cast aside with victory in sight, and a mid-season slump in the John Player League left them with just too much ground to make up. A case of so nearly, yet not quite.

Yet we are running ahead of ourselves, so first let us retrace our steps to the aftermath of 1977.

The following summer witnessed an excellent defence of the title in which Middlesex scored 255 points, 28 more than the previous year's triumph. There was one more win than the previous summer, ten as opposed to nine, and more batting and bowling points were accrued, yet they finished third behind Essex and Kent, who having been forced to share the spoils with the north Londoners the year before took them outright.

It was the start of the campaign which would cost Mike Brearley and company with only two wins and four defeats coming in the first nine games. Thereafter eight victories allowed them to surge up the standings, albeit a little too late.

If 1978 could be regarded as a stout if ultimately unsuccessful defence of their crown, 1979 was little short of calamitous. At one stage they were rock bottom and looked destined for the wooden spoon. Three wins in quick succession raised hopes of respectability, but these faded as quickly as they had appeared as none of the last five games were won and they trailed in 14th in the standings.

Against that, there was some joy in the shorter formats. Middlesex were fourth in the John Player League and reached the semis and quarter-finals of the Gillette and Benson & Hedges cups respectively. That said, both those knockout games ended in heavy defeats after horror-story displays with the bat.

Such a decline was both dramatic and unexpected, but there were some mitigating factors, most significant of which perhaps being the absence of Brearley for swathes of both the 1978 and 1979 campaigns on Test duty and in the case of the latter season the 1979 Prudential World Cup. In the former of the two seasons he played nine of 22 County Championship fixtures, while amid Middlesex's travails in 1979 he played only eight. To lose someone of such a standard of leadership – never mind his weight of Championship runs – for an extended period was quite a burden to bear.

Philippe Edmonds and Mike Gatting were also members of the World Cup squad, while the former was a key member of the subsequent Test series against India, so missed over half of the County Championship fixtures.

Whatever the mitigating circumstances, it was clear some changes were needed ahead of the 1980 campaign, as Brearley recorded in the club's minute book for that season, 'There was much to put right and I was able to give the committee assurance that I was wholly committed to the job. I decided to start the season with a clear framework of discipline and routine. I ran the nets myself and intervened more with comments on technique and insisted on punctuality. We had fielding and warming up sessions before each day's play in the first few weeks of the season and talks about the opposition before each match.'

It's interesting to see Brearley's plans written down in this way, not least because in the modern era all such things would be considered sacrosanct or fundamental to a team's preparation. Most counties in recent years have had players back in for training from November onwards – those not involved in international or franchise cricket overseas anyway. However, as we've alluded to previously, 40-odd years earlier cricket was still in an era of summer contracts where players had winter jobs, so extra preparations meant additional time commitments.

In terms of personnel changes since the 1977 success, Norman 'Smokey' Featherstone's 11-year stay at Lord's came to an end in 1979 as he headed west to join Glamorgan, putting more pressure on the Middlesex middle order and depriving them of his more than useful off-spin.

However, ahead of the start of the season, Don Bennett, Brearley and the club had a more pressing matter at hand – or at least so they thought. Wayne Daniel was expected to be named in the West Indies' tour party to England that summer, making the need for a replacement urgent. The man coach and captain alighted on to fill the void was the giant South African Vintcent van der Bijl.

Standing almost 6ft 8in, Van der Bijl had been a keen rugby player and shot putter in his youth, but settled on cricket as his number one sporting passion after meeting former South African Test star Trevor Goddard while at university.

Financial considerations meant his cricket appearances for Natal had to be fitted in around his professional careers, first as a schoolmaster and then at the paper firm Wiggins Teape.

Nevertheless, he was the *South African Cricket Annual's* Cricketer of the Year in 1971, such was the devilry of his medium-quick bowling coming down at the batter from a height in excess of nine feet. His figures in Currie Cup cricket compare with greats like Procter and he could also employ his long levers to good effect with willow in hand, so was a fearsome striker of a ball.

'We'd heard about Vintcent and I'd heard about him a lot because I'd been coaching out in South Africa from 1965 to '75,' ventured Clive Radley. 'I'd seen him on the scene and he was clearly a phenomenon, a freak. I believe he'd got 330 wickets in Currie Cup cricket at about 14 apiece – something like that.'

Talks were had and Van der Bijl's services were secured. Daniel void filled, thought those in charge, except in the end there was no void anyway as to Middlesex's surprise and no doubt Daniel's disappointment he wasn't selected by the West Indies after all. From a Middlesex perspective it meant that all of a sudden it wasn't a matter of either/or, but both/and. The men of Lord's suddenly had arguably the most fearsome new-ball pairing, certainly in the club's history and maybe that of the County Championship too.

Van der Bijl, however, had never played outside of South Africa and knew nothing of English conditions, so how would he make the adjustment? A solitary wicket in a pre-season match against Lincolnshire suggested he might need a bedding-in period and according to Radley, the right-arm bowler was 'panicking a bit' in the wake of the warm-up game. However, with his skillset and sheer physical presence it wasn't long before batters were falling victim to his wiles with monotonous regularity.

'I can't think of any medium to fast bowlers better than him ever and we didn't even see the best of Vince,' offered Roland Butcher. 'We saw him at the end of his career and he was still unbelievable. Vintcent was a huge man in every sense of the word. He was a big guy and tall, but again another guy, although at an advanced stage of his career, you could just give him the ball and he would bowl and bowl and bowl and he got the results. Great competitor with a huge desire to win. He was magnificent, there's no question about that. He only lasted one year, but that was the best year, no doubt about it.'

Nottinghamshire were the first to face the new-ball threat of Daniel and Van der Bijl, and while the loss of all but 75 minutes of the opening day of the season led to an inevitable draw, both took four wickets each to serve notice of what was to come. And there were four more apiece against Lancashire next time out at Lord's though the visitors, aided by some bad light on the final day, batted out for a draw. Brearley made the first of his five Championship centuries in this game, in a year where he would be Middlesex's leading run-scorer. Middlesex's first competitive win of the season came in their John Player League game with the Red Rose county over that same weekend, the hosts squeezing home in a high-scoring encounter by seven runs thanks to 70s for Radley and Graham Barlow and three wickets for Mike Gatting. This was the first of six wins in a row to open up their JPL campaign.

Middlesex largely breezed through their Benson & Hedges Cup group over the following couple of weeks to maintain their interest in all four competitions, the one exception being a thriller against Somerset. Middlesex posted 282 thanks to 90s from Barlow and Gatting, but a century from Indian legend Sunil Gavaskar saw Somerset apparently coasting to victory at 217-1. However, Phil Edmonds returned to have Gavaskar stumped as he took three wickets in a hurry as well as catching the dangerous Ian Botham off Mike Selvey's bowling. This set up a dramatic finish in which two run outs allowed Middlesex to win by one run.

The return to Championship cricket brought the first win in that competition and an emphatic one at that as Sussex were beaten by an innings. The fearsome power of Middlesex's speedsters was seen as Sussex wicketkeeper Arnold Long was put out of the match after being struck on the head by Daniel while batting in the first innings. Peter Graves, meanwhile, cracked a finger after being hit on it twice, first by the Barbadian and then shortly afterwards by Van der Bijl.

Credit though went to Barlow for his 128, while Radley fell three short of a century.

They, along with Gatting, Brearley, Butcher and Paul Downton – more of whom shortly – would average over 40 in 1980, with the captain and senior pro Radley topping 1,000 runs. Butcher said that level of reliability played its part in giving their peerless bowling attack a bank of runs to play with.

'The batters did their job,' he added. 'For six to average 40-plus is excellent and shows that there was no over-reliance on one or two players. And it meant whatever situation we got into, somebody would put their hand up and do the job. That was a really good thing for us that runs came from many corners.'

Radley would star again with a century in the draw with Worcester, Middlesex batting themselves out of trouble on the final morning before just coming up short in their bid to bowl the Pears out for a second time.

What proved a career-best 4-24 for Bill Merry, in a game sat out by Daniel, was enough to see off Somerset with some comfort before a crucial meeting with Surrey took place at Lord's.

The Brown Hats would prove to be Middlesex's closest challengers in the title race, but they were swept aside thanks to a fourth-wicket stand between Radley and Gatting of 248, which helped secure a lead of almost 300. The spin twins Emburey and Edmonds wrapped up an innings win giving Middlesex 20 points to Surrey's two. The winning margin at the end of the season would be 13 points, so showing the true value of this result.

The draw with Yorkshire witnessed pretty much Groundhog Day as Radley made 136 for the second game running and shared another monster stand with Gatting, who clocked up 110. However, the match was petering out into a draw long before rain brought an early finish.

Safe passage to the Benson & Hedges Cup semi-final was secured at the expense of Sussex, before the reverse Championship fixture with Surrey at The Oval ended in a draw. There was a little bit of niggle between the captains when Brearley, feeling his opposite number Roger Knight should have declared Surrey's first innings earlier to give both sides the chance of a win, forfeited Middlesex's second innings, forcing Surrey to come out and bat for the last eight overs. Knight suggested afterwards that Brearley's actions had been 'churlish', or words to that effect.

When Van der Bijl's eight wickets in the match helped beat Essex by eight wickets, Middlesex had reached mid-summer day unbeaten in all competitions. However, their aura of invincibility was about to be shattered by a form blip which ended their hopes of all four trophies.

A dramatic collapse with victory in sight meant they lost their B & H semi-final to Northamptonshire by 11 runs, despite a valiant 91 from Gatting, and a belligerent hundred from Warwickshire wicketkeeper Geoff Humpage ended their unbeaten run in the John Player League too. It was the first of five defeats in the next six Sunday clashes, the other being abandoned, which ultimately cost them the title.

The dip in fortunes might have extended to an embarrassing exit at the hands of Ireland in the first round of the Gillette Cup had it not been for a virtuoso performance from Van der Bijl. He was at his best with ball in hand, returning 5-12 in the best part of 11 overs as the visitors were rolled over for 102.

However, what should have been a routine chase got a little sticky as Middlesex slumped to 67-5. Only Barlow of the top order remained and he compiled a patient unbeaten 39, while Van der Bijl clubbed 25 in quick time to save his side's blushes.

There were as always contributory factors behind the slump. Brearley's captain's report to the committee recorded, 'We lost John Emburey and Mike Gatting to England and crucially, Phil Edmonds suffered a knee injury from which he never fully recovered. Therefore for much of the time we were without our two spinners, both high-class bowlers.'

Even back in the Championship, Brearley's side were not quite themselves for a while. Barlow made a fine century but Edmonds's absence was keenly felt as Middlesex narrowly failed to bowl Warwickshire out on the final day of a rain-affected match at Edgbaston. The left-arm spinner returned for the game with Northamptonshire at Lord's but rain, which arrived part way through the second day, washed out day three altogether.

It had been an uncomfortable two weeks on the field and it would take some extraordinary batting from Roland Butcher to change the fortunes of the Seaxes against Hampshire at Lord's. This was another game that the weather looked to have ruined with no play possible on the opening day. By the end of the second the hosts were 87-4 in their first innings, trailing by 128.

Typically, Brearley opted to give the match a chance of life, declaring first thing on the third morning and Hampshire entered into the spirit, making quick runs before leaving Middlesex a target of 296 against the clock.

Brearley, who had been forced to retire hurt in the first innings after being hit on the head, opened as normal second time around. Would concussion protocols allow such an eventuality now? However, he failed and the target was looking out of reach when Butcher strolled out to join Radley at 54-3.

What followed from Middlesex's middle-order enforcer was what *Wisden* termed as an innings of 'unusual violence'. Butcher sent the members scattering for cover more than once as he cleared the ropes with regularity. He and Radley added 177 for the fourth wicket, after which wicketkeeper Ian Gould proved a good foil for Butcher's explosive hitting.

Butcher produced nine sixes in all and though he lost Gould just short of the target, the hosts scampered home by five wickets. His tally of 153 not out was his career best at that time, but it wouldn't stand for long – only 12 days in fact, by which time Middlesex had sped up the M1 to Scarborough to face Yorkshire.

Again Middlesex were in early trouble at 64-3, but Butcher, adrenaline still apparently coursing through his veins after his Lord's effort, flayed the home attack to the tune of 179 to rewrite his personal stat book once again. It lifted the visitors to 391 and Mike Selvey's four wickets pressed home the advantage, forcing Yorkshire to follow on. David Bairstow took a leaf out of Butcher's book with a thrilling 145, Daniel in particular on the receiving end of the onslaught, but Brearley's men knocked off the 98 needed with few alarms.

Butcher's big hitting and fast scoring had come to the attention of the England selectors and within a month he was making his one-day international debut against Australia at Edgbaston. He made a good first impression with 52 made in 38 balls, yet he revealed that he was almost the last to know of his call-up,

'Back in those days, communication I guess between administration and players was not perhaps as good as it should have been. In my case the way I found out was quite strange actually.

'I got a call from my wife. I was at Lord's training because we had a match coming up. She gave me a call around 1pm to say, "Is it true that you've been selected for England?" I said to her, "I've no idea. As you know I'm training, we've just finished practice and I'm going to lunch, nobody has said anything to me, so I have no idea."

'She told me, "Well, my boss heard it on the news, on the radio."

'I felt that was strange because if it was the case someone at Lord's would have told me what was happening.

'So, I forgot about it, got home in the evening about 6pm and my father called and asked the same question and I told him, "Well, not as far as I know, nobody has told me anything."

'It was not until about nine O'clock when the news came on the TV and there it was on the news. So, that was the first I knew about it. Nobody had been in touch to say, "You have been selected."'

This in turn would lead to Butcher's historic selection for the tour to the West Indies in the winter of 1980/81 where again lines of communication were far from ideal and he was on the other side of the Atlantic when a sports hack tracked him down to break the news.

'The season finished and I then took a break with my family and went to Canada to stay with my cousin. I didn't leave any forwarding address or numbers or anything like that. I just took a break.

'I was at my cousin's house one day when the phone rang and she said, "It's for you." I said, "But I haven't given this number to anyone. Who are they and how did they know I was here?" But on the phone was a reporter from England saying I'd been selected to go on the tour to the West Indies.

'I thought, no one has been in touch with me and they wouldn't know how to get in touch with me anyway, but this reporter had managed to track me down in Canada to tell me I had been selected.'

Initially, the news was cause for personal celebration for Butcher having fulfilled every schoolboy cricketer's dream. It wasn't until sometime later when the press and others began drawing attention to him being the first Black cricketer to play for England, he began to appreciate the enormity and wider significance of his selection. He admitted that it was a weight which sat heavily on his shoulders.

'I would say it took quite a long time for the wider significance of my selection to sink in because I don't think that was in my mind at the time,' he reflected.

'My thoughts as with all cricketers who play the game were I'd had a desire from a very young age to play international cricket. That is why we all play the game, so here was my opportunity to play Test cricket. It was something I had dreamed about as a youngster in Barbados and here I was getting selected. That was first and foremost in my mind and it was all I was really interested in back then. I was fulfilling the dream I'd had as a little boy and it was really just a case of me wanting to play and do well.

'It didn't occur to me at all that I was the first Black player or what that meant. Nothing like that. So it took quite a while before that actually sunk in.

'Later on, people were making a big fuss of that and with the fuss then comes a lot of pressure and responsibility.

'The responsibility did weigh on me because suddenly you've got everybody looking at you as a role model and what happens to them depends a lot on what you do. The fact that people were now depending on you to lead the way, that is a lot of responsibility and a lot of pressure as well.

'Being selected, what it actually did was to give a lot of other Black players the motivation to believe they could make it as well. That was the good side of that, that suddenly the likes of Wilf Slack, Norman Cowans, Neil Williams, Devon Malcolm and others felt if he can do it, I can work hard and I can do it as well. From that point of view that perhaps was the easy part.

'The hard part was trying to do well to ensure that those guys coming after you had the opportunity.'

The impact Butcher's selection had on others was captured by Norman Cowans, by now a member of the MCC Young Cricketers, who had chatted to Butcher occasionally when they were training at Lord's.

Cowans said Butcher was 'like the Godfather really' in respect of Black cricketers,

'He was the one who'd been there the longest and was an astute man, very knowledgeable about everything – a great reader of people.

He was a pioneer for Black cricketers.'

So taken was Cowans with Butcher that when that weight of expectation led to Butcher struggling on that same West Indies tour, the youngster felt compelled to get in touch with his elder statesman to offer encouragement. Of course this was long before the days of social media and therefore the still teenage quick had to resort to carrier pigeon.

'I remember Roland wasn't doing particularly well in the Caribbean and you feel so helpless because you're back here and it was hard to find a way to encourage him,' said Cowans.

'So I thought, "Let me write a letter." So I wrote a letter to Roland Butcher c/o the England cricket team, saying, "Come on Roland, you can do it."

'It was a big thing because it made me think if Roland can get picked for England maybe there is a chance that I can.'

'I'm glad Norman didn't say I was the grandfather of Black cricketers,' laughed Butcher, confirming he did receive Cowans's letter all those years ago.

'I'm delighted that I played a small part in him wanting to pursue his ambition and then him finally achieving it, as did Wilf Slack and Neil Williams a little later.'

Regardless of his Test career having been a short one, Butcher is indelibly imprinted into the history of the game as a pioneer and a forerunner for others to follow. Over 40 years on, that list is still a relatively select band, too few in number, especially on shores as diverse as these.

However, in tribute to and as an indication of Butcher's legacy, here's a list of others who have been able to follow where the Middlesex man first trod, by playing Test or ODI cricket for England.

Cowans, Slack and Williams were among the first to step through the door Butcher had pushed ajar.

Gladstone Small, Phil DeFreitas, David Lawrence, Devon Malcolm, Chris Lewis and Monte Lynch were others on the early roll call.

Since then have come Joey Benjamin, Mark Alleyne, Mark Butcher, Dean Headley, and Alex Tudor – the 99 not out man, the highest score ever made by a nightwatchman in Test cricket.

In more recent times we have seen Michael Carberry, Chris Jordan, Tymal Mills and most latterly of all, Jofra Archer.

We should of course salute two more fine cricketers who are part of Butcher's legacy. Firstly, Ebony Rainford-Brent, the first Black woman to represent England, and after retirement the founder of Surrey's African-Caribbean Engagement (ACE) programme of which Butcher is a proud patron, giving Black youngsters more opportunities to play the game and a player pathway to elite level.

And coming into the present day, Sophia Dunkley, the first Black woman to play Test cricket for England. Will she be the first Black woman to captain her country? Time will tell, but Butcher says Dunkley should set her sights high, 'The last 20 years has been a bit barren [in respect of Black players achieving England status] but now the ACE programme is very much in place and looking to produce players, maybe the playing field is a bit more level and that might give them the encouragement to put in the hard work to try and achieve what we did all those years ago.

'I know Ebony very well. I'm a patron of the ACE programme, so I'm very close with it. She has done a great job along with the team involved with that. There is still a lot of work to be done as currently we are only scratching the surface. There is a tremendous amount of work to be done, but a lot of progress has been made. I think you will see the fruits of that labour perhaps in the next five years plus.

'It would be something for Sophia to lead the England team and she really should have that ambition. She has proven herself as a player. Her next ambition should be to continue in that vein but at the same time wanting to be a leader as well.

'I speak to Sophia often and she has done really well, certainly in the last couple of years. I can see her getting better as she gets more experience and yes, she should have that ambition to lead England. I would imagine by the time she gets the opportunity she will be well suited.

'I think also the fact someone like Jofra Archer is in the England side now makes a difference. OK, he didn't learn his cricket in England like the rest of us, but he still has an important role to play in ensuring that he is now the role model for future players to look up to.'

Some of the Championship-winning side of 1980, including the giant Vintcent van der Bijl (back row fourth from left).

Regardless of what the future holds for Black cricketers in the English game Butcher will forever stand as the seed of change, the catalyst for all that follows.

For now though duty calls us to return to the events of the summer of 1980 and Butcher and Middlesex's quest to recapture the County Championship title.

Next stop on the route was a journey to Tunbridge Wells to face struggling hosts Kent. Rain washed out the first day, leading to a dull and inevitable draw, but the match was a significant one in that it witnessed a change behind the stumps for Middlesex in a move which caused a fair amount of angst.

Paul Downton made his debut as wicketkeeper against his former employers, his pathway at Kent having been blocked by the legendary Alan Knott. Downton had been recommended to Middlesex, by Knott as much as anyone, and Brearley was keen to get him on board, as much for his batting as for his glovework. Mike Smith was coming to the end of his Middlesex tenure and other options such as Slack, though he had been getting some appearances, were somewhat raw, the youngster still finding his way in the game.

It wasn't, certainly at first, a universally popular decision. Gatting and the sitting tenant behind the stumps, Ian Gould, were the best of friends having come through the ranks together and it's clear the future captain found the move a surprise, particularly when Gunner was immediately usurped by the new arrival.

Roland Butcher became the first Black player to represent England in 1980.

Gatting reported, 'Somebody turned up and said to Brears, "Paul Downton is available and is a good wicketkeeper batsman, Knotty rates him very highly." So for some strange reason we got rid of Gunner and Paul came in.'

Gould couldn't recover his spot and headed south to Sussex to continue his career at Hove, going on to win 18 one-day international caps for England from 1983 onwards.

He returned to Lord's in 1991 for a stint as coach, before going on to be a successful Test match umpire.

Emburey expressed his disappointment that Gould gave up on life at Middlesex quite so readily, but also admitted that Downton filled a crucial role at that time and for almost a decade afterwards,

'When Paul [Downton] got selected, Gouldy said "I knew this was going to happen as soon as he came. I knew he'd get in the side straight away and that was it."

'I was a little bit disappointed that Ian didn't fight back for his place, but he ended up leaving instead and going down to Sussex at the end of that year. But Paul worked his way up the order and started to open the batting. Brearley was quite keen on his technique and the way Paul played. He had a habit of scoring twos. He was perhaps not strong enough to hit fours but enough to beat the in-field and get twos. He probably got as many twos as all the other players put together. It appeared to be like that. He would just clear the in-field and it would go for two.

'He was a good player when he got in, gritty, solid, valued his wicket, didn't have a wide range of shots and I think that is why Brears liked him because he would see off the new ball. It meant with him and Mike opening we didn't score runs quickly up top, so you were then looking at Gatt, who was becoming a more senior player and Butch, who was naturally a good striker of the ball to accelerate things.'

Downton did plenty to justify his selection at Gould's expense against his former county. Thrown in at the deep end and asked to open with Brearley, he made 64, more than double his previous highest first-class score of 31. Then with the game dead on the third afternoon he added a further unbeaten 46 to underscore the earlier effort.

Three more half-centuries, including an unbeaten 90, meant he finished the season averaging 40 and his first taste of Test cricket came that winter in the West Indies.

Rumblings over the wicketkeeper position appeared to continue behind the scenes, meaning Brearley addressed the issue in his end of season report, now part of the Middlesex minute book for that year.

He acknowledged the decision was tough on Gould, but felt it was justified given Downton's greater batting prowess, writing, 'Another area in which competition proved controversial was the wicketkeeping position. The committee are aware of the background to the eventual selection of Paul Downton for it must be stressed he was told he would have no guarantee of selection when he opted to join the club. He began to keep well and score runs at a time when we needed an opener in the county side.

'The tragic part is that Ian Gould was left out when he had been, earlier on, playing better than at any time in his career. A lot of members felt strongly that we were wrong in our decision to include Downton. There was little to choose between the two as keepers but Paul fitted our needs at the time as his runs proved.'

The clash with the soon-to-be-deposed champions, Essex, at Lord's looks an easy victory at first glance, an innings and four runs the winning margin, but that doesn't begin to tell the story of a real cliffhanger in which both old and newer faces came to the fore.

With Van der Bijl's arrival and Daniel still pounding down the overs, opportunities had been fewer and further between for Selvey, something else Brearley acknowledged in his end-of-season report to the committee. However, his first-innings five-wicket haul, his only one of the Championship summer, gave the hosts a firm grip on the game.

Not content with that, Selvey then produced his best effort with the bat of 40 not out, allowing Barlow to reach an unbeaten hundred. Their efforts followed half-centuries for Butcher and Downton, the latter raising his career best again, this time to 67.

Essex began the final day 271 behind with all their second innings wickets intact and there was little sign of the drama to come when they reached 226-3 shortly after tea. Even though a breakthrough came, at 255-5 the match still appeared destined for a draw when Daniel blew the game open with a spell of 4-11 in 25 balls.

The last pair came together with Essex 11 short of Middlesex's score, and John Lever chalked seven off that tally while David Acfield hung on at the other end. With only four overs left and two to come off for the break between innings the visitors were potentially one blow from safety when Simon Hughes produced the perfect yorker to scatter Acfield's stumps and seal a priceless win.

Brearley took time in his report to acknowledge the efforts of stalwart Selvey and to flag up the potential of Hughes, the two having often competed during the season for the third seamer spot in the XI.

'With the new ball in such capable hands Mike Selvey's opportunities were unfortunately limited and he found himself contesting the third seamer's place, first with Bill Merry and then Simon Hughes,' he wrote.

'Naturally enough he became frustrated at getting so much less bowling. However, he played a vital role, especially in the one-day matches and also improved with the bat.

'Simon, whose university commitments will continue to restrict his appearances next year, looked at 20, one of England's best bowling prospects. He has a touch of flair, a fine action and, although erring on the side of complete attack at times, does get good players out.'

Just when it seemed normal service had been resumed after their earlier blip, Brearley's side, shorn of Gatting, Emburey and Van der Bijl and with Edmonds again on the sidelines, were thrashed by an innings by Leicestershire, never recovering from Butcher running out first Radley and then himself in a disastrous first-innings effort.

With Van der Bijl back in harness for the trip to Cheltenham, they looked set to resume normal service when setting Gloucestershire 270 in the last innings, this after rain produced limited action on the second day.

However they'd reckoned without Mike Procter, who smote the visitors' attack to all parts. It could have been different had Brearley clung on to a hard edge at slip when the South African all-rounder had made 58, but the chance went to ground and Procter went on to make 134 not out as Gloucestershire skated home by six wickets.

It was hardly ideal preparation for their Gillette Cup semi-final with Sussex which came up 24 hours later at Hove.

Bad weather forced the game into a second day, but Middlesex struggled again with the bat, looking in need of inspiration. It came from an unlikely source – Sussex all-rounder Imran Khan.

The Pakistan quick made the mistake of forgetting the rules of the fast bowlers' union and bounced Daniel, removing the tailender's helmet and coming within inches of taking his head off. The indiscretion clearly upset the usually genial quick who had a Dr Jekyll and Mr Hyde moment, as clearly livid, his eyes widened and turned red with fury.

Khan brushed it off and soon pinned last man Hughes lbw to leave Middlesex 179 all out, not many to defend, or so onlookers probably thought.

Daniel, though, had not forgotten the incident and was still smarting when he got ball in hand. Tearing down the hill like a man possessed, he promptly laid waste to the top order.

John Barclay was first in the firing line and lasted only two balls before he was beaten for pace and bowled, one of the stumps ending all the way back at the feet of wicketkeeper Downton, who understandably was a long way back.

Soon afterwards Gehan Mendis was also castled, and anger not satisfied Daniel had Paul Parker caught by Van der Bijl for just a single to leave Sussex 18-3.

Khan and Colin Wells briefly threatened a fightback when Daniel took a breather, but Khan completed an injudicious afternoon by running out his partner before nicking Van der Bijl through to Downton.

Daniel returned still spitting fire and venom, forcing Colin Phillipson to depart hit wicket, before rearranging Garth Le Roux's stumps and pinning Arnold Long in front. His final figures of 6-15 from ten overs meant Sussex were rolled over for 115, so sending Middlesex to the final for the third time in six years.

This was one of only two occasions all season that Daniel claimed a five-wicket haul, so it's a mark of his consistency that he got 118 in all competitions across the course of the summer.

Selvey could only remember one brief spell in Daniel's 12 years at Middlesex where his radar was a little off.

'He went through one bad trot for about a fortnight to three weeks where people were banging the ball back past him and hitting him all over the place,' said Selvey. He was getting driven a lot and that wasn't Wayne. We couldn't work out what was happening until we discovered the *Sun* newspaper was offering £500 for "Demon Bowler of the Year" which would be the one who hit the stumps the most often.

'Wayne had got his eye on trying to hit the stumps and getting the 500 quid, so, we told him, "Wayne, we'll double that amount if you start hitting people on the head again," and we got him back on track that way.'

Returning to the Championship, Middlesex's batting woes surfaced again when despite 54 from Radley they found themselves 86-6 on the first day of their match with Nottinghamshire at Lord's. They could ill afford a third Championship defeat on the spin, so needed two batters to stand up. That pair turned out to be Barlow and Van der Bijl, who shared a seventh-wicket stand of 152, the latter making his highest score of the season, 76, while Barlow fell three short of a century.

The rest of the game was the story of one of Emburey's greatest days on a cricket field. The off-spinner bowled almost 53 overs on the second day of the contest, claiming six wickets in the first innings and another half a dozen in the second after Nottinghamshire followed on.

Over 40 years on Emburey revealed that his preparations for that day's cricket had been far from textbook,

'I remember getting the 12 in one day against Notts in 1980. I had a late night the day before. A couple of my wife Susie's friends had come over from Australia and they wanted to go out. We didn't get home until 2.30am!

'I wasn't a happy bunny so drove like a bloody madman getting home and then had my best day ever.'

To continue their Championship challenge, Middlesex would have to make a rare excursion away from Lord's which was being prepared for the Centenary Test between England and Australia.

Therefore, the setting for the game with Derbyshire was a maiden first-class fixture at the Uxbridge Cricket Ground in the extreme west of the county. The national papers at the time recorded a keen interest by fans to see Middlesex play beyond the walls of Lord's and that the match was therefore well attended. This writer can confirm the fact as I was one of those spectators. Uxbridge wasn't far from my family home and being almost 16 by then I was allowed to travel by myself. It was the school summer holiday too, so to the best of my memory I attended most of the game, leading to my own encounter with Wayne Daniel.

During a break in play, whether it was at the end of Derbyshire's second innings or one of the scheduled intervals, I remember running on to the outfield – we'd been given permission, honest – clutching my book of signatures and shouting after Daniel who was scurrying off, 'Wayne, Wayne, can I have your autograph? Wayne, Wayne, sign my book.'

Daniel stopped dead in his tracks with his back towards me, before slowly turning round. I wasn't the biggest of 15-year-olds, so as you can imagine he towered over me. For a moment I wondered what he would say. I didn't have to wait long. 'Say please, man,' came the response as he did a brilliant job of keeping a straight face.

'Sorry Wayne, please sign my book,' I responded, by now afraid I had offended him by forgetting my manners in my youthful enthusiasm.

I needn't have worried as 'The Diamond' slowly broke into a huge grin from ear to ear, before holding out his hand and saying, 'Give us your book.'

Some may argue I'd plumped for the wrong fast bowler as Van der Bijl completely overshadowed Daniel over the course of the match, having his best game for Middlesex in bowling terms.

His five wickets in the first innings enabled the hosts to bowl Derbyshire out for 220, but Geoff Miller struck back with five of his own to earn the visitors a lead of 56 early on the second day.

Undeterred, Van der Bijl charged in again, ripping out the Derbyshire tail on the third morning to bag a second five-for and ten in the match. Much to everyone's surprise, despite being on an out-ground, the pitch held up really well and Middlesex made light work of knocking off the runs thanks to an opening stand of 138 by Brearley and Downton. The wicketkeeper would post a third career best with the bat in just a few weeks, reaching 90 not out as the champions elect stormed home by nine wickets.

Emburey, who we should remind ourselves played some part in all seven Championship-winning sides of the golden era, was in no doubt that Van der Bijl was that extra sprinkling of stardust which made the 1980 team a cut above all the others he was privileged to be involved with,

'Vintcent rounded off the best side I played in. Wayne had the pace, Vintcent had the height and the bounce, not quick, but he had great control and got movement off the seam. We had Mike Selvey who swung the ball and we had two good spinners, so we had a very rounded side. We had someone who could bowl well and perhaps get a five-for in all conditions which makes it enjoyable.

'It got to a stage where the players believed whatever we scored we'd bowl them out cheaper because we had a good bowling attack.'

Van der Bijl continued his form into the next game against Sussex at Hove, his 6-47, a career best in his year in NW8 building on another fine century from skipper Brearley and allowing Middlesex to enforce the follow-on. He would add three more in the second dig, but victory hopes were thwarted by a brilliant double hundred from Kepler Wessels, meaning any celebrations were put on hold for a few more days at least.

Van Der Bijl played all his best cricket during his nation's period of exclusion from the international cricket community because of apartheid. He had been selected for the series against Australia in 1971/72 which was cancelled in the wake of the Basil D'Oliveira affair, or should that be controversy?

D'Oliveira, a Cape Coloured man of Portuguese/Indian ancestry, had moved to England from South Africa six years previously and played for England since 1966. He was initially omitted from the tour party to South Africa, but called into the squad at the 11th hour following an injury to Tom Cartwright. Several South African politicians insisted this late inclusion was politically motivated and despite attempts to find a compromise the tour was cancelled.

Radley argued that Van der Bijl's absence from that arena made the game poorer. The Middlesex stalwart made his highest Test score against a New Zealand side including Richard Hadlee in his pomp, so knows a good bowler when he sees one and is qualified to comment, believes that his 1980 team-mate may have eclipsed the Kiwi and all other bowlers of his type had he been given the chance,

'He came over for a one-season blast to see how he'd do outside of the Currie Cup and it was clear to me he was the best there was. The last two overs of the Sunday League stuff, you knew. These days it is a different ballgame and they might even smash him around now, but you could guarantee he would get every ball of those last 12 in the blockhole and they were coming down from a huge height.

'By the end of the season he'd shown what a great bowler he was. He could bat a bit as well and he was a good fielder for the giant of a man that he was. He was a fantastic bloke to have in the side.

'When people ask about the best bowlers you played with or against Van Der Bijl always comes up in my estimation as the number one. He and Richard Hadlee were similar sorts of bowlers, but obviously Vince didn't have the opportunity to do it on the international scene because of Apartheid. That's why when he came over he was a little bit nervous because he'd got all his wickets in Currie Cup cricket, but hadn't been tested on the international scene.

'Comparing eras is an impossible thing, but in the era in which he played I would say he is comfortably the best of the lot of them. Hadlee and others were tested and you can see the number of Test match wickets that they got and how good they were. Vince through no fault of his own born in South Africa and bought up under the apartheid system, and so he was kept out of international cricket during his playing career. We'll never know but my hunch is he would have got a lot of wickets.'

Middlesex celebrate their Championship win at Buckingham Palace.

1980 Championship winner's plate.

With the Gillette Cup Final looming and a County Championship still to be won, Middlesex's players hit the M4 to head to Cardiff where they were soon in trouble at 15-3 after being put in, with Brearley, Downton and Barlow all back in the pavilion. The rain came down soon afterwards preventing any further play on day one, but even after the clouds rolled away the visitors struggled to 163 all out. With not many to defend but keen to move the game on, Middlesex's bowlers hit back, Van der Bijl and Hughes taking four apiece as Glamorgan were bowled out for 140.

Middlesex stretched that lead to 48 by stumps and with Brearley making a quick hundred by his standards on the final morning, the hosts were set 235 to win.

Such a scenario never looked likely as Hughes quickly removed the top order, Daniel rooted out the middle and Edmonds cleaned up to secure victory by 72 runs with time to spare. The win put Middlesex 27 points clear with one game to go, meaning they were out of reach of closest pursuers Surrey, and the title was theirs for the third time in five seasons.

Surrey narrowed the margin to 13 points by winning their final game while Middlesex drew with Kent, but in perhaps what was a gentle jibe at their rivals, Emburey admitted he wasn't aware they'd even come second,

'Surrey had Sylvester Clarke, who bowled pretty rapidly at that time and they had a good attack with Robin Jackman who was still there, Pat Pocock and Intikhab Alam would have still been there. So they had a good team. But I never remember who came second – who cares if we'd won.'

Surrey would have an early chance to get even as it was the London sides who met at Lord's in the Gillette Cup Final which brought the curtain down on the 1980 season.

As so often in the past on the big occasion, Selvey bowled magnificently, completing his full allocation of 12 overs for just 17 runs and the wickets of openers Alan Butcher and Grahame Clinton. Hughes too got wickets, albeit at much greater cost, so restricting Surrey to 201 all out with last man Jack Richards run out off the final ball of their 60 overs.

For once, Radley failed with the bat on the big occasion, but Brearley played the required innings of substance with an unbeaten 96, while the acceleration came courtesy of Butcher, three big sixes helping him to an unbeaten 50 at comfortably more than a run a ball as Middlesex cantered home with 37 balls to spare.

Brearley was named player of the match by Ian Botham, the man he would replace as England captain in the Ashes series the following summer. The Middlesex skipper had kept his word of the previous winter to the committee to resurrect the county's golden era. We didn't know then, but 1982 was to afford Brearley one last hurrah.

CHAPTER 7

1982

'Comfortably before lunch on Tuesday, 14 September 1982, at Worcester, Mike Brearley made the final run in Middlesex's ten-wicket win over Worcestershire. He had been applauded on to the field at the start of the match; and he was applauded of it into the retirement he had planned and announced. He walked into the pavilion for the fourth, and last, time as captain of the county champions.

'In his 11 years as captain of Middlesex, they won the County Championship three times and shared it once, against five and one shared in their previous 89 years in the competition. They were twice winners and once losing finalists in the Gillette Cup; once Benson & Hedges finalists; once runners-up and twice third in the John Player League … The salient points of his make-up are intellectual quality, clarity of mind and common sense – which are by no means the same thing, nor always found in the same person – and human perception. It is as certain as may be his was the most effective intellect ever closely applied to the game.

'His understanding – both intuitive and tutored – of human beings proved a major asset in his captaincy. He was able to reach, sympathise with and – in the current term motivate cricketers as few, if any have done.'

The above is a snapshot of the 1983 *Wisden Cricketers' Almanack*'s reflections on Mike Brearley, who to the backdrop of Worcester Cathedral exited stage left, having orchestrated the greatest period in Middlesex's history.

Wisden naturally enough was keen to highlight his record with England, having relinquished the captaincy 12 months earlier after relieving Ian Botham of the burdens of leadership, so unleashing the beast that was Beefy for a summer of exploits a then teenager such as myself will never forget.

However, to dwell on that is not my brief here as our focus is on Brearley leaving the domestic game with the due respect of his peers after bringing the curtain down on his episode of sporting theatre in the grand manner.

This last of his four County Championship triumphs – three outright, one shared, as with that of two years previously – represented something of a turnaround in fortunes given the underwhelming 1981 domestic summer which preceded it.

Brearley, as we've just alluded to, missed almost half of the Championship season in 1981 while on his England rescue mission, which no doubt had an effect. Middlesex could also point to their May fixture with Sussex being abandoned without a ball being bowled, the last home match to be entirely lost to the elements for 33 years until a washout at Merchant Taylors' School in 2014 – Sussex again the unlucky opponents. As a journalist by then, I remember the latter 'game' to my cost, having to venture to Moor Park on all four days in the rain knowing full well there was no prospect of seeing bat on ball.

That in all likelihood cost Brearley's men a place in the top three, although they finished fourth – no disgrace. Rain also ruined their Benson & Hedges Cup campaign, but the John Player League bid never got off the ground, while the Gillette Cup witnessed a limp first-round exit at the hands of Lancashire. All this despite a brief tenure at Lord's of fearsome Australian quick Jeff Thomson, who admittedly was not quite the bowler he once had been and in any event, injury ended his stay early.

It was all in marked contrast to the all-conquering exploits of the class of 1980, but as with any era, there had been changes among the men of Lord's since that heady triumph.

Most notably of course, Vintcent van der Bijl's stay had been for just the one year in what proved to be the twilight of his career before returning to South Africa to resume his work with paper manufacturer Wiggins Teape.

Replacing the 85 championship wickets he took was never going to be a quick fix, especially with Mike Selvey's influence on the wane and prospect Bill Merry plagued with injuries. Simon Hughes, to quote the title of his subsequent book, was getting through 'A Lot of Hard Yakka', but fresh faces were needed and fortunately for Middlesex, thanks again in no small part to coach Don Bennett, they were beginning to emerge, with Norman Cowans at the front of the queue.

Born in Enfield in the parish of St Mary, Jamaica, Cowans moved with his family to England at the age of 11 and was playing at colts level for Middlesex in his under-15 year.

The young paceman knew he wanted to get into professional cricket and so immediately upon leaving school he wrote to Middlesex and asked if he could come for a trial. His prayers were answered with the club quick to respond to his request and invite him to Lord's at the end of the 1977 summer.

Bennett himself took charge of the proceedings with the then first-team wicketkeeper Ian Gould the man with bat in hand.

When the trial concluded, Bennett told the young hopeful, 'We don't usually take youngsters on at your age. I suggest you go for a trial with the MCC Young Professionals and we will give you some games for the second team.'

Cowans took the advice on board, got through his subsequent trial and signed to play for the MCC YPs for the 1978 summer. Not that he got much chance to shine in that role as true to his word, Bennett was always on the phone, calling the speedster up for second XI duty. So keen was Bennett to have Cowans's services, he volunteered to drive him all the way to his debut game with Glamorgan at Barry Island in the early spring of 1978. It wasn't the most auspicious of first appearances as Cowans went wicketless, but his promise didn't take long to show its head as four first-innings wickets next time out against Warwickshire allowed him to take another important step on his sporting journey.

His maiden first-class wicket would come almost two years later when he pinned Oxford University opener James Rogers lbw in a midsummer game at The Parks.

By this time Cowans had taken up a few chances to observe fellow West Indian Wayne Daniel at work and while he gleaned some pointers by watching on, he said Daniel was a man of few words and that his main advice in those early days came out of a chance meeting with another of his boyhood heroes, Australian fast-bowling legend Dennis Lillee.

Cowans said, 'During my time on the MCC staff we used to be able to be very close to the Middlesex players and I remember watching Wayne bowl and prepare and stuff. It was always great to see what was required from a senior player.

'I remember being 12th man one game at Lord's when Wayne was bowling and it was the first time I'd actually been on the pitch with him. It made me realise how much effort and hard work it was to be a fast bowler. He was a very strong man and he showed me what was required. So, I learned a hell of a lot just from watching really.

'Wayne wasn't the type of character to give you tips. He just let you get on with your game really. He wasn't like a Dennis Lillee, who was like an artist of a fast bowler really. Lillee came over one summer when I was on the MCC staff, so I used to go and talk to him about fast bowling and he'd give me a few tips. He was an amazingly generous man. He was one of my heroes anyway, Dennis Lillee, so when I had the opportunity to meet him I took it.

'He came to Lord's and wanted to have a bowl in the nets, so I went over and joined him and started picking his brains. He was so generous and down to earth. Four years later I was playing against him for England.

'It was a hard school at Middlesex, with quite a hard coach. They wanted you to learn – nothing was ever given to you. At the end of the day, once you are out there in the middle, it is just you and the opposition. One of their things was if you are in the first team you should know what you're doing and a lot of the time you were left to do stuff and learn from your own mistakes.'

Another 15 months would pass before Cowans's promotion to the first XI arrived in a late-season trip to face Leicestershire at Grace Road. He remembered waking up on the first morning of the game with a stiff neck, but when asked by Brearley if he wanted to play he made light of any discomfort for fear he wouldn't get another opportunity for some while. The cricket gods though were with him as Middlesex batted first, racking up a big score, giving him a chance to get loose again.

With most of the second day lost to rain, Cowans's first championship wicket – that of Nick Cook, caught behind by Paul Downton – didn't arrive until the third morning. Not the most glamorous of scalps then, but with the visitors able to enforce the follow-on, Cook's wicket proved merely the hors d'oeuvres to a superb afternoon for the now 20-year-old as he ripped out the top five to set Middlesex on the road to an innings victory. Among his scalps that afternoon were the illustrious trio of Chris Balderstone, Nigel Briers and best of all David Gower, who he trapped in front.

'I found it pretty challenging trying to bowl against the likes of Gower, so he was a good scalp to get for a young player trying to make his way in the game,' Cowans said. Although we were chatting on the phone, it was clear that the recollection has him grinning from ear to ear.

'I remember meeting David at Lord's when he was trying to establish himself in the England team back in the late '70s when I was on the MCC staff and I've always been a fan of his anyway. I just loved the way he played, but as with a lot of left-handers, if you can get the ball to come back into them or swing it in, then you've always got a chance. I always had that in my locker.'

It was clear from listening to Cowans that he was another youngster to benefit from having Brearley as his skipper, even if it was in his case only for a short time. He was part of a tour to Zimbabwe undertaken by the county and led by Brearley in the winter of 1980/81 and it didn't take long for the captain to leave a strong impression on Cowans,

'It was a fantastic experience to come into the team with Mike as captain.

'The great thing about Mike was he made you feel immediately that you were part of the team rather than just a youngster coming in. He made you feel you were just as good as any one of them really and he trusted you to do a job.

'He used to talk with me and try and educate me on the game. I'd be watching the game and he'd come out on the balcony and say, "Norman, watch the first few overs and see how the wicket is." He just wanted you to feel included. That was one of his biggest strengths and I was very fortunate he was captain when I made my debut and got into the team. He understood us and the players really respected him. As soon as he walked into the dressing room it was clear they all respected him.

'When he was on the field, Mike was a very hard man who knew what he wanted, but a guy you could talk to and tell him anything. He was perceptive, knowledgeable and encouraging.'

While the pace attack was in the process of being rebuilt at the start of Brearley's final season, the spin twins John Emburey and Philippe Edmonds were largely reunited thanks to the former's international ban, more of which in the next chapter. Edmonds played in the Test against India and so missed a few games, but was left out of the subsequent series with Pakistan, increasing his availability to Brearley.

As for the batting, it had a familiar look to it, though Graham Barlow missed most of the campaign struggling with injury.

The season-opener with Essex at Lord's was troubled by rain which caused much of the second day to be lost. However, this gave Brearley a chance to show that the advancing years hadn't affected his sense of daring in the quest for a result.

The visitors, led by skipper Keith Fletcher's 120, posted 355-8 declared and with the rain interrupting play, Middlesex were only 8-0 in reply by the close. Never afraid to take chances, Brearley declared immediately on the final morning and to his credit Fletcher then forfeited Essex's second innings, leaving the hosts 348 to win.

Fortunes swung first one way and then the other in the chase as Middlesex reached 200-3 before subsiding to 246-7 with Gatting gone for 90. Essex were now favourites but Emburey the burgeoning all-rounder turned the tide with an unbeaten 67, and with first Selvey and then Neil Williams (27 not out) providing valuable support in a ninth-wicket stand of 59 Middlesex squeezed home.

It was reward for ambition and adventure in the season's opening game, something seen rarely, certainly at Lord's, in the modern era. I say that with a match between the same two counties in 2017 firmly in my mind.

Middlesex had gained sufficient first innings lead to enforce the follow-on but declined to do so, then ended up batting for too long in their second innings and making a declaration which was too safe, enabling Essex to escape with a draw when the light closed in with them eight down on the final evening.

The gist of the explanation given at the time was Middlesex's bowlers had bowled 95 overs in the first innings and it was too early in the campaign to take chances.

In mitigation, you could argue in a modern era of two divisions the threat of relegation meant risk-taking may be kept to a minimum early in a campaign. However, the contrast in outcomes was a stark one. Brearley was brave and won the title, while the class of 2017 were ultimately relegated by a point.

Buoyed by this opening success, Brearley's men comfortably saw off Northamptonshire by nine wickets at Lord's. Key to the win was their first-innings score of 379-5 in which Brearley himself led the way with 165. However, the innings was most noteworthy for Emburey's maiden first-class hundred, the hosts declaring as soon as he reached the landmark.

Emburey had been challenged by Brearley as far back as 1977 that if he improved his batting he would get a Test call-up for the winter tour to Pakistan and New Zealand. Evidently, despite all his wickets and Middlesex winning the title back then, Emburey lost out for a place on the plane to Geoff Cope, though the Yorkshire spinner came home early from the tour having been called for throwing. Emburey's first Test cap came the following summer against the Kiwis and he was selected for the 1978/79 Ashes tour that winter.

However, according to Emburey, it wasn't until the rebel tour to South Africa in 1982 that he made a breakthrough with his batting,

'When I went to South Africa my whole philosophy changed. Before that, I could occupy the crease, but I couldn't score runs very quickly as I didn't have many shots. South Africa changed the whole philosophy of the way I batted. Instead of standing in the crease with not much of a backlift where I used to shovel everything over midwicket, I thought sod it and started to walk down the wicket against the medium-pacers and the quicker bowlers.

'At times that was a bit silly as they were a little bit too quick, but all of a sudden I was coming down and as soon as you make a forward movement you automatically pick up the bat, so you have a bit of a backlift.

'I was skewing the ball off over the top of extra cover or over gully. I hit a couple of good shots and all of a sudden I was scoring runs at a decent lick and I just continued in that vein.

'I became a better player and a valuable player by playing like that for Middlesex on bad wickets where a 30 or 40 was a decent score. And because I became an orthodox player it actually worked. I didn't have the responsibility of a top-order batter who had to rely on technique, I had a good eye and a different thought and mental process. It proved fruitful as I started to win the occasional game or change a game with the bat.'

While the increased batting contributions were appreciated, Emburey's primary role, certainly at this time, was as an off-break bowler and as one half of a great partnership with left-arm spinner Philippe Henri Edmonds to give him his full title. The two had been in harness for several summers now, but 1982 will go down, statistically anyway, as their most successful bowling in tandem. Emburey would take 74 Championship wickets to Edmonds's 71, but the latter in a spirit of healthy competition which existed between them will point out he bowled fewer balls, had a higher strike rate and a lower average per wicket.

It's high time we talked about these spin twins, who are surely up there with Laker and Lock, and Young and Sims when it comes to discussing the great slow bowling partnerships.

According to Emburey the pair were Ying and Yang, the Laurel and Hardy of the cricket world with Emburey happily, or perhaps not so happily cast in the role of straight man (he winced slightly at my suggestion that his bowling was 'mean' or 'tight'). He expressed it using a slightly different analogy, but maintained that however you look at it the pair complemented each other perfectly,

'The secret to my spin partnership with Phil was we were very different. I always alluded to the two of us as Phil being the Cavalier and me being a Roundhead. I was the boring one and Phil was the one who would give it a bit more air. He had really good flight, he got dip, he spun the ball more than me, so he was the more exciting to watch, whereas I was length and line, control, trying to squeeze all the time.

'It's interesting you would call me mean and tight because others used to say it and I would reply that I didn't bowl bad balls. And because I bowled a good length I didn't get hit. I bowled variety in terms of length and pace but because I didn't get hit people perceived me as a defensive bowler, so I didn't get the credit I deserved for that control.

'Phil was an aggressive individual. He was a big bloke, so he had presence and he was aggressive. He wanted to get a wicket every ball. One of his faults was he always wanted to bowl on middle or middle and leg and hit the top of off. He wanted to bowl the miracle ball all the time, whereas I was quite happy bowling maidens.'

Mike Gatting, who would inherit the joy of having these two masters of their craft bowling in tandem, agreed that they were different bowlers, who shared a tallness of physical stature they used to enhance their respective bowling styles.

'They complemented each other, especially with Philippe bowling it away from the bat, while Embers would wheel away in nagging fashion just back of a length,' he said. 'And because of their height they didn't have to loop it up because it was coming down from a height anyway. It was coming down more quickly at the batsman and was therefore more difficult to play I suspect. They were high-quality bowlers and when it turned they both got wickets.'

It wasn't just the spinners who appreciated each other's art. The other members of the bowling attack, while operating at a different pace, could still find themselves transfixed out in the field as the two wheeled away from their respective ends.

Cowans said that watching them operate was a real education and that the duo not only complemented each other, but the rest of the bowling unit, who had different responsibilities at different times of the year and in differing conditions.

'You can learn from very different bowlers to you, absolutely you can,' he asserted. 'Middlesex had such a good attack. We knew in the first half of the summer the seam bowlers were going to do the bulk of the bowling because conditions would suit us much better, but that as the season progressed, Phil Edmonds and John Emburey would do a lot more. The fast bowlers would then be strike bowlers. We all knew what our roles were and it was a joy to know when those guys came on they would do a great job.

'When you have good spinners like Phil and John, you had time to recover. If you have a spinner who's not doing the job you know you're going to be asked to bowl more than you should in conditions that don't really suit you. So, Phil and John were a great foil for the fast bowlers and you learned from how they went about their business, the field placings, the tactics. They would get world-class players out and you knew you had to be alert as any ball there could be a catch coming towards you. They were masters of their craft really and we trusted them as a team.'

The two spinners were always fiercely competitive, as much as anything because they were competing for one England spot for much of their careers. You get the impression too there was some good-natured point-scoring that went on between them with Edmonds alleging that he got more proper batters out than his partner in crime. Interestingly Emburey, rather than refute that charge, offered a theory as to why he was better at cleaning up a tail. And in any case, he ventured, it all came out pretty even in the end.

'If you look at our careers, Phil's and mine, although I played more games than him at the end, our figures are very similar. I got more wickets, but I played more games. If you look at everything else and you worked it out on an average, wickets-wise we were very similar.

'I think that's where we complemented each other. On certain pitches Phil got the wickets and in other matches I got wickets. But Philippe would always say, "Why is it you always get the lower order out and I always get the top order out?"

'He wondered why he couldn't get tailenders out and I did and I think it is because of the way he bowled. I bowled with control, so I had men in front all the time. I forced them into playing big shots, otherwise there would be a little bat-pad and you're gone. I would have a couple of men out, so I had an in/out field which stopped them playing the big shots and brought the two men in front of the wicket into play. Then they are in two minds and they neither attack or defend properly.'

The two shared plenty of good natured banter while watching from the balcony at Lord's or in the visiting dressing room on their travels. Emburey recalled one quip from Edmonds during a match with Surrey where he addressed why their art hadn't resulted in even more wickets for both of them,

'Keith Medlycott got a couple of our wickets with drag-down long-hops where batters went back and cut upwards and got caught at backward point. We were near each other and he turned around to me and said, "Do you know our problem?" "No." "We don't bowl enough s**t balls."'

That said, Edmonds had bowled a few such s**t balls at the beginning of the previous summer in 1981 where he lost his action for a while, suffering cricket's equivalent of the 'yips'. It's a term usually applied to golfers who are having trouble on the greens, whereupon it's a cue for them to revert to a long-handled putter to give them more control. I've never played golf seriously, but was a keen left-handed darts player in my younger days. I was fairly decent at it as a youth, developing a free-flowing action with good rhythm. That is until one day someone made the mistake of telling me I was good and from that moment on in any competitive situation I was done for. I would stand at the oche completely unable to let go of the dart and on the rare occasion I managed to do so I developed left-hander's hook. For those of you who know your dartboards, that's never going to end well.

By all accounts Edmonds suffered in similar fashion, struggling to release the ball. When he did so it could end up just about anywhere. For a man who had always had such control and rhythm this was a baffling state of affairs. Yet Roland Butcher, who used to change alongside Edmonds in the Middlesex dressing room, said it was not a phenomenon unique to Edmonds but something he'd seen afflict other bowlers of his type.

Middlesex spin twin, Phil Edmonds the charismatic Cavalier and John Emburey the 'Boring' Roundhead.

'I don't think Phil could quite understand it. He wasn't the first one it happened to as I know it happened to a lot of left-arm spinners. Maybe it is something left-arm spinners are susceptible to because there are a tremendous amount of left-arm spinners who have had the same problem where you suddenly cannot land a ball on the pitch.

'He was bowling head-high full tosses or three-quarter length long-hops. He just could not get it on a length. Sometimes he would be three foot wide of the off stump and he couldn't work out why it was happening. It got to the point where he even tried to bowl off of one step. It was not nice watching him suffer because nobody knew the answer. Through my career I saw a lot of left-arm spinners, Keith Medlycott and others who at some point went through that same thing. I never saw right handers have that problem. That was quite a rough time for Phil.'

Edmonds's dilemma was perhaps best illustrated by an early season encounter with Essex at Chelmsford where Keith Pont was the batter on strike. Spin twin John Emburey took up the story.

'Philippe bowled a ball which was a rank long-hop and then the next ball went over Keith Pont's head and the head of the wicketkeeper [Ian Gould]. Then the next was the perfect ball, pitched about middle, turned sharply and took the edge. Pont shrugged as if to say how do you play that sort of thing. But Philippe went through that for the majority of that summer and he really struggled.'

It seems Edmonds did manage to keep some sense of perspective and a sense of humour about it all. Clive Radley recalled a moment after another couple of stray deliveries where Edmonds, tongue in cheek, claimed to have finally found the cure for his bowling ills.

'He came up a third time, stopped in his delivery stride, looked over his shoulder down the wicket and said, "I've cracked it. Brears, (Mike Brearley) every time I get in this position the only thing I can see is you. So if you wouldn't mind moving to cover I wouldn't have to look at you."'

This incident perhaps hints at the slightly tricky relationship between Brearley and Edmonds which we've already seen evidence of and as we'll see later, his relationship with Mike Gatting could also be difficult, so it seems he wasn't great with authority figures.

From Butcher's perspective though, he never had any issue with the talented spinner, though he felt Edmonds didn't make the most of his vast natural talent.

'Phil was a guy that I liked. We shared a couch together in the dressing room and used to get changed side-by-side. One thing I would say about Edmonds is he was a winner. He didn't like mediocrity. He always believed he could win in any situation. He didn't like weakness, or people he considered to be weak. He liked strong people.

'He was not your typical team-mate. He was not a socialiser in the sense that you would see him in the bar having a drink with the lads, or that sort of thing. At the end of the day Edmonds always had something else to do. Or, early in the morning he would go and do what he had to do in the city before coming to Lord's. I had no difficulty with him at all.

'If he was more dedicated to the sport, if he'd worked a lot harder on his fitness, I truly believe he would have been one of England's greatest ever spin bowlers. He had that amount of ability. He wasn't a big trainer; he didn't like training and stuff, but give him the ball and he was different class. He had stardust. He was charismatic. I liked him. I didn't have a problem with him at all.'

Edmonds certainly stole the limelight in the 68-run victory over Sussex which made it three wins from three to start the season, with 12 wickets in the match. His 8-80 in the second innings was at that time a career best, though he did trump that analysis two years later when returning 8-53 against Hampshire at Bournemouth.

Middlesex's batting effort at Hove had been led by Wilf Slack. The left-hander had begun the year in sparkling form with a ton in the match with Cambridge University at Fenner's, before recording his second career double century, against Oxford University at the Parks.

The 85 against Sussex turned out to be his highest Championship score of a summer that did not quite match that of 12 months previously. Gatting revealed that Slack struggled against spin in his early years at Middlesex and was encouraged to turn to Edmonds and Emburey for help,

'They helped Wilf a hell of a lot because when he first came on the staff he couldn't play spin bowling very well. He asked Don Bennett what to do and Don told him, "See those two blokes over there, whenever you have free time and they're not doing anything ask them if they'll bowl you a few." That's what they did. They were good like that, both of them.'

The visit of Derbyshire to Lord's at the start of June ended the winning sequence, though not through any lack of enterprise on anyone's part.

The first day was curtailed with the visitors only able to reach 150-4 after winning the toss. They declared on day two at 228-9, Emburey having taken five wickets for the hosts, and Middlesex, looking to make up for lost time forfeited any thought of batting points, declaring at 89 for no loss.

Overseas star John Wright's century then allowed Derbyshire to declare again, setting Middlesex 348 in 66 overs. Brearley and Radley fell early on and all looked lost at 88-4, but there was no thought of shutting up shop as the hosts continued to chase. With Gatting making 140 at better than a run a minute and first Emburey and then Edmonds providing support, Middlesex reached 322-5. Suddenly the highly improbable looked, well, probable. However, Gatting and Edmonds fell in quick succession amid a late collapse, meaning last pair Williams and Daniel had to bat out the final ten minutes to save the draw, Middlesex finishing eight runs short.

Winning ways were soon restored as Kent were crushed at Tunbridge Wells. Gatting's form carried over from the Sussex run chase as he made another hundred, while Clive Radley's 141 not out was his highest score of an underwhelming season by his standards. Emburey got five wickets in the first innings and Daniel five in the second. In the case of the latter, his efforts served as a prelude to what would statistically be his greatest performance on a cricket field.

The setting was the St Helen's Ground in Swansea where Daniel returned 9-61 in the second innings of a ten-wicket win. Mike Selvey wasn't selected for that game, but clearly enjoyed recalling their bowling partnership together, remembering his friend with a real sense of affection,

'Wayne had a lot of fun, he was a wonderful bowler, a perfect foil for me. He was very fast. He didn't know how to bowl slow. If you asked him in the nets to bowl slower he couldn't do it. He gave absolutely everything.

'There is no question it was a good partnership between me and Wayne. If the wind was blowing, I would do the hard yards into the wind and Wayne would come storming down the hill.

'I have some wonderful pictures of Wayne, one in particular that I treasure of him leaping into the crease. It's just the epitome of a powerful fast bowler. You just know he is going to bowl the heaviest ball you ever felt. He bowled a very heavy ball and it was a nasty length. He bowled a ball that was a bit more than five and three quarter ounces. It was like a cannonball – horrible. It was the sort of ball that would take your fillings out or give you an electric shock down your arm.'

Rain and an-over cautious approach from hosts Yorkshire meant the game at Abbeydale Park was drawn, but Middlesex's first innings batting collapse proved a forerunner to the Benson & Hedges Cup quarter-final back at Lord's which followed it, where, having sailed through the groups, they made a mess of chasing 192 to win, Clive Radley's 66 the only resistance as they lost by 52 runs to Lancashire.

A quirk of the fixture list meant that the Red Rose county remained in London for the next Championship fixture, which the rain returned to spoil and it petered out into a draw. It would mark the last appearance in first-class cricket of medium-pacer Bill Merry, who had a one stage been highly thought of in Middlesex circles. However, having failed to establish himself over four seasons he returned to the minor counties scene with Hertfordshire.

The bad weather followed them across the Thames to The Oval where Middlesex made 330-9 between the downpours of the first two days, thanks to Gatting's magnificent 192 – at that stage a career best.

Captains Roger Knight and Brearley did their best to breathe life into the contest with imaginative last day declarations, so leaving the hosts 250 to win in 44 overs. Surrey were never really in the hunt, but six wickets for Daniel meant Middlesex had more than a sniff of victory late on. However, those hopes were dashed as ninth-wicket pair Grahame Clinton and Robin Jackman batted out for a draw. Disappointment at not getting the extra 16 points was tempered a little by victory over their London rivals in their John Player League clash, a sixth win in their first seven games in that competition, so putting them in early season title contention. Sadly that form would falter through July where batting failures led to three successive defeats, a run which left a gap to eventual champion Sussex they were unable to bridge and they ultimately finished runners-up.

The batting frailties surfaced in the Championship too where Middlesex suffered a first defeat, by six wickets to Leicestershire at Uxbridge, in a game where they were forced to follow on. Unlike in the John Player League, however, they recovered quickly to record back-to-back innings victories over Nottinghamshire to get their title charge back on track. The second of these witnessed Keith Tomlins's highest Championship score of 138, just short of his career-best 146 made earlier that summer against Oxford University. The right-hander spent 11 seasons at Lord's and while he was only a regular in County Championship cricket in 1983 he played some valuable hands when others were away on Test duty, a fact appreciated by Roland Butcher.

'Keith Tomlins and all those guys came in with us together,' he said. 'Guys like him and Simon Hughes meant we were fortunate not to have to rely on one or two people to be effective because somebody with bat or ball would produce something and quite often more than one would.'

Two dull draws followed before something of a coming-of-age match unfolded for Cowans against Somerset at Weston-super-Mare. His five-wicket haul in the second innings meant the hosts were bundled out for only 57, Simon Hughes taking the other four to fall to bowlers as the two bowled unchanged.

For Cowans though, his highlight of the innings victory came in the first innings where he claimed the scalp of one of his heroes, Isaac Vivian Alexander Richards, caught by Edmonds.

'That was pretty special to me because it was a great way to test yourself against the best of the best,' he said.

'I was in good form at the time, bowling pretty good away swingers at a decent pace. The wicket was quite helpful as well which made a huge difference. It wasn't a flat track and had a bit of bounce.'

Unbeknown to Cowans, the dismissal caused quite a stir in the Somerset dressing room with even Richards himself impressed by the youngster who claimed his wicket. And they didn't go unnoticed either by Somerset opener Peter Roebuck, who flagged up the incident in an article for *The Cricketer* shortly afterwards.

'Roebuck wrote a piece about young fast bowlers to keep an eye on,' recalled Cowans. 'I remember the part of the article where he said, "Norman Cowans is a bit of a dark horse. He bowled against us at Weston-super-Mare and got Viv Richards out. When Viv came back to the dressing room he announced, 'I smelt the leather, man.'"

'I had no idea he'd said that, but was quite chuffed to read it. It was a pretty special game.'

Such an endorsement from a player of Roebuck's standing may have proved instrumental in Cowans's selection for the Ashes tour of 1982/83. It was in the wake of the tour party being announced that Cowans's nickname of 'Flash' first came to public prominence. As Cowans explained, until then it had been something that arose during his time with the MCC Young Cricketers and not a tag used in the dressing room at Lord's.

'My name, Flash, came when I was at MCC from a guy called Mark Scott who I was bowling to in the nets. Some of the lower order guys came for a net and couldn't lay a bat on me, so Mark said I was "quick as a flash".

'From then on Mark used to call me Flash, but he was the only one really. Then when I got picked for England, Ted Dexter was trying to find out about me for his piece in one of the papers. He rang Don Wilson, my old MCC coach, and he said, "Oh, you mean Flash."

'So he (Dexter) wrote the article calling me Flash and that's how I got known on the tour. I'd never been known as Flash to my Middlesex team-mates – it all came up out of Don Wilson's interview.'

As with the circle of life, while Cowans's career was on an upward curve towards its zenith, another was about to see the sun set on his illustrious years as a Middlesex player.

Mike Selvey had continued to play a valuable part in the golden era of success despite being a less-regular member of the side in Championship cricket at least. However, his long innings at Lord's came to an abrupt end in mid-August against Warwickshire at Coventry, a match otherwise famous for a 17-ball over by a young Gladstone Small plagued with issues of no-balls and wides.

Selvey had thrown his elbow out while bowling and while he was keen not to advertise the fact he was in pain, he elected not to drive to the Sunday League game at Edgbaston against the same opponents. He therefore left the vehicle at the team's hotel at Kenilworth for Wilf Slack to drive over the next day, while he caught a lift.

Arriving in the dressing room on the Sunday lunchtime, Selvey called to Slack, 'I just need to go and get my kit out of the car.'

To his horror, back came the reply, 'I got a lift in.'

Selvey, whose weekend was about to get worse, bellowed back, 'What do you mean I got a lift in, the car has got my kit in it!'

He took up the story when we spoke, 'I had to go back to Kenilworth to get my kit and by the time I got back the game had started and we were batting. In the course of that game I threw my arm out again and made it even worse.

'On the Monday I was supposed to bowl again and didn't tell anyone my arm had gone. So I strapped it up so that it was straight and took two wickets, but then said I can't do this any more, so took myself off the field.

'My elbow locked in that position for a fortnight and I never bowled another ball until January or February the following year.'

By that time Selvey had departed through the Grace Gates to take up the captaincy of Glamorgan, but his years of toil across the country and from the Nursery End at Lord's had taken their toll and his body began to fail, meaning he hung up his boots a year and a half later.

His tally of 101 first-class wickets in 1978 remains a record to this day for a Middlesex pace bowler in a single season. And while he cherished the three Test caps he won prior to that year, he believed in many ways they came too soon.

'I don't think I became a proper bowler until 1978 which was when I was at my best,' he concluded. 'Even when I played for England I was very naive. If I'd played for England in 1976 knowing what I knew in 1978 I'd have been twice the bowler I was.'

Even without Selvey's services for the second innings up at Coventry, Middlesex duly won by an innings with Daniel again among the wickets, but as someone who had remained a strong part of their one-day team, the seamer was missed in their Nat West Trophy semi-final with Surrey at The Oval which followed 24 hours later.

Selvey had returned figures of 1-17 from a full 12 overs as Middlesex won a thriller against Lancashire in the competition's second round, though he had been absent from another nailbiter in the quarter-final with Gloucestershire at Bristol, three runs the winning margin on that occasion.

There would be no such close call against the Brown Hatters. The bowlers looked have done a good job in restricting the hosts to 205-9 in their full 60 overs, Daniel the star turn with 4-24, while Emburey was as miserly as ever with 1-25 from his 12.

Hopes of another final, though, were blown away by a devastating new-ball burst from Surrey's West Indian paceman Sylvester Clarke, whose 4-10 in seven overs reduced Middlesex to 17-4. It proved a point of no return and they were bundled out for 80 in an ignominious display.

After only two days in which to lick their wounds, it was back to Lord's to entertain Yorkshire in what turned out to be a special game for Butcher – though not as special as it could have been. The White Rose county were hustled out for 182 on the opening day, but the hosts lost Brearley and Radley cheaply before the close and when Slack fell early on the second morning they were 68-3.

They needn't have worried as Gatting and Butcher first rebuilt and then took charge in a stand of 237. Gatting was stumped in the quest for runs, but Emburey provided good support as Butcher got closer and closer to his first double hundred. However, it never came as he was run out by a direct hit three short of the landmark. What you're all dying to know is whose call was it? Butcher said it was Emburey's, but there were no hard feelings.

'They were trying to give me a bit of time to get to 200 because we were looking to declare,' he advised. So we started to take unnecessary risks for singles and twos. Embers called me for a single and they scored a direct hit, so that was it. We wouldn't have been batting for a lot longer.'

The shame for Butcher was that rain washed out the final day, meaning the hustle for those quick runs was fruitless and he never did get that double hundred. He was however one of four players to pass 1,000 runs that season along with Gatting, Slack and Brearley.

Points having eluded them against Yorkshire, Middlesex were keen to consolidate their position at the top in the reverse fixture with Surrey and it was here fate gave them a helping hand.

A quick look at the wicket suggested it would be one for the spinners, never a bad scenario with Edmonds and Emburey in your ranks, but they were to receive unexpected help when Fred Titmus, now 49, put his head into the dressing room to say hello ahead of the toss.

'Fred had retired and had a couple of years coaching down at The Oval,' said former travel buddy Radley, taking up the tale. 'This particular day he was on his motorbike to go to a meeting in the city with somebody and he called in to see how the boys were going before the game.

'Titmus was sat in a chair on one side of the dressing room, smoking his trusty old pipe as ever and passing the time of day, when Brearley, sitting over the other side calls out, "Fred, we've just had a look at the wicket and it looks like it's going to turn square. Are you still registered?"'

With Fred keen to oblige, someone was despatched to the Middlesex office to see if they could locate the paperwork and it was soon established Titmus was still a Middlesex player. However, there was the small – or not so small – matter of the fact that he had no kit.

'He ended up borrowing my boots and trousers because they were the only ones that fitted him,' grinned Radley.

The punt on playing the extra spinner didn't pay immediate dividends with Titmus bowling 15 wicketless overs in the first innings. Added to that, Edmonds and Emburey bowled 86 overs between them for a mere wicket apiece as Surrey declared only three runs behind.

Slack and Tomlins both made half-centuries in the Middlesex second innings before, with time running out, Brearley showed his willingness to gamble once more, declaring and so setting Surrey just 161 to win.

As it had more often than not, the gamble paid off. With the wicket turning sharply as had been predicted, Edmonds and Emburey quickly removed the top order to leave Surrey floundering at 49-5. West Indian quick Sylvester Clarke produced a few big hits, but the wily Titmus came on to lure him into an indiscretion too many and he holed out to Cowans in the deep. Two more wickets would come for a man now bowling into his fifth decade in the sport before Emburey got the final wicket to clinch victory by 58 runs.

Cowans, as a much younger player, had heard dressing-room talk of the legend that was Titmus and they'd met a couple of times, but he had never had him as a team-mate until that moment.

'People always mentioned Fred Titmus and his legacy at Middlesex,' he said.

'He used to pop in every so often with his pipe and then disappear and then for one game I ended up playing with him. It was a turning wicket and Mike wanted three spinners so called for Fred. It was like a different age. He was such a cool character in the dressing room. He'd seen it all and done it, so he knew exactly what was required.

'Watching him bowl he made it look so easy. The way he held a ball back, teased the batsmen and set traps, always with fun, he was clearly enjoying it. He wasn't fazed about not having played for so long and then coming into an important game. It was like he'd been playing all season.

'I remember taking a catch off his bowling at long-on and I was thinking, "This guy is a legend. He comes on to bowl just like he's drinking a cup of tea." It wasn't hard work for him at all, it was phenomenal and playing with a legend like him was amazing.'

With Titmus withdrawing graciously back into retirement, this time for good, there would be one more spoke put into Middlesex's Championship charge down by the sea in Sussex over the August bank holiday. As always seems to be the way with the summer long weekend, part of it was wet, rain seriously curtailing play on day two, the Saturday. Declarations were made by both sides on the Monday, so setting Sussex 252 to win and that looked a formality when Allan Green and Gehan Mendis piled up 168 for the first wicket.

Daniel and Emburey struck back with three wickets apiece and Paul Parker was run out to put matters back in the balance at 201-7, but Alan Wells and Chris Waller joined forces to see Sussex home. It completed a miserable 24 hours for the Seaxes, whose dwindling hopes of overhauling their hosts in the battle for the John Player League title ended when Sussex won their encounter on the Sunday by 23 runs.

Mike Brearley leaves the field at Worcester after clinching his fourth title as Middlesex skipper.

The County Championship defeat, though, would prove just a blip when, a little over a week later Middlesex saw off Hampshire at Uxbridge to move within touching distance of the title.

Edmonds's six-wicket haul earned Middlesex a small first-innings advantage and Hampshire's eventual victory target bore a spooky similarity to that of Sussex's the previous weekend – 245.

The outcome though was never in doubt as Edmonds claimed his 850th first-class wicket when pinning diminutive middle-order batter David Turner lbw for a duck, one of four in the innings to swell his swag bag for the match to ten. Daniel weighed in with another four as Hampshire succumbed to 138 all out.

With the cushion of a 21-point lead, Middlesex headed to New Road to face Worcestershire only a small step from giving Brearley the perfect parting gift of a fourth County Championship crown in seven years.

The task was clear – bowl out Worcestershire in their first innings and that title was theirs regardless of anything chasers Leicestershire achieved away against Kent at Canterbury.

With Worcestershire opting to bat after winning the toss, Middlesex had an early chance to claim those ten wickets and they wasted little time. On a lively wicket, Cowans removed both openers in his new-ball spell and Slack, bowling his more than useful medium-pacers, soon nipped out two more. Only David Humphries with 56 held up the charge for long, Emburey's three wickets removing the tail to sew up the title by mid-afternoon.

From there it was a matter of whether they could win the game. Despite a fiery burst from a 17-year Ricky Ellcock, Butcher's 90 not out had Middlesex over 50 in front by stumps and though he fell early on day two, Edmonds produced a belligerent 92 to carry the advantage beyond 200.

Four wickets for Gatting meant it was almost over by stumps, Slack and Brearley knocking off the 50 required, with the latter fittingly making the winning hit.

'It was Mike's last game as captain and we really wanted to win the Championship for him. So, everyone was really up for it,' recalled Cowans.

'I remember it was misty and the wicket was doing a bit.

They tried to give us a hard time, but it was an amazing occasion really to win that. It was my first Championship and I don't think I realised how significant it was. It was fantastic to contribute to that and for Mike Brearley to bow out with winning the Championship.'

This was one of the few occasions when Middlesex's players actually celebrated a title won on the road, something recalled by Radley, who was also part of celebrations with the 2022 team when they were promoted from Division Two at New Road.

'We were having a drink at Worcester when the lads got promotion and Brears sent a WhatsApp round saying well done to everybody,' he recalled.

'I sent him one back saying it wasn't like the real thing when we quaffed champagne the day we won the Championship.'

And so it was one era closed and another was about to open. The baton of leadership would be passed on, but not as originally planned.

The 1982 County Champion's Plate complete with Middlesex crest.

CHAPTER 8
1985

After four County Championships in seven years, Mike Brearley had departed in the wake of the 1982 triumph to pursue the world of psychoanalysis and other ventures, leaving a huge void at the top of the side. Standing in the gap he left may have seemed a daunting prospect. There were surely no philosophers of the game like Mike Brearley in the Middlesex ranks; no one as tactically astute. No one with the degree in people and how to make them tick. Brearley's gifts were indeed many and considerable.

Ultimately of course the committee in situ at the time would alight on Mike Gatting as the man to try and continue a truly golden era in the club's history, but originally destiny beckoned to another who had emerged during Brearley's 11-year reign – John Emburey.

The off-spinner was considered the obvious successor and wheels were set in motion for him to assume the role, but his decision to undertake the rebel tour to South Africa in 1982 changed the course of Middlesex history.

Emburey recalled, 'In India in 1981/82 I got a telegram from Middlesex saying would I accept the vice-captaincy for Mike Brearley's last year in '82. I sent back a reply saying yes and then when I got back from India and Sri Lanka and headed out three days later to the rebel tour in South Africa they took the vice-captaincy away from me.'

With Emburey out of the running, focus switched to a choice between Gatting and the more experienced Phil Edmonds. In the end the lot fell with Gatting, partly because of the perception of Edmonds as not being captain material, despite him having fulfilled the role on more than one occasion in Brearley's absence on Test duty in 1981.

Gatting was as surprised as anyone to get the honour, but it seems his experiences performing the role in grade cricket down under in 1980 had stood him in good stead.

'It wasn't going to be me; I was never going to be it,' revealed Gatting. 'It was either going to be Philippe Edmonds or John Emburey. Embers went on the rebel tour of South Africa and the boys felt Philippe probably wouldn't be a good captain. Fantastic cricketer, but probably wouldn't make a good captain. Philippe thought he'd be the best captain in the world, as you would.

'I'd been over to Balmain [in Australia[and in my last year over there in 1980 I'd captained the team and we'd won the club championship. They also had a thing in the *Sydney Morning Herald* where you got points for batting, bowling and fielding and I managed to win that, which hadn't been done for a while by an Englishman. It was in those days where all the Test players played, so it was a fantastic standard, like playing county cricket if not better.

'Obviously, somebody rang up Balmain and said, "How was he as a captain?" When it came to making a decision in the end I think they wanted to give Embers a go and if he did OK then fine and if not I was the fallback sort of thing. Then that didn't come about because Embers went to South Africa and I think he was going to be banned for three years or whatever by England, so the committee asked me if I would do it.

'It was a bit of a sad way to get it, but it meant I was never really thinking about it to be perfectly honest with you. I was just enjoying my cricket, getting runs and we were winning games, so it didn't really worry me.'

Gatting clearly inherited an excellent team, a winning team, and such a scenario potentially brings extra pressure with it. Succeed and well, you're supposed to succeed, Brearley left you with a great team after all. Fail to add to the string of trophies of your predecessor and you become an easy fall guy.

Gatting claimed that he never saw it that way, but he nevertheless had to try and lead his way and some of the lessons he learned both in Australia and on his first England tour helped inform his style and approach.

'I think because I'd captained out in Australia which was quite tough, you had to earn the respect of the people out there, but I had to do it my way,' he said. 'I would try and be honest with people and open with them.

'What I did make a very big mental note of was, I went on my first trip with England while the Packer series was on. I went instead of David Gower when I was 20, but I felt a bit left out and it wasn't because they weren't nice people who were on the tour, it was just they got with their friends that they knew and I didn't really know anyone.

'Even though Mike Brearley was there he was trying to make sure everybody else was OK. I was going to be peripheral as opposed to mainstream, but it was a bit strange because of the way Mike had worked with us at Middlesex.

'So, I felt if ever I became captain I would make everyone on the periphery feel part of the team. I never really thought about captaining England either to be perfectly honest, but that came about too, so again I was very much aware of what I needed to do with guys on the outside.

'The rest was about captaining a very good team, having two of the best spinners in the world and three or four of the best seam bowlers in the County Championship. I'd say it was an easy team to captain because they all wanted to win and we'd built up a way of playing.'

Inevitably, Gatting's tenure saw a different brand of leadership. He was a very different character. He was less privileged than Brearley, no Harrow School or Cambridge spires for him. He was state-educated at John Kelly Boys' School not far from his family home in Kingsbury.

It soon became evident that Gatting was a natural leader, one who wasn't afraid to make decisions or own his mistakes. Perhaps most significantly, he didn't expect anyone to go anywhere he wasn't prepared to go first.

Roland Butcher said that consequently, Middlesex was a very different ship under Gatting compared to his predecessor.

'Brearley and Gatting were two different characters, so you wouldn't expect them to lead the same way,' he admitted.

'Gatt was more of an up-front guy. He wanted to lead from the front. He would have been the first one over the wall if there was a war on. That was him, he was that type of person.

'We used to say he was like a bull in a china shop. That was his approach. Brearley was more reserved, more thoughtful. He used more psychology really, where Gatt was lots of energy.'

Clive Radley endorsed this view of Gatting, also drawing on military metaphors to describe the new man at the helm's style,

'To this day you'd have Gatting in the trenches with you because you knew he would lead by example. Tactically he was good and got better and better, but you certainly followed him because you knew if he wanted something done he would do it. He was top-drawer, Mike.

'Brearley was renowned for being the most astute person on the circuit captaincy-wise so they were big boots to fill, but he [Gatting] did that well. He didn't give much sympathy if he didn't think people were trying their hardest because he would be.'

As for Emburey, having seen the dream of captaincy removed from him, the transition from Brearley to Gatting was probably a more difficult one. Now vice-captain, not to an older and wiser head like Brearley but to a contemporary, he admitted in our interview that the first season or so their communication wasn't always easy.

He revealed it was an exchange one day between him and wicketkeeper Paul Downton which changed the dynamics between the pair for the better.

And although Gatting being selected over the top of him probably cost Emburey a proper run at the England captaincy a few years later – Gatting got that too – 'Ernie', as he was affectionately dubbed, admitted that it was in fact the right choice for Middlesex.

'As vice-captain I remember making suggestions to Gatt saying, "We should do this," or "We should do that," without saying "What do you think of this, what do you think of that." It was almost as if I was telling him,' Emburey said.

'One day I was at first slip and Mike at second and when he moved away at the end of the over I remember I said to Paul Downton, "Gatt never listens to me."

'I remember Paul turning around to me and saying, "Perhaps it is the way you speak to him." That may have been a year or a year and a half later, sometime in 1984, but I never forgot that and I totally changed because I thought, he's right actually.

'Gatt was probably the right person for the job. I don't think I would have been hard enough. I think I would have been a good enough captain tactically, but I wouldn't probably have been as hard as Gatt. So, in the end it was probably a good choice, although I was very disappointed not to get it.

'I probably got the right position as vice-captain because I think we complemented each other with me in that role.'

While Emburey reconciled to being second in command, Edmonds appeared not to take the snub so easily, continuing to be as much of a challenge to Gatting as he had been to Brearley in times past.

Gatting admitted that he didn't always see eye-to-eye with Edmonds when it came to tactics and that his slow bowler was not always as focused on the cricket as he might have been, preferring to be the showman. However, his talent with ball in hand made those challenges worth facing.

Gatting acknowledged, 'Philippe didn't play as much as he should have done for many reasons, so he was a good one to have in the team when he did play. He hated losing, so you can say he was awkward in many ways, but everybody is different and the fact is he was really a very good cricketer you'd love to have in your side all the time.

'It's not always the nice ones you've got to have in your side. There will always be some difficult people you have to handle.

'Why was Philippe so difficult? Because he was Philippe. He felt he should have been captain of the team. That's what he wanted to be. He wanted to be in charge which is fair enough. People have ambitions like that. He felt he never got a chance and he should have done.

'Philippe was the first cricketer to walk out with a Swatch watch on his arm. You'd always see it even on a cold, long-sleeve sweater day.

'He was also the first person to sit in the Lord's pavilion with one of those brick phones as well. That was always one of his tricks. He'd say, "I've got to make a phone call."

'You'd tell him, "Philippe, lunch is at 1.15pm you can make it then." But it was, "No, no, I've got to do it at 1pm." And it was only because he wanted to go sit there get his brick phone out and parade it, so he could go to the sponsors and say, "There we are, here's me, I've just promoted your phone, blah, blah, blah." Sometimes it worked and sometimes it didn't. He was always wheeling and dealing.

'He wanted to do it his way when he came on to bowl as well. He wanted to bowl the way he wanted to bowl which is fair enough.

'One day it was turning square, so we had a short extra cover in and Phil said, "I want a midwicket."

I told him, "You don't need a midwicket. Let's have somebody stopping them getting leg-side of the ball or coming in at short leg. You've got your man on the off-side, so let's do away with midwicket."

"No, I want a midwicket."

"I'm going, "It's turning square. I want him to try and hit you through midwicket because you've got a short extra cover, a slip and a gully.'

Gatting got his way, but not for long and very nearly at serious personal cost, as he explained,

'He bowled these three full tosses and nearly killed me with one of them and said, "Told you I needed a midwicket. I don't want to be hit through there."'

The shakedown of the captaincy issue had other tough implications for Emburey too, seriously impacting his relationship with former best man Edmonds and indeed the relationship between their spouses too.

Emburey admitted, 'Philippe thought he should have got the captaincy for 1983 and that of course never happened. But he thought I'd gone behind his back over the vice-captaincy and our relationship fell out for about three years off the back of it.

'We had a close relationship, Philippe, his wife Frances, and Susie and I, and then there was no communication with Frances for about three years. Philippe blamed me and yet all I did was say yes.'

The new regime of Gatting and Emburey made a stout defence of the title in 1983. After a wet start they won ten games out of the first 12, losing only one. However, just one win in the next eight meant they needed cricket's equivalent of snookers to overhaul leaders Essex by the time they headed to Trent Bridge to face Nottinghamshire in the season finale. And those hopes of a miracle were doused by rain which washed out almost the entire first day's play, after which a draw was all but inevitable.

The following year, 1984, was almost the reverse where, after winning their opening encounter with Glamorgan, Gatting's men didn't taste victory in the next ten, losing five. Seven victories in the remainder of the campaign lifted them to a creditable third, but they were well adrift of the top two, Essex retaining the crown after a close fight with Nottinghamshire.

While success eluded him in the longer format, Gatting was still able to keep the trophy cabinet stocked and therefore retain the sense of a golden era courtesy of two of the most memorable one-day victories those who saw them will ever be privileged to have witnessed.

First came the 1983 Benson & Hedges Cup Final against Essex – another powerhouse of the era complete with Graham Gooch, Keith Fletcher, Stuart Turner, rising star Neil Foster and others.

After losing the toss, Middlesex stumbled to 74-4 and only a typically stoic unbeaten 89 from Radley carried Middlesex to 196 in their allotted 55 overs. Despite the veteran's heroics, the total looked dangerously slight, even more so when Essex raced to three figures for the loss of just Graham Gooch for a forceful 46.

'It was one of the best games of cricket I've ever played in,' recalled Norman Cowans.

'We had a very low score and were up against a phenomenal Essex side really. So we were very much up against it and didn't have the best start when we bowled. I was hoping to swing the ball, but Goochie whipped me through square leg a few times for four. That was the first time I'd bowled against Goochie and it was a lesson to be learned.'

Cowans produced a magnificent diving catch at cover to remove the dangerous Ken McEwan but with 69 needed and half the overs left, hope was fading both on the field and among the home support in the stands, before a huge moment changed the mood.

'A lot of the crowd left because they thought we were going to get hammered,' Gatting recalled.

'The wicket that probably got people believing was Keith Fletcher. Phil Edmonds was bowling and Clive Radley was asked to go to silly mid-off. Keith was one of the best players of spin of all time but the boys said, "We've got to get some wickets here. He's just come in, let's get a man in front and see what happens."

'Phil went up to bowl, Fletch got just one side of it and it must have seamed up the hill a bit and he nicked it straight out to Radders [Radley]. I'd never seen Fletcher get out that way before because he played back to spin all the time, but he got half forward and Philippe bowled it a little bit quicker than most other deliveries.'

Emburey agreed that this was a moment which fanned the dimly burning wick of belief back into flame. 'All of a sudden, you think, hello,' he said.

A final seemingly surging to an inevitable conclusion slowly but surely unfolded into a piece of sporting theatre which had spectators, whether lucky enough to be inside the Grace Gates, or like the author huddled around his television set at home – we had colour by then, though it was getting so dark you barely noticed – utterly transfixed.

Edmonds and Emburey squeezed for seemingly over after over, the off-spinner going wicketless but bowling his full allocation of 11 overs for just 17 runs as Essex's earlier cavalier approach gave way to circumspection bordering upon fear.

Amid the rising tension, unusual happenings unfolded, such as Keith Pont dropping his bat on to his off bail after being struck on the helmet by a rising ball from Neil Williams.

Brian Hardie's innings of 49 ended soon afterwards, but even so, England all-rounder Derek Pringle and Turner carried Essex to within 12 of victory, albeit with overs beginning to run out.

Wayne Daniel pinned Pringle lbw and then came two pivotal moments as substitute fielder John Carr plucked one out of the sky to remove Turner, and David East middled one straight to Gatting at midwicket – a foot either side of the skipper it would have been four.

Every cricketing soap opera needs a run out and Ray East became the fall guy, wandering beyond the safety of the crease distracted by optimistic shouts for leg before.

It left the last pair, Foster and John Lever, needing five from the final over, but Cowans brought one back off the seam to castle a crestfallen Foster as Middlesex somehow won by four runs in the gathering gloom – no floodlights back then.

Radley, without whom there would never have even been a contest, was named player of the match, the second time in three finals of this golden era in which he'd scooped the accolade.

Yet, when it came to honours handed out by the press, it was Gatting and Emburey who were both listed among *Wisden*'s five Cricketers of the Year in the 1984 edition.

Speaking of Gatting's first triumph since inheriting the Brearley mantle, *Wisden* scribe Mike Neasom wrote, 'He was expected to extend Middlesex's 'golden age' by presenting their somewhat fickle supporters with a trophy. He did so too, and it was the first one available. He revealed the Brearley touch by forcing the Essex batsmen to panic as Middlesex, losers all day, pinched a cliff-hanging victory in the Benson & Hedges Cup Final.'

Emburey's frugal bowling in the final was symptomatic of a season where he took 96 Championship wickets and scored 772 runs to boot. *Wisden*'s citation included the following on the spinner's bowling wiles, 'Though he relies less on variations of flight than most great off-spinners, Emburey's high arm, poise in delivery stride, and extreme closeness to the stumps when he lets the ball go make him in other respects a classic bowler of his type.

'A big spinner when conditions call for it, his wicket-to-wicket line of flight allied to steady length and drift from leg to off earn him many successes, either bowled off stump, caught at slip or at the wicket against batsmen playing for the ball to turn.'

As if like clockwork it was Radley again who took the starring role in the 1984 NatWest Trophy triumph over Kent.

Thanks to Chris Cowdrey's 58 at better than a run a ball, Kent made 232-6 despite typically frugal bowling from Emburey (1-27).

Kent looked favourites when in reply Gatting fell to leave Middlesex 124-4. However, Radley (67) stood firm as ever, he and wicketkeeper Downton (40) finding the gaps and running hard in a fifth-wicket stand of 87.

Both fell in quick succession to put the game in the balance and six were needed from the final over with spin twins Emburey and Edmonds at the crease and darkness closing in.

'That was another late finish where it was getting dark and it would have been more difficult for the fielders fielding square of the wicket, whereas, with the ball coming directly to us, you adjusted to the light,' recalled Emburey.

With one needed off the final delivery, Richard Ellison strayed on to Emburey's pads allowing him to guide the ball down to long leg for the winning hit. Emburey remembers sprinting off 'swinging my arms in celebration' as the crowd streamed on to the field, the custom in those days.

Radley duly collected his latest gold award and his skipper was quick to acknowledge the value of the man who was for so long his senior pro both on and off the field.

'Rads had an incredible habit of making runs on the big occasion,' Gatting said.

'I remember the first time he did it in 1977 against Glamorgan where he got 60 or 70 in such a low-scoring game and got us over the line.

'You can't underestimate the influence Radders had on a lot of people, especially the young kids, because he was always happy to talk to the youngsters. He would always be there or thereabouts and would always do it his way.

'He hated losing and he was just a lovely man who you would want to have in your side because you knew he would take it through and finish it off. He would very rarely get out once he got in and in finals like that it was what you needed.'

The latter win especially enabled Gatting and company to carry momentum into 1985 which would prove a challenging one for the Lord's tenants on many different levels.

Mike Selvey was the notable name missing compared to the class of 1982, but Norman Cowans and Neil Williams now had two extra summers of experience to draw upon and the presence of Simon Hughes further bolstered the seam options.

Middlesex, though, were in many ways the victims of their own success, the England selectors regularly pillaging their ranks for the Ashes series against Australia.

Gatting, Downton, Edmonds and Cowans were heavily involved in the one-day internationals which preceded the Ashes and when the Tests got under way, Gatting, Downton and Emburey, whose ban for the South Africa rebel tour had now expired, played all six, Edmonds five and Cowans also graced the first game at Headingley.

The impact on Middlesex domestically was considerable with Gatting and Downton missing ten Championship games, while Emburey and Edmonds sat out nine. The absences would make Middlesex's title challenge all the more laudable, meaning as they did others would need to step from the shadows and fill the void.

There would be five games before the international season got going and Middlesex made a positive start, beating Worcestershire by eight wickets. It sounds like a routine win, but in truth it was anything but.

Star Indian all-rounder Kapil Dev blazed a century on the opening day in only 78 balls, with Cowans in particular feeling the force of the onslaught. In reply, only half-centuries from opener Slack and Emburey got Middlesex to 195, but they trailed by 106. Their response to such adversity was impressive, bowling Worcestershire out a second time for 103 before chasing down the victory target courtesy of a swashbuckling 80 not out from 62 balls by Roland Butcher. This would be the second of three successive seasons when Butcher made more than 1,000 first-class runs, most of them in an aggressive see-ball, hit-ball style.

'We used to say Brearley filled bars and Roly emptied them,' Selvey told me.

Not for the first time on a visit north to play Yorkshire, Middlesex came out on the wrong side of a thriller, but Slack's early season form continued with scores of 86 and 99. Games with Kent and Glamorgan were drawn, the former when the visitors declined a last-day run-chase, while in the latter the Welsh county batted comfortably to safety after being asked to follow on. Every Middlesex player, including wicketkeeper Downton, was called upon to bowl in Glamorgan's second innings.

With the first ODI on the horizon, Sussex were duly despatched by an innings thanks to nine wickets in the match for Cowans. According to Emburey, Cowans was a top-class performer, especially from the Nursery End at Lord's, but he sometimes needed to be cajoled out of a tendency to bowl within himself. Emburey recalled one such occasion when during an interval in play there was a frank discussion in the toilets, which apparently were quite often the scene of strategy meetings at Lord's,

'Norman was a crackerjack bowler, but Gatt got annoyed with him occasionally because he felt he should bowl quicker because he could be genuinely fast. Norman had this thought process which we pinned him down about in the bloody toilets at Lord's one lunchtime.

'Gatt said to him, "Norman, you've got a new ball, why don't you always run in and bowl quick?" Norman replied, "Well, if we don't get wickets, later in the day I'm still going to have to bowl and we'll get a second new ball."

'So Gatt told him if you bowl quick when you've got the new ball at the beginning of the day, you won't have to bowl later in the day because they'll be all out. I think that got through to him a little bit.

'Norman was a great bowler bowling at the Nursery End because he had the ability to make the ball nip up the slope. He could swing the ball away and then all of a sudden he would get one that would nip back. He got lots of wickets bowled or lbw where people were letting the ball go. He was a much better bowler than people give him credit for.'

With Sussex vanquished, it was time to sample life largely without Gatting and the rest of the England brigade in attendance.

Save for one match where Emburey did the honours, the burden of captaincy fell on senior pro Radley, who to a large degree had to rely on pacemen Daniel, Cowans and Williams in the absence of the spin twins. Perhaps the wet weather helped in that regard by keeping the pitches greener.

With resources stretched, it seems that Middlesex abandoned their policy of attacking and finding creative ways to win matches in favour of a more conservative approach

Wisden reported that Radley's thinking was, 'We didn't expect that the makeshift side could win much, but we looked for every bonus point and tried to make sure that no challenger took advantage of us being under strength.'

The plan largely came off as although only one game was won under Radley's leadership, only two were lost with bonus points steadily accrued.

Radley was a key part of the run-making process, amassing his highest number of first-class runs in a season since 1972 and averaging over 50. Clearly the burdens of captaincy merely heightened his survival instincts.

Graham Barlow, too, rediscovered his form – a visit to a faith healer having apparently rectified a hip injury which had plagued him throughout the previous summer. Cowans said that Barlow was something of a superstitious type,

'We called Graham Barlow "Gladys". He was in phenomenal form that year. It was amazing to watch his preparation. Everything had to be just so before he went out and he had his rituals when he got out there too, but when he was in form there was no better player to watch. He used to be such a great competitor as well and a great runner between the wickets.

'He used to take us on our fitness training as well where he was very enthusiastic, and would gee the guys up. What a great team man. Watching him and Wilf bat together was a joy.'

Slack and Barlow formed a formidable partnership at the top of the order, the St Vincent man enjoying his best season yet for Middlesex. He would pass 50 13 times in first-class cricket in 1985, going on to make a hundred on three of those occasions.

Middlesex's West Indian-born contingent were stalwarts of that class of '85. Slack and Butcher played every one of the 24 Championship fixtures, Daniel all but two and Cowans and Williams 19 apiece. If you add in Zambian Edmonds and Kenyan Rajesh Maru, though the latter had left by 1985, Middlesex were surely the most culturally diverse team, not only in county cricket but in sport in general in the 1980s.

Cricket has been rocked in recent times by Azeem Rafiq's allegations of racism shown towards him during his time as a player at Yorkshire, the hearings into which having been concluded during the writing of this book. So it is interesting to reflect for a few moments on what it would have been like for this quintet, four of whom had come to England with their families as children or young teenagers, both inside and outside the Middlesex dressing room, back in the 1980s.

Cowans was clear that those who shared his cultural background and came before him were both an inspiration and eased his path.

He spoke of what was then regarded as good-natured banter on both sides, though he admitted that it may not be regarded as such today and said cultural differences sometimes showed themselves in amusing ways.

'The likes of Wayne Daniel, Roland Butcher and Wilf Slack who were there before I came definitely helped me to settle and to feel part of it,' he reflected. 'There was no barrier to getting in the Middlesex team regardless of whatever colour you were.

'We were all very good cricketers and that helped a lot that we were so good at what we did. It was a very diverse dressing room where we all came from different backgrounds. We had this dynamic in the dressing room where we used to pull each other's legs. The politics is different now, so it might not be seen as banter today, but we took it in the spirit in which it was meant.

'I was just aware we were a team of great players and it just happened that half the team were Black. When we crossed the line we just played really well together while in the dressing room we had a different way of doing things.

'For instance, the white players, as soon as the game was finished they'd shower and be gone, where the Black players would be putting all our moisturiser on our skin, doing all our pampering and they'd be ready to go. It was a completely different way of doing things where we all had our own quirks. The white players couldn't wait to get down to the Tavern and have a beer and we were like, "No, man, we've got to make sure we cream the skin and then go."

'We liked our music and had our food spicier, but at the end of the day, when we crossed the line to go out there we were just one team.'

Butcher said those like him of Black culture stood out when it came to attitudes towards drink, though he was also clear that the team was diverse in other ways beyond skin colour,

'We weren't only diverse in having five Black players. If you look at the backgrounds of others in the Middlesex side, you had guys from Oxford and Cambridge, John Emburey from Peckham, Gatting from up the road in Brent in with Neil Williams and Wilf Slack from St Vincent, Cowans from Jamaica, Edmonds from Zambia, Norman Featherstone [from] Rhodesia as it was then and me from Barbados.

'None of us Black players were drinkers though. Wilf didn't drink, I didn't, Norman didn't drink, or Neil. Wayne would have one now and again, but we were not people who spent a lot of time in the pubs or that sort of thing.

'At the end of a day's play, I wanted to get home as quickly as possible – that was me. Obviously, in the early days up until 1979 I was in London, I was a single man, though I met my wife in 1976, so things started to change then. When I got married in 1980 was when I moved out of London, so now I was going further out, which meant when play finished I was heading home.'

Others in cricket from beyond the home dressing room (Middlesex players who contributed to this book didn't wish to identify who in light of current sensitivities) tagged Daniel and co. as the 'Jackson Five'. It's in the same vein I guess as how West Bromwich Albion's trio Cyrille Regis, Laurie Cunningham and Brendan Batson were christened the 'Three Degrees' in that same era.

According to some it was a label which caused offence, Cowans indicating that there was an element of upset. Others perhaps viewed the label as a back-handed compliment, a great band being compared to a great band of cricketers – a mark of grudging respect if you will.

There was, though, definitely a darker side. Cowans spoke of turning up at an unnamed ground to hear comments like, 'Oh, are we playing the West Indies?' and worse still, there were occasions when some players had things thrown at them which indicated they were being subjected to racist abuse.

Mike Selvey, who had seen the beginnings of these things before leaving Middlesex for Glamorgan in 1983, felt more could have been done to challenge those responsible and to support their team-mates.

'None of us in our side ever thought, "Aren't we a diverse side." All we saw were five wonderful cricketers. That's who they were to us. That's not strictly true of other teams who saw us differently. It is certainly a regret of mine that I didn't speak up more. I didn't used to like it when people used to say 'here come the Jackson Five or 'here come the Three Degrees'. It is only now I start to realise.

'It was overtly racial and I didn't like it. I wish we collectively had spoken up more about it back then, rather than laughed along with it. The game has got to get back to understanding that is how the game has to be and should be. It's not about where you come from; it's about whether you can play cricket. We were very fortunate we had five great cricketers there.

'I was very proud of our team in that regard. Neil was a slinky, slippery bowler. You had Butch in the side because you knew you were getting someone who would win two or three games a year because of how he could play. That's what you wanted from Butch and he used to deliver it.'

Three wins in a row in late June and early July would be the ones to propel Middlesex into title contention in 1985.

The first saw Nottinghamshire swept aside by ten wickets at Trent Bridge. Daniel, bowling off a shorter run than in previous years but with no discernible drop in pace or hostility, took four wickets to restrict the host to 202 in their first innings, a tally Barlow and Slack almost overhauled by themselves in an opening stand of 171. Slack went on to make 112 and with Barlow and Gatting making 70s Middlesex were soon well in front. Three characteristically big sixes from Butcher in his 71 ensured Notts were over 200 in arrears by the time they batted again.

Daniel was unable to bowl in the second innings because of a stomach upset, but Cowans and Williams brilliantly filled the void between them, taking four wickets apiece, and it was only some late belligerence from last man Kevin Cooper which forced Middlesex to bat again to knock off the 15 required for victory.

Daniel's stomach complaint was slow to clear up meaning he wasn't fit to take part in the visit to New Road to face Worcestershire two days later. His absence was a double blow for Middlesex, who had Gatting and co. away on Test duty, so Keith Tomlins, Colin Metson, Jamie Sykes, Simon Hughes and Graham Rose were all called into the first XI.

Tottenham-born Rose would enjoy a remarkable debut which puts me in mind of a non-cricket-related story I have both heard and indeed retold many times. So, please indulge me.

There was once a young man who was part of a very famous orchestra. This particular orchestra got to play regularly at the best venues in the world. It had everything. There were stringed instruments galore, violins, cellos, double bass, even a harp and a sitar. There was brass, trumpets, trombones tubas and cornets. There were wind instruments, saxophones, flutes, oboes, clarinets, and of course there were drums.

This young man often looked around the orchestra pit before a performance – you name it, this orchestra had it – wishing he could play this or that instrument.

Why so melancholic, you might ask? Well, this young man was the triangle player. His role was to play one note in one piece of music in the entire performance.

Yet every night he would still dress up in his shirt and bow tie, polish his shoes to a fine mirror shine and take his seat in the orchestra pit. And each night when his time came he would play his one note perfectly and at exactly the right time.

The young man in the orchestra pit in that game at Worcester in 1985 was Graham Rose.

He experienced an anti-climax on day one as the rain came down and washed out play. His maiden Championship wicket was former England seamer Neal Radford and Middlesex declared their first innings early on the third morning 88 in arrears in a bid to make up for lost time, meaning Rose didn't get a bat.

Like my man in the orchestra pit, he kept waiting for his moment which arrived soon after Worcestershire went out to bat for a second time, when he had Pears' skipper Phil Neale caught by Butcher. It proved to be the start of something special as one wicket didn't bring two – it brought six, 6-41 to be exact, including the prize scalp of Kapil Dev.

Rose's heroics set up a run chase in which he missed out, scoring only four, but by then he had more than made his mark. Butcher though thrashed 120, while, following a late wobble, Sykes, more of whom later, and Metson shared an eighth-wicket stand of 31 to get Middlesex home by three wickets.

Gatting believed that players stepping up in the way Rose did at New Road was pivotal to Middlesex's success, and an example of the talent they had to call upon outside of the first XI.

'1985 was another of those times when we had some really good people on the fringes, in and around the team, young guys who came in and did a job while we were away,' ventured Gatting. 'Then, when the Test guys came back we made sure we won the matches.'

Sadly, many of those talents ended up having to go elsewhere to play cricket, or drifted out of the game altogether because there weren't sufficient opportunities for them at Lord's.

Rose was one such player. He appeared only once more in the Championship-winning side of 1985 and made five outings the following year. Unlike some others he did get a chance to play a prominent part in another cricketing orchestra, that of Somerset, taking over 600 wickets and scoring in excess of 8,000 first-class runs, achieving the feat of finishing his career with a higher batting than bowling average, so he can be classed a genuine quality all-rounder.

Other future stars forced to move on included Phil DeFreitas and Chris Lewis.

'The CEO at the time told them to go because they weren't going to get an opportunity,' revealed Gatting. 'He was probably right, but it's sad to see people of that much talent have to leave.'

Test players restored to the fold and with Daniel fit and firing again, Middlesex completed their hat-trick of wins on the road at Northamptonshire's County Ground.

They were on top from the start thanks to the latest century stand for the opening partnership between Barlow and Slack, the former this time being the one to push on to three figures once the pairing was broken.

One of only two five-wicket hauls for Edmonds that season then secured a winning lead of over 140 and after half-centuries for Radley and Downton, the left-arm spinner took four more to make it nine in the match.

The return with Northamptonshire at Uxbridge would be the only win in the next nine Championship games and it was one which would be remembered for a special reason by Radley.

Now 41 and in the twilight of a career with the Seaxes stretching back 19 years, Radley had clocked up in excess of 25,000 first-class runs, yet his highest score had come on Test duty with England in New Zealand in the winter of 1977/78 – a marathon innings of 158 in over ten hours.

A double century had long eluded him but it finally came, not in the grand surrounds of Lord's but at Uxbridge Cricket Club. Yet it might have all played out very differently as Radley himself explained.

'You'd think if you'd played as many games as I had as a batter you'd have got a double century or two, but my only one was that one at Uxbridge,' he reflected.

'There are funny things that you remember. I remember Wayne Larkins dropping me on nought or certainly before I got to double figures and it was quite an easy one at slip. It was a nice place to bat at Uxbridge in as much as the ball came on to the bat and went over the outfield like a tracer bullet. I would have got a few runs there over the years.'

Radley certainly made Larkins pay for his drop; his milestone innings made batting at five was spread over more than six hours. He shared a fifth-wicket stand of 289 with Downton – still a Middlesex record for that wicket against Northamptonshire to this day. Emburey weighed in with 68 more as the hosts built up a massive score of 567-8 declared.

They had been able to accumulate runs in leisurely fashion thanks to bowling out the visitors for only 191, shortly after lunch on the first day. The morning's cricket was enlivened by West Indian spinner Roger Harper, who plundered eight sixes in a whirlwind 97, with Daniel, unusually for him, being particularly harshly treated. However Daniel bounced back quickly, his four second-innings wickets – including that of Harper – helping Middlesex wrap up an innings win.

Clive Radley made his one and only double hundred of a glittering first-class career, aged 41.

The victory was the last for some while as Middlesex went winless through August, but they were still well in contention when journeying to face Leicestershire in early September where it was two of their bowlers who once again took centre stage.

First to catch the eye was Cowans. Back on the ground where he'd claimed his first Championship wickets for Middlesex four years earlier, he continued his love affair with Grace Road by recording what would be a career-best 6-31. In another nod to the events of 1981, he again included Chris Balderstone, Nigel Briers and perhaps most notably, David Gower among his wickets – quite an illustrious trio.

Cowans admitted to fond memories of the Leicestershire pitch, but he cited two other performances as surpassing his efforts that September day in 1985, with the latter perhaps surprisingly trumping the former,

'The wicket at Leicester always gave you a bit of a chance because they had some decent seamers themselves. During a season you come up against different conditions and sometimes those conditions suit a pace attack more than the spinners.

'On paper, my 6-77 against Australia in the Boxing Day Ashes Test [of 1982] would be better, given it was my first Test series and a baptism of fire in front of 90-odd thousand

Norman Cowans – a 'Crackerjack' bowler in Middlesex's title-winning side of 1985.

people. That's pressure, so getting man of the match and helping England to win the Test in Melbourne would be the pinnacle of anyone's career.

'However, even better was helping England to win in India in 1984/85 when I was the main strike bowler as there was no Bob Willis or Ian Botham. Being able to perform on dead wickets and helping us win the series was more satisfying,'

Cowans's efforts justified Gatting's decision to put the hosts in as they were hustled out for only 158. Radley stuck his hand up in reply with a typically resilient 87 and with four other batters getting 30 or more, Middlesex led by 140.

Then it was time for Daniel to take centre stage, ripping out Leicestershire's top order before later mopping up the tail to record his best figures of the campaign, 7-62.

Daniel's team-mates confirmed that he wasn't just a big personality on the field, but also the life and soul of the dressing room off it. Several of them made mention of the big red phone in the changing room at Lord's which would be glued to the paceman's ear as he tried to surreptitiously whisper sweet nothings to whatever young lady he was courting the attentions of at the time. Needless to say, a good many of those team-mates were hanging on to every word spoken.

It wasn't only those conversations involving Daniel that the rest of the squad listened to. Roland Butcher, who shared a flat with Daniel at one stage in their Middlesex careers and therefore knew him better than most, relayed how his fellow countryman would entertain an increasing number of willing listeners, not to mention Harry Sharpe, the then Middlesex scorer, during rain breaks and intervals.

'Wayne was the best story teller. Most of it was lies, but the way it was told he would have the dressing room in stitches,' Butcher laughed. 'Harry Sharpe used to hang on to every word. He knew they were tales from afar of course. Wayne was so funny, so very funny.'

Victory at Grace Road sent Gatting and company to the summit of the County Championship table and five wickets for Williams at next to no cost to shoot Essex out for 92 in their first innings in the penultimate match at Chelmsford raised hopes of wrapping up the title with a game to spare. It didn't though play out that way. An accomplished century from Gatting consolidated their strong position and despite a later collapse they led on first innings by a little shy of 200. However, centuries for Graham Gooch and David East meant Middlesex had to chase 274 to win very much against the clock, and in the end they needed an unbeaten 83 from Gatting to emerge with a draw

This sent them into the last game with Warwickshire up at Edgbaston with a one-point lead over Hampshire in what was a straight fight between the two.

According to Gatting, his side could scarcely believe their luck when they turned up in Birmingham to find a wicket more than amenable to spin bowling,

Mike Gatting and team-mates spray the champagne at Edgbaston.

'Any pitch would have been good really apart from a bland, nothing sort of pitch which you can sometimes get at Edgbaston, but Warwickshire produced an absolute Bunsen Burner for us. It was unbelievable.

'I know it was the end of the season, but we couldn't believe it when we turned up there. I think they had Norman Gifford and someone else as spinners, but I remember thinking we couldn't have asked for a better wicket. I think even their players thought, "Fancy having a turner for Edmonds and Emburey." I don't quite know what happened, but it was the perfect pitch for us really.'

Hampshire kept up the pressure on their rivals by bowling out hosts Nottinghamshire on the first day of their final fixture, but Middlesex retained the upper hand by dismissing Warwickshire cheaply despite losing the toss, and rattling up 64-0 in reply by the close.

On day two, half-centuries for Slack, Brown, Gatting and Emburey, the last with the aid of four sixes, led Middlesex to 445 all out by the close, a lead of 258, while Hampshire had to declare behind, forfeiting a batting point in the process.

For Gatting's men the task for the last day of the season was clear: bowl out Warwickshire and they would be champions regardless of what happened in the East Midlands.

In truth the result was never really in doubt as, despite an opening stand of 56 and some stubborn resistance from former England opener Dennis Amiss, the visitors claimed the laurels by soon after tea, Edmonds and Emburey doing the business with four wickets apiece on the turning pitch.

Up the road at Trent Bridge, Hampshire made a heroic attempt to chase down 280, finishing 12 short with their last pair at the wicket, leaving Middlesex champions by 18 points.

As a footnote to 1985, there was a first Championship appearance for one Angus Fraser. It would be five years before Middlesex lifted the trophy again, by which time Fraser would have served his apprenticeship and made his first forays into the Test arena, but more of that presently.

The intervening period would also witness a change in the playing laws, while tragedy visited Middlesex's doors with the loss of a much-loved team-mate.

CHAPTER 9
1990

Their 1985 County Championship triumph meant Middlesex had won a trophy in every year of the 1980s bar 1981 and while it would be another five years before they could again claim domestic cricket's biggest prize, there were still, even amid something of a transition in player terms, successes along the road.

The 1986 summer witnessed them drop to 12th in the Championship, but they reached a third one-day final in as many seasons in the Benson & Hedges Cup and in the words of the then BBC television cricket anchor Peter West, 'After a largely quiet and unglamorous day, it produced a rousing finish.'

The mere mention of it being an unglamorous day hints at the fact that Middlesex's veteran warhorse Clive Radley might have been somewhere in the thick of the action – and so it proved.

Now in his seventh final, the senior pro was required to once again steer the tenants of Lord's from the perils of 85-4 to the calmer waters of 199-7, his typically gritty top score of 54 at least giving them something to defend.

Tremendous pace bowling from Wayne Daniel and Norman Cowans reduced Kent to 20-3 in their chase and an astonishingly frugal spell of 11-5-16-0 from John Emburey meant that Kent still needed 99 from the final 12 overs. It's incredible to think in these days of heavy bats, white balls and brutal six-hitting that it had taken 38 overs of a chase to raise 100. Graham Cowdrey's excellent 50, ended by Radley's catch at midwicket and some big hits from Richard Ellison got Kent closer than some believed possible and when Steve Marsh pulled Simon Hughes into the Warner Stand for six midway through the last over, for a moment they looked favourites. But needing to hit the last ball for six, Graham Dilley, who had earlier bowled magnificently, could only manage two, meaning Middlesex had beaten their rivals off the last ball in a Lord's final for the second time in less than two years.

Emburey took the Gold Award, not only for his tight bowling spell but also for 28 useful runs and a spellbinding slip catch. For Radley, who played for one more season before the years caught up with him this was something of a last hurrah, so it seems fitting to allow Cowans to pay him one final tribute.

'Clive Radley, what can you say about this amazing player,' he said. 'He was very unorthodox, but got the job done. The beauty of playing with someone like Clive Radley was he showed you didn't have to look pretty to score your runs – just look in the book. He was so knowledgeable about the game. He knew the bowlers inside out and he was such a fighter. What a player. Always did well on the big occasions and never let Middlesex down.'

The following season produced a dramatic downturn where a mix of England call-ups and losses of form meant Mike Gatting's side finished one off the bottom of the Championship and made no impression in the one-day competitions.

But as the next generation of talent began to establish itself, so things improved once more in 1988 with Middlesex back in the top half of the table and semi-finalists in the newly instituted Refuge Assurance Cup after finishing fourth in the standings.

A near miss there then, but silverware would be gleaned in the final one-day showpiece of the season, the NatWest Trophy. It was a game which really introduced Mark Ramprakash to a national cricket audience.

Born in Bushey in 1969 to an Indo-Guyanese father and English mother, Ramprakash learned his early cricket at Bessborough CC, where he dabbled with fast bowling before devoting himself to batting. He would be another discovery of Don Bennett, who didn't need much convincing he had uncovered a rare talent.

'I hadn't seen Ramps play, but I remember Don Bennett saying to me ,"Norman, I've seen this guy called Mark Ramprakash,"' said Cowans. '"I tell you what, he's the best batsman I've seen since Gatt. He's the best young player I've ever seen."

'I think he'd played a second team game against Leicestershire at Hornsey and Don had been to watch. Phillip DeFreitas and all these sorts of guys were playing for Leicester and Ramps hooked them all over the place. He made them look ordinary and he was probably only 16 at the time. It made me think I can't wait to see this guy.'

Cowans didn't have to wait long as Ramprakash made 63 not out on his Championship debut against Yorkshire in 1987, aged only 17 and still a schoolboy at Harrow Weald College. Another half-century would soon follow.

He still wasn't a regular in the 1988 season, but made over 400 championship runs in 11 innings, including three further fifties, one of which came at Hove in early September immediately prior to the NatWest Trophy Final date with Worcestershire at Lord's.

Cowans and Ramprakash were travel companions back then and the paceman recalled vividly their conversation on route back to London from the south coast on the eve of the final,

'Ramps said to me, "If I get picked, what do you think?"

'So I told him, "If you get picked just go out there and enjoy yourself. Just enjoy playing and the occasion."

Ramprakash clearly took Cowans's words to heart – and Middlesex would need him to.

All appeared to be going to plan when despite 64 from their skipper Phil Neale,

Worcestershire could only scrape together 161-9 after Middlesex put them in, Hughes picking up four wickets, while Cowans bowled his full 12 overs at less than two an over, plus the early wicket of Steve O'Shaughnessy.

That score looked a lot more when Graham Dilley, who had moved from Kent to Worcestershire the previous summer, ripped out Middlesex's top three and skipper Gatting was run out for a duck, meaning two days shy of his 19th birthday Ramprakash was making his way through the Lord's Long Room and out in front of a packed house with his side 25-4.

What happened over the next two hours was a precocious young talent enchanted a spellbound crowd, not with a series of huge shots, but with an innings which defied his years. In company first with Roland Butcher and then Emburey, Ramprakash, who knew run rate was not an issue, made a half-century to take Middlesex to the brink of a victory, eventually achieved by three wickets with four and a half overs to spare.

According to Gatting, even at that stage it was clear that Ramprakash was going to be no run-of-the-mill county cricketer,

'You could see he was going to play for England. When he walked out and won that match against Worcester in a one-day final at Lord's. I wouldn't have been able to do that at his age I don't think.'

Just over a week later back at Lord's, Wilf Slack, who had played in the above final, walked off the ground having made 80 in the second innings of the final County Championship match of the season against Kent.

He'd chalked up more than 1,000 Championship runs for the eighth season in a row and was a fixture at the top of the order. Only Gatting that year had made more runs in a Middlesex shirt. But no one could have imagined then that it would be Slack's final innings for the county.

Four months later, the devout Christian was batting in the Gambia on a Christians in Sport tour when he collapsed at the wicket. The emergency services were summoned, but Slack died on the way to the hospital less than a month on from his 34th birthday.

Numbingly shocking as this was, there had been warnings. Cowans remembered him collapsing or 'fainting' several times on the field of play, and Gatting recalled him keeling over in the nets on the 1986/87 tour of Australia. The St Vincent-born left-hander always seemed to recover quickly and tragically, no test carried out got to the bottom of what ailed Slack until it was too late.

'It was where his valve had closed and he would collapse and black out,' said another of his team-mates, John Emburey. 'Then the valve would open again, which meant when they did tests on him everything was normal. So they never really got to the bottom of it.'

Players were speedily informed of Slack's passing, Gatting relaying the tragic news to several of his stunned team-mates.

'I think the club were pretty good dealing with Wilf's death,' reflected Gatting. 'They sent out messages to everybody, so there wasn't much more you could say, apart from just utter devastation. You talk about Wayne [Daniel] being a lovely man. Wilf was from St Vincent as Neil Williams was and sadly, I went to both their funerals. They both died at a very young age and it was just so sad because they were both wonderful human beings and fantastic cricketers as well.

'All I remember is it was unbelievably devastating. It was a bit like when my son rang me and said, "Have you heard Shane Warne has died?" I was like, "What, don't be so stupid." This was an even earlier death because Wilf wasn't even 40. It was a very sad day, for Middlesex, for everybody.

'He was quietly competitive. He loved batting and that is all he wanted to do. He also bowled some very good medium-pacers I might add.'

The players and staff would turn out *en masse* at Slack's funeral a few weeks later as Emburey explained:

'It was very, very sad. I remember going to the funeral which was here in London and it was an open coffin. So everyone got up and filed around it and it was awful. He was a man of strong faith as was his sister, his sister was a lovely woman. To me Wilf was a big loss.'

Perhaps hit hardest by the tragic events was Butcher, who had a strong bond with Slack right from when he first arrived at Lord's:

'Wilf was a great friend, probably my best friend. From the time he came to the club we got on really well. Wilf, Wayne and me actually lived together. We shared a flat in Finchley. Then after that Wilf and myself shared another flat in Hammersmith, so we were very close friends. He wasn't just a really fine player, but a really nice guy.

'He was the ultimate nice guy. Good with kids, good with women, good with old people, young people. He had time for everybody.

'It was very sad when he died. I remember it like yesterday because that was the start of my benefit year at Middlesex and he was due back pretty soon to start coming to some of the events. It wasn't a great way to start the year.'

Slack's untimely passing had ramifications for life on the pitch too as it left a void at the top of the batting order which would take some filling. The committee alighted on the 32-year-old West Indian Test opener Desmond Haynes as the right man to inherit the mantle.

Your author has vivid and almost very painful memories of Haynes from several years prior to this. As a 15-year-old I won a competition which carried as a prize three tickets to the one-day international between England and the West Indies at Lord's on the 1980 tour. My friends and I sat in the Grandstand at a time when Old Father Time was perched on top of it in the years before he was moved to his current location. I know that because Andy Roberts slogged a delivery from Ian Botham over Old Father Time and on to the concourse – but I digress. Earlier in the West Indies innings, Haynes hooked a ball from Chris Old. My thought process went something like this,

'That's a good shot … It's going for six … Oh s!?! it's coming straight for me!'

Everything was scattered everywhere as I dived for cover. I'd like to tell you I dived because this was long before the days where they offered money for crowd catches. I strongly suspect it was more the thought of not wanting to go home with another broken pair of glasses which meant discretion triumphed over valour.

Haynes's arrival had other seismic repercussions as in days when only one overseas player was permitted it meant an end to Wayne Daniel's 12 seasons with Middlesex. Emburey suggested that it was 'harsh' on Daniel after the years of service he had given, suggesting he was perhaps the overriding influence of Middlesex's golden era, an influence for which he has paid a heavy physical price today,

'Wayne was the biggest influence we had, going through from 1977 to 1988. He bowled and bowled and bowled. He really bowled his heart out for us and if you see him now, walking, he's struggling. First of all he blames Mike Brearley because Brearley used to bowl him and bowl him and bowl him. If we wanted a wicket we always went back to Wayne to try and scare the living daylights out of them. He was the best overseas player we had.'

Haynes though made an immediate impact in the 89 season, topping the County Championship run-scoring charts with in excess of 1,400 as Middlesex finished third in the standings.

The Barbadian also had an enormous influence on their run to another NatWest Final with three scores of 80 or more.

He would make 50 in the Lord's showpiece too, but Warwickshire overhauled Middlesex's total of 210 with two balls to spare to break their sequence of six one-day final wins in a row.

By the time 1990 dawned county cricket was in the middle of a five-year experiment in terms of its playing conditions. You'll recall back in our first chapter the Middlesex board rejecting an MCC proposal to increase county games from three to four days. Some 85 years later, the beginnings of that vision came to pass when the powers that be proposed that matches be a mixture of three and four days' duration. Middlesex welcomed the change, by this stage believing it played to their strengths.

'We felt that it would suit us because we had players with Test match experience who had played over a long period of time,' said Emburey. 'We had a good bowling attack and good batters at the top of the order. Ramprakash's arrival had strengthened that obviously.'

There had been several other changes in personnel apart from Haynes from the class of 1985, with the batting ranks in particular having an unfamiliar look.

Radley had called stumps on his long innings in 1987, while Graham Barlow, Slack's long-time opening partner had been forced into retirement by long-term hip and back injuries and Butcher, another mainstay, was now very much a veteran out on the fringes.

In the stead of these three stalwarts, Ramprakash and Mike Roseberry had now established themselves as fixtures in the roles of middle-order batter and opener respectively, while Keith Brown would rise to greater prominence in this Championship-winning year. Both he and Roseberry were awarded their county caps that summer.

On the bowling front, Phil Edmonds had traded left-arm spin for business life in the City three years previously which meant a very different left arm-spinner, Phil Tufnell, would fill the void left behind.

Daniel's shoes though were harder to fill, particularly given that Angus Fraser had risen from novice in 1985 to Test level over the intervening five years.

Cowans said it wasn't straightforward for Lancashire-born Fraser when he first came on the scene in the mid-1980s, when his fitness wasn't the highest level, earning him an unflattering pet name,

'When I first saw Angus I thought he had a lot of work to do. At the time he was carrying a few pounds. His nickname was "Lardy".

'He was tall and a very accurate bowler, but he needed to get himself fitter really. He went over to New Zealand during the winter of 1987/88 and worked really hard on his fitness.

'I remember him coming back at the start of the season to the indoor nets and he looked a lot fitter – a lot leaner. With his height and ability to bowl a heavy ball I knew he had a lot of potential.'

Early physical challenges or not, Fraser had what all bowlers need, that insatiable thirst for wickets, which would bring out his competitive steak, even when it came to his own team-mates. Cowans remembered an early occasion where they bowled in tandem against Cambridge University back in 1985. The pair took a stack of wickets, yet Fraser, who acquired a reputation for being grumpy, was apparently far from happy.

'Mike Atherton was playing for Cambridge at the time. We opened the bowling and I got five wickets and Angus got four,' said Cowans.

'Angus came up to me afterwards and said, "I'm getting five next time." I knew then there was something about him and that he was ambitious. I liked the attitude that he wasn't happy that I got five and he only got four.'

Gatting too confessed that Fraser could be grumpy, but that was what drove him on as a bowler, so it had more upsides than down,

'Angus Fraser hated losing. If he bowled a bad ball it was the end of the world, but again another wonderful competitor. That's what seemed to come through over that era, you had people who always wanted to win and were prepared to practise hard for it. The culture was good.'

Despite all the comings and goings, it is important to stress that of all Middlesex's title wins, 1990's was achieved by the most stable team. Both Gatting and Emburey were banned from Test duty that summer having been part of the second rebel tour to South Africa in the winter of 1989/90, meaning both played all 22 County Championship matches, so providing a consistency of leadership.

Haynes, Roseberry, Ramprakash and Brown were four others not to miss a single fixture, so giving a familiarity to the top six.

In addition Tufnell played 20 times and Williams 19, making therefore almost eight ever-presents in the XI.

Given a full season to be present with his men, Gatting thrived, making almost 1,700 Championship runs at an average of 58, while providing a constant lead voice when his team were in the field.

Gatting believed he was lucky enough to enjoy the pressures of captaincy rather than them being a burden to him, though he admitted that his straight-talking approach sometimes left coach Don Bennett mending fences,

'It didn't affect my game being captain. If anything it probably helped me I suspect. Sometimes it helps people and sometimes it hinders them.

'I enjoyed being captain and having a chessboard with chess pieces on it you could move about, use and know they were going to do you a good job whenever you asked them to bowl – that was always great. There were not many counties who could look at having five international bowlers to pick from. So, when you wanted something done, you knew they could probably do it.

'People do talk about my field placings, the spinners do especially, but then I was probably thinking about the way I would play them and what I wouldn't like to be trying to have to do if I was facing them. That's all I would be thinking as a batter.

'Don used to mop up behind me as when I was young I was probably a bit too honest with some of the kids. How do you tell someone they're not playing? Well, you're not playing because you haven't been bowling well enough – simple as that. How else do you tell somebody? But I was probably a bit harsh sometimes and Don would always mop up the tears or the anger, do the arm around the shoulder bit.

'But, nobody really held grudges within that team. They were all professional enough to know if you had a difference of opinion you could come out and say so and then get on with it. They knew I was captain, so I had to make a decision. We would try it my way and if it didn't work we could go back to the way they wanted. It was better than always plodding along doing the same old same old. If you needed to change it a bit, if that caused a few ructions then so be it. At the end of the day, if you don't say anything you won't ever know. There is no point in just holding on to it.'

Fraser missed the opening game of the campaign against Essex at Lord's where even with four days it petered out into a draw, mainly because almost all of the first day was lost to rain.

Even so there was time for Brown to make a strong first impression courtesy of a career-best 141 – a sign of things to come that summer.

With Fraser still unavailable, Middlesex's first win of the campaign came at the expense of Kent at Lord's thanks largely to two extraordinary bowling performances, one a good deal less predictable than the other.

It was Neil Williams who gave the hosts the early initiative with figures of 7-61. While these didn't quite match his 7-55 taken in Zimbabwe some years earlier, they were his best in England at that time.

Williams's exploits with the ball earned him his only Test call-up later that summer. His figures against India at The Oval were an unremarkable 2-148, but his two scalps were skipper Mohammad Azharuddin and a youthful Sachin Tendulkar, so not a bad double. He also made 38 as nightwatchman, but with the usual suspects all available by the time of the Ashes tour to Australia that winter, Williams was dropped and never played for England again. He would however better his career-best figures two years later when returning 8-75 in a win over Gloucestershire at Lord's.

Half-centuries for Roseberry, Gatting and Brown had given Middlesex a first-innings lead of 76, but the visitors were almost 200 to the good second time around when they reached 260-6.

Emburey pointed out that Gatting, despite being a more than competent medium-pace bowler at county level, was more often than not reluctant to bowl himself and that he as vice-captain would on occasion cajole his skipper into doing so. Perhaps this was one such occasion and it brought instant and dramatic results.

Gatting had twice taken five wickets in an innings, but as far as impact goes this probably trumped them both as within two overs he blew away the Kent tail to finish with 4-2, before leading the chase with 87 not out as Middlesex romped home by eight wickets.

Roseberry's 122 was the highlight of an uneventful draw with Surrey, before Middlesex's fourth home game in a row – against Gloucestershire – proved something of a classic.

The three-day fixture on a good batting wicket required three declarations before the visitors embarked on a chase for 272 to win. Bill Athey's 69 kept them in the hunt and with the late Kevin Curran, father of Ben, Tom and Sam, going well, they looked favourites at 229-6.

But Emburey and Tufnell, more of whom shortly, took four wickets apiece to remove the tail and leave Curran stranded on 53 not out as Middlesex squeezed home by ten runs.

A promising first month in the Championship was being replicated in the Refuge Assurance League 40-over competition – something in which Middlesex had rarely flourished in previous years – four wins out of five putting them among the early frontrunners.

The one big disappointment in May came in the Benson & Hedges Cup where, having come strongly through their group and bowled out hosts Somerset for 183 in the quarter-final at Taunton, the batting misfired in the subsequent chase and they went down by 22 runs.

His century in the season curtain-raiser apart, the first month of the championship season had been a quiet one by Haynes's standards, but the trip to Valentine's Park for the return fixture with Essex proved the catalyst for his remarkable summer.

He and Roseberry shared an opening stand of 306 at the start of the match, Haynes going on to make 220 not out.

It wouldn't be the last time he would make an individual score of over 200 in 1990, a season in which he passed 2,000 Championship runs.

Gatting witnessed first-hand how intimidating a presence Haynes was at the crease, but he believed his influence went far beyond just events on the pitch,

'Dessie, what an absolutely amazing cricketer. He helped Mark Ramprakash enormously when he was with us as he did a lot of the bowlers.

'He certainly helped Mickey Roseberry who ended up opening with him and having him up the other end was a pleasure.

'I know when I was batting with him the guys who were bowling just didn't want to bowl, basically. Dessie had relaxed a bit and expanded as a player. His contribution was enormous.

'You forget he played five or six years for us in the end and time flew by. He was again a huge, huge impact on a lot of the young kids, especially the Ramps of this world and others. It was good for them, rather than them having me at them all the time, to have some senior guy like Dessie come in and just reinforce what we were saying, but in a different way. It wasn't the same old same old like me.

'It was a different way of saying the same thing, but probably getting it across better. So to me Dessie, when you talk about Wayne Daniel, he was in the same class as a player and in the contribution that he made. Absolutely incredible.'

Roseberry's innings of 135 in the stand at Valentine's Park would mark the highest of his three Championship centuries that season, where he formed a prosperous partnership with Haynes at the top of the order, the pair developing a great understanding running between the wickets.

County Durham-born Roseberry had his best season two years later in 1992 where he made nine first-class hundreds in a run of inspired form. It earned him a place on the England A side's tour of Australia the following winter, but he would never hit those heights again, either in a spell with his native Durham or a second stint at Middlesex where he was given a testimonial year in 2002.

Despite Haynes and Roseberry's efforts and managing to enforce the follow-on thanks to Emburey's 5-61. Middlesex were held at bay by Graham Gooch's second-innings century as the match was drawn.

Gatting's men were on the thin end of a draw against Warwickshire, but enterprising captaincy from both he and counterpart Nigel Briers enabled them to grab victory against Leicestershire at Grace Road after most of the second day had been lost to rain.

West Indies great Desmond Haynes had a huge impact on and off the field.

The latter game witnessed the first appearance for Middlesex of wicketkeeper Paul Farbrace. The future England assistant coach and head coach of Sussex stepped into the breach following a serious injury suffered by Paul Downton while keeping wicket in a Refuge Assurance League game against Hampshire on the May's Bounty Ground at Basingstoke.

Mike Gatting goes on the attack at Uxbridge.

Downton was standing up to the wicket when a beauty from Emburey hit the top of the stumps, causing the off bail to fly up and catch him in the eye, resulting in a trip to hospital.

The injury would prove to be more serious than feared with damage to the cornea being diagnosed. Downton spent six weeks on the sidelines before returning in late July to keep for the remainder of the season. He started the next campaign too, but it became clear that the game was now a struggle for a man who had been highly competent at his craft, so much so that he had accrued 30 England caps among over 300 first-class appearances, and he was forced to hang up his gloves and retire.

'He had problems after that with perception of depth and as a wicketkeeper that's not great,' reflected Emburey. As for Farbrace, he became the regular wicketkeeper in 1991, taking the gloves in 20 first-class games. However, in what would become an all-too familiar story for specialist keepers, his lack of runs – a first-class average of 15 – eventually told against him, meaning Keith Brown, previously a specialist batsman, took over the role for 1992.

More enterprising captaincy would be needed in the next Championship outing up at Old Trafford against Lancashire, where thanks to plenty of rain the hosts didn't reach 300 until the third morning.

A deal was struck between the captains to forfeit the next two innings leaving Middlesex to chase 302 against the clock. After Roseberry and Haynes set another solid platform, Gatting's 95 ensured a fourth win in the first eight games.

Wardown Park in Luton was the stop-off point on the way home from Lancashire and it proved to be the setting for Edmonds's replacement, Phil Tufnell, to claim his first five-wicket haul of the season in a 79-run win.

Barnet-born Tufnell trained to be a quantity surveyor, but gave up that career path to pursue his sporting ambitions, making his first XI debut for Middlesex in 1986, aged 20.

According to Cowans, it was immediately clear that Tufnell was a different breed to cricketers he'd been used to and that his presence in the dressing room was something of a shock to the system for him and his team-mates.

'I remember Phil well from when he first came into the side. I don't know whether it was a societal thing, but youngsters coming in then had a different way about them,' he said.

'My generation were very respectful towards our senior players. We made sure we always turned up on time and did what we were supposed to do. Tuffers though came in and was a completely different character. He smoked, his kit wasn't always the cleanest. He wasn't one to say "let's go for a run" or "let's do some shuttles" to get fitter. He and some of the other youngsters didn't seem to have the same attitude.'

Among the 'other youngsters' Cowans made reference to was Jamie Sykes. An east Londoner from Shoreditch, Sykes made his Middlesex debut a few years earlier than Tufnell aged 17. He showed plenty of promise in the years that followed, making a first-class hundred against Cambridge University at Fenner's at the start of the 1985 campaign. So, clearly a better batter than Tufnell, he could have developed into a more-than-useful all-rounder courtesy of his right-arm off-breaks.

However, he and Tufnell were thick as thieves and by all accounts an extremely bad influence on one another. So much so that come the end of the 1989 season something had to be done to address the situation.

'Tuffers and Jamie Sykes were just messing around, being unruly and not really concentrating on their cricket,' continued Cowans, 'so, one had to go to let the other one fulfil his potential.

'So they got rid of Jamie Sykes and kept Tuffers, who then didn't have any distractions. At one time I think the club were thinking of releasing both of them, but Mike Gatting pleaded Tuffers' case.'

Emburey backed up this theory of both careers having been in jeopardy, suggesting the lot may have fallen with Tufnell because of the prevailing spin bowling situation at Middlesex at that time:

'We had to make a decision between Sykes and Tufnell. I think because I was always there as a spinner and Philippe [Edmonds] was toying with the idea of retiring they kept Tuffers on instead of Jamie. Had I been 37 or 38 it could have gone around the other way.'

So, while Sykes drifted out of the game and became a London cab driver, Tufnell stayed and began to develop his own brand of left-arm spin. Discipline remained an issue to some degree, especially when it came to batting at net practice. Considering the career he has gone on to develop as a TV and radio commentator on the game, not to mention his stint as a captain on *A Question of Sport*, it seems hard to believe he struggled for self-belief on the field, something which manifested itself in a multitude of ways and could make it very difficult for Gatting, or whoever was skipper, to manage him.

'There are many stories about Phil,' said Gatting. The fact of the matter is you wouldn't mind picking a fight with Phil Tufnell, but you wouldn't want to pick one with Philippe Edmonds. Philip Tufnell was a very funny man. After a match he was fantastic company. During the match he was frustrating as hell. He never turned up on time. If someone got after him he wouldn't want to bowl and then as soon as a wicket fell it would be, "I'll have a bowl now skip," and I'd be, "No you won't Philip."

'I'd say, "Set the field, Philip," and he'd say, "No, you're the one with the three lions on, you set it."

"Philip, you've got to learn.""

"No, no."

'He didn't want to take any responsibility at all.

'He got better by talking with Ernie [Emburey] and he learned a little bit more discipline – not very much but a little bit more. He would still be very difficult, but he would bowl the overs in the match and that is where you are going to learn basically. He had that ability.'

Emburey and Tufnell slowly struck up some sort of partnership, but with the latter having a very different approach to bowling from his predecessor Edmonds, things were never easy, especially if they were required to bowl in tandem.

Emburey said, 'Tufnell was awkward for the captain at times like Philippe [Edmonds] had been. When he established himself after two or three years, if a side were coming in to get some quick runs, he didn't want to bowl. He was a bit of a fair-weather sailor in that respect. If the shit was hitting the fan he didn't want to bowl. He'd say, "Let the young bowlers bowl, give them some experience."

'He'd be told no, that's the senior players' role to soak up that and bowl well and take the onus away from the other players.

'I remember under Mike Brearley, he'd bring me on when I was young in situations where I wasn't going to get slogged around and more senior bowlers would bowl in those situations.

'Then, if a wicket went down he might throw me the ball and allow me to bowl where they were looking to just play.

'I always had a situation where you work in partnerships. If Phil [Edmonds] was at one end I was at the other. We'd have this thing where if a number 11 was in and a number six was in, if the six was facing for the last couple of balls of an over you would squeeze and make sure he didn't get a single, so then the other guy would have six balls at the number 11.

'It didn't happen with Tuffers as they often got a single the last couple of balls of the over and I would have to bowl to the established batter. Then last couple of balls I'd make sure I kept him at my end so Tuffers could bowl at the other guy. This happened for years over lots of matches. It used to piss me off, so when people ask me who I'd prefer to bowl with Edmonds or Tufnell – always Edmonds.

'Edmonds and I complemented each other more I think because we were competing for an England place. We didn't play too much Test match cricket together. In all of our years we played cricket I think we only played ten or 11 Tests together, mostly against Australia rather than other countries.

'Tuffers was a more fragile character. Edmonds didn't mind experimenting, but Tuffers didn't like getting hit. Edmonds didn't mind getting hit as long as he felt he had a chance of getting a wicket. Tuffers didn't want to get hit and if he was getting hit he felt, "Why am I bowling?"'

Despite their obvious frustrations regarding Tufnell and his frailties, Gatting and Emburey were nevertheless in agreement as to his abundance of ability. Gatting said, 'He was so talented,' while Emburey gave insight into what made his second spin twin such a force to be reckoned with.

'Tuffers' great ability when he bowled was he could make the ball hang in the air and land on a good length and whatever. He had great flight.'

Tufnell would take 74 first-class wickets in all in 1990, 65 of them in the County Championship, numbers which brought him to the attention of the England selectors who named him in the Ashes party of 1990/91. He would claim a five-wicket haul in the third Test in Sydney.

Cowans recalled that the wages from that tour were used to satisfy Tufnell's thirst for a flash set of wheels which he wasn't slow to show off.

'He used his tour fee to buy a 911 Porsche and he said to me, "Norm, I've got a Porsche." I'd never been in a Porsche before so asked him if he'd give me a spin, and he took me out. He'd gone from not having a car at all to having a Porsche.'

Worcestershire would cling on for a draw despite having been asked to follow on at Lord's at the start of July, but the winning feeling was quickly regained when Yorkshire succumbed to defeat at Uxbridge.

The latter fixture was the first of two games in a row at the out-ground as part of what was termed the Uxbridge Festival with the second match against Somerset producing a thriller.

The visitors, inspired by Stephen ('Jimmy') Cook's century dominated the opening day, going on to post an imposing 445-6. Thanks to Gatting's rapid 170, Middlesex were able to save the follow-on and they bravely declared 140 behind.

Their final chase was a daunting one as they required 369 to win with time against them. Haynes made a century, but it was Ramprakash who produced the match-defining innings, his 146 not out allowing the hosts to gallop home at a rate of more than five an over.

The Uxbridge match set a trend for the next few weeks where Middlesex became engaged in several nerve-shredding encounters.

The clash with Kent down at Canterbury was almost a rerun of the Somerset game. Simon Hinks and Neil Taylor's monster partnership of 366 for the second wicket led Kent to 449-2, but Ramprakash's second hundred in successive games helped them to 308-3 in reply before they again declared behind to keep hopes of a win alive.

Three wickets apiece for the trio of Williams, Cowans and Emburey meant Kent were then shot out for 140 second time around, leaving Middlesex 282 to win.

Yet another hundred for Ramprakash and one for Gatting – they added 198 for the third wicket – raised hopes of another successful chase, but they came up six runs short with their ninth-wicket pair at the crease when the overs ran out.

From there, the squad travelled straight up to Trent Bridge where another epic encounter unfolded, Chris Broad – father of Stuart – leading Notts to 336-8 courtesy of his 140. Middlesex's batting misfired in reply and they found themselves more than 100 in arrears.

Their target this time would be 354 in 70 overs and they promptly lost Haynes and Roseberry both without scoring.

Gatting though embarked on a scintillating innings and with first Ramprakash (52) and then Brown (55) lending support Middlesex looked favourites at 244-3. However, the fall of the latter's wicket saw momentum shift again and although Gatting batted through until stumps they were 25 runs shy with again only two wickets left standing.

Back home at Lord's the following week, roles were reversed in another cliffhanger with Glamorgan. Centuries for Haynes and Brown enabled Middlesex to pass 400, but despite five wickets for Williams, Hugh Morris's ton kept the Welsh side's deficit to 87. The hosts rattled up quick runs on the third morning before declaring soon after lunch, leaving Glamorgan 251 to win.

The Seaxes chipped away as the visitors never really took up the challenge, but time looked to be running out before four wickets fell for no runs – Fraser proving to be the architect of the collapse with a season's best 6-30 – but Middlesex saw the extra 16 points snatched away at the last moment, as tenth-wicket pair Steve Watkin and Mark Frost batted out the remaining balls to save a draw.

The failure to secure that last wicket would usher in the most frustrating few weeks of the Championship campaign for Middlesex, beginning with the trip to Bournemouth to face Hampshire, where despite a century for Emburey and six first-innings wickets for Tufnell, once Hampshire avoided the need to follow-on, the game petered out into a draw.

Back at Lord's a similar story unfolded against Sussex where having posted a first-innings score of 449, the hosts allowed the south coast side's tail to wag so that 203-7 became 387 all out and so another match was drawn.

It would be wrong though to race off from this game without paying tribute to Haynes's majestic unbeaten 255, the highest score of his entire first-class career.

Knocks like this carried him to over 2,000 first-class runs that season, earning him a place in *Wisden*'s five Cricketers of the Year for 1991.

Part of the tribute read, 'It was not just the runs he scored, it was the way in which he scored them. Never slowly and always most attractively, without a slog in sight. His cover driving a combination of timing and barely evident power remained in the mind's eye as a particular adornment of his batting.'

The downturn in form culminated in a heavy loss to Derbyshire at the County Ground where Middlesex were bowled out for 99 in the fourth innings. Before coming down heavily on the batters, we should note that umpires Chris Balderstone and Peter Wight reported the pitch as substandard for a match of this level, meaning the hosts were docked 25 points, three more than they got for winning the game.

This unhappy few weeks in August also saw Middlesex miss out on another Lord's one-day final, after failing to defend a score of 296 in their semi-final with Lancashire at Old Trafford. Haynes's 149 helped them post the imposing total, but Gehan Mendis's 121 enabled Lancashire to make light work of the chase as they galloped home with more than four overs to spare.

Fears that Middlesex had terminally lost momentum at a crucial time were eased when they closed out a frustrating month on the field with victory over Yorkshire at Headingley. Haynes was back to his imperious best with another cultured century, while Gatting made 91 and Tufnell 37, the highest first-class score of his career to that point and one which would remain so until the tailender made his only half-century some six years later.

Hughes got five wickets in the first innings, while Cowans and left-arm quick Charles Taylor each got a handful each second time around. Taylor's 5-33 would prove his best in Middlesex colours in a career cut short by injury.

Momentum restored, the Seaxes returned to London to entertain Nottinghamshire in a game which produced a red-letter day for another of their unsung heroes, Keith Brown.

State educated in Enfield, north London, Brown was the sort of professional any other county would give their eye teeth for. A gritty dependable character on the field who was seven or eight out of ten most weeks, this particular week he'd be a ten, making the only double hundred of his career. A mark of his innings was that he proved the senior partner in a stand of 188 with Ramprakash, who himself made a century, before adding another 168 with Downton in a mammoth stay of six hours.

Despite not being the most glamorous of cricketers to watch, Brown's batting exploits were appreciated by the likes of Haynes, who told *Wisden*, 'Keith Brown doesn't get the credit he deserves and I would single him out for special mention. He is reliable, difficult to get out and always seems to be able to play the right sort of innings for the situation.'

Middlesex declared on 510-5 as soon as Brown's landmark was reached and with the platform built, their bowlers did the rest. Dismissals were shared around as Middlesex secured victory by ten wickets and took a maximum 24 points.

This was a big moment in the title race as the leaders before that round, 1989 bridesmaids Essex, were being thrashed by 276 runs by Northamptonshire at Chelmsford, meaning Middlesex leapfrogged them at the top of the standings.

Cowans understood how crucial the back-to-back wins were in the scheme of the season and said they were typical of the Middlesex teams of that era,

'The win at Yorkshire where I got my five-wicket haul was a significant one. We needed to win and you get those occasions where even though your body is tired you need to go to a different gear and find that extra bit of energy.

'I remember Martyn Moxon trying to hook me and getting caught and then getting a few others bowling down the hill there at Headingley.

'And Nottinghamshire where I got four wickets and broke Paul Johnson's thumb, so he had to retire hurt and didn't come out again, was significant too.

'That can happen when you are going for the Championship as opposed to being in the middle of the table. You just go that extra mile. We were good at that at Middlesex when we smelt blood.'

Now it was a straight shoot-out between Middlesex and Essex with two rounds of the Championship to go and Middlesex 14 points to the good.

Essex played host to Kent, while Middlesex entertained Surrey in matches which proved to be runfests. Essex briefly sniffed victory when their visitors stumbled to 129-4 second time around, just 30 ahead, but the benign pitch won out as the game petered out to a dull draw.

For their part, Middlesex were under pressure when Surrey racked up 480 after winning the toss. In reply, the champions elect found themselves 267-5 with skipper Gatting having retired hurt without scoring. Still over 200 in arrears and with no guarantee Gatting would be fit to resume his innings, Middlesex found an unlikely batting hero in Angus Fraser, who launched five sixes in a blistering 92, more than twice as many as he'd ever made previously. The seamer would only make more than 50 on one other occasion in his first-class career, making this effort all the more remarkable. Fraser's assault on the Surrey bowlers got Middlesex to within 55 of their opponents, after which the game was only ever going to be a draw. No damage done though for Middlesex, still 14 points ahead with one to play.

Before the Championship finale could play out, Middlesex had the chance of another piece of silverware in the Refuge Assurance Cup. 1990 marked the first time it had been run as both a league and a knockout competition, Middlesex having qualified for the latter by finishing third in the table despite a mid-season slump.

They'd extracted revenge for the NatWest Trophy semi-final defeat by beating Lancashire by 45 runs in the last four thanks to 86 from Roseberry and four wickets for Emburey.

The final at Edgbaston pitted them against league winners Derbyshire, who they restricted to 197-7 thanks to Paul Weekes's 2-35.

Haynes, Gatting and Brown all made 40s in the reply where Middlesex reached 191-5 with balls running out.

As so often in the past, Emburey came to the wicket for the thrilling finale, reverse sweeping Adrian Kuiper to the fence for the winning hit with two balls to spare.

'It was the first time I ever remember trying the shot,' he said.

So with one trophy safely stashed away, Gatting and company set out for Hove to regain the County Championship. Their 14-point lead was a good one, but only a win would guarantee an 11th title. Anything less and Essex could steal the glory with victory over Surrey at The Oval.

The chasers did all they could to keep the pressure on over the first seven sessions of play. A huge hundred for Nasser Hussain and another for Jonathan Lewis helped them pile up 539 before they bundled out their hosts for 140, making a maximum-points win look likely, though in the end it didn't materialise

As it turned out, any Essex victory would have been immaterial as in Sussex, Middlesex were facing a team destined for the wooden spoon and always had the upper hand after bowling out their hosts for 187, led by 4-34 from Simon Hughes.

By stumps, Roseberry and Haynes had knocked off 88 of those without being parted and on day two the visitors turned the screw. Roseberry made 83 and Gatting 51, but the star again was Brown who finished unbeaten on 116 as Middlesex built a lead of 224.

The title would be won on day three as the three seamers worked their way through the brittle home line-up. Alan Wells produced the only real resistance with 50, but Fraser took 4-47 before Hughes struck with successive balls to set the champagne corks popping before tea. Cowans retained fond memories of those celebrations.

'It's always good when you come off the field and there's champagne,' he said.

'It's a long season and when you get something at the end it's so rewarding because you know what it's taken to achieve it. There were so many great players that we played against in that era. Every team had great bowlers and great opening batters, so it was a long slog to end up winning the Championship because they are not easy to win. So when you get to the final day and you win these things it's a great feeling.

'Sometimes you try and reflect on it and even now looking back you don't always realise the magnitude of all these things, or the era we played in and how significant it was.

'At the time you just do it because it's your job, but when you step back and think of all the travelling and the hard slogs, days in hotels away from everyone, driving up and down the motorways, it's a lot. You don't think about that as much when you're young as you do looking back.

'You reflect on it and think wow. So, we had to at least try and savour the moment down there.'

So, a sixth title in 15 years was relished and there would be a magnificent seventh before the curtain fell on the golden era of Middlesex's history.

CHAPTER 10
1993

At first glance, Middlesex's seventh and final County Championship win of their golden era appears something of an anomaly.

Seemingly, it came out of the blue after two years of being very much in the doldrums as far as the longest form of the domestic game was concerned. The title defence of 1991 had been a non-event with only three matches won as they finished 15th. It was a year to draw a veil over quickly with the team also making little or no impact in any of the one-day competitions.

It's true that 1992 was an upgrade with a first Sunday League title added to the trophy cabinet – in a year where it ran without a sponsor for the first time – Desmond Haynes spearheading the victory charge with ten half-centuries as he rattled up almost 900 runs in the competition.

The improvement Championship-wise, though, was marginal with the Seaxes still languishing in the bottom half after finishing 11th.

Yet 1993 would arguably be the most dominant County Championship win in their history with the laurels destined for Lord's well before season's end.

A closer look reveals there were mitigating circumstances for the two-year lull in Middlesex's fortunes.

1991 had seen Haynes called up to the West Indies tour party for the series with England, so depriving the team of the 2,000-plus runs he'd made the previous summer, not to mention breaking up the thriving partnership he'd established with Mike Roseberry at the top of the order. The enforced retirement of Paul Downton further destabilised the batting ranks and altered the balance of the side as Paul Farbrace, good keeper though he was, couldn't replicate the runs that Downton had consistently churned out over a decade.

Batting wasn't the only issue that year with Angus Fraser sidelined almost entirely with the hip injury which blighted that time in his career, and Simon Hughes was also hardly seen in what would be his final year at Middlesex before heading north to Durham, so putting pressure on Norman Cowans and Neil Williams, plus Charlie Taylor and a young Dean Headley, who made a breakthrough aged 21.

By 1992 Haynes was back in harness, and with stalwart Keith Brown having taken up wicketkeeping duties the side was never short of runs. It was an especially golden summer for Roseberry with more than 1,700 coming from his bat helped by six centuries – only Mike Gatting was ahead of him in the run-scoring charts.

However, Fraser was still severely restricted and bowling resources were even more stretched with Cowans missing the campaign with a hernia issue. And although John Emburey was a constant presence due to still serving his ban for the second rebel tour to South Africa, his spin partnership with Phil Tufnell was disrupted by the latter's Test call-ups.

By the time the sun rose on 1993, Fraser was emerging from his injury nightmare, all-rounder Mark Feltham had crossed the river from The Oval to Lord's and as it transpired, Tufnell only donned his England cap twice during the Ashes mauling by Australia, while Cowans was also fit for the odd game, bringing the bowling resources back towards full strength.

The timing was perfect too as after five years of dovetailing three- and four-day Championship cricket, the governing body opted exclusively for the latter, some 90 years after the idea was first mooted.

While four-day cricket suited Middlesex's make-up, the prospect of extra days away from home cooped up in hotels was not an appealing one for Emburey, who despite his travel travails of our 1977 chapter often allowed as the expression went back then, the train to 'take the strain'.

He explained, 'If games went to the fourth day you would have the extra night in a hotel, but a lot of the away games I didn't always travel the night before. I would travel in the morning on my own. So, I wouldn't be one of the official cars and I wouldn't take players.

'I even remember travelling to Manchester on the morning of the Championship match, leaving at 6am and getting to the ground at ,nine, 9.15am. I think a lot of that is because Susie and I had young children and you already spent a lot of time away during tours and whatever. And I just wanted to spend more time at home.

'Four-day cricket played to our advantage because we still had the bowling attack to take 20 wickets and now just had longer to get them.'

The opening game took Middlesex to Bristol to face Gloucestershire where a first-innings collapse from 142-3 to 180 all out left them 119 in arrears. The spin twins got to work to skittle the hosts for 95 second time around, but even so a target of 215 looked unlikely on a pitch increasingly favouring the bowlers.

Mark Ramprakash produced an innings unlike any played in the match to make 75, but the visitors still needed an unbroken seventh-wicket stand of 60 from Brown and new boy Feltham to start the season with a win.

In the week leading up to the first Championship fixture at Lord's, the Seaxes entertained the Australian tourists for a 55-over encounter, which they lost by 69 runs. However, what hurt Middlesex and their skipper in particular was his altercation with a dressing room door – a reaction to being run out. The damage suffered to his hand ruled out of the Kent clash.

In his absence the captaincy reins were taken up by John Carr, who had only returned to the sport 12 months previously after three years away working in the banking sector. Soon to turn 30, Carr rose to the occasion, making an unbeaten century to carry the hosts to a first-innings lead before adding 70 not out in the second as the game drifted to a draw. It would appear that Carr had modified his unorthodox approach to batting during his three-year sabbatical from the sport.

'John Carr was back because he missed it so much,' said Gatting. 'He wasn't batting front on, he was batting side on by then.

'He was another one who could catch pigeons. He was a great slip catcher and was a very talented cricketer. He could and probably should have played for England the way he played at times, John.'

It wasn't just at slip that Carr had a great pair of hands; he also caught blinders fielding close to the wicket in front of the bat according to Emburey, though the spinner revealed he wasn't always the bravest.

'John was a good player – great hands. He always used to field short leg to me and didn't always feel comfortable there. He always used to look over his left shoulder and he liked to see a deep midwicket out there because then he felt the batsman wasn't going to have a big slog.

'If I didn't have a man out there he felt less comfortable because he felt the batter would have a big swipe. He took some great catches.'

The Kent draw produced another incident which raised a laugh or two. Ramprakash, batting in the second innings, called for play to be halted as he was having difficulty sighting the ball at one end of the ground due to a lady sitting in front of the sight screen wearing a red jumper. There was a slight pause in play while the said lady was persuaded to don a white cardigan instead.

We are pleased to report that there were no such issues with any lady's attire in the next game at Lord's, but it began badly for the hosts when Roseberry broke a finger while batting early on the first morning. He later returned to the crease against the advice of the medics and top scored with an unbeaten 79. He batted down the order second time around, lasting only three balls and making nought, but was still fit for the next match. This one, too, proved a dull draw.

Bowling injuries to others over the previous two years meant much of the seam burden had fallen on Neil Williams, who was now in his 12th year as a first XI player.

The St Vincent-born quick had born the weight of responsibility well and he would be pivotal to Middlesex crushing Sussex over the late May bank holiday weekend. Williams returned figures of 6-61 in the first innings to bundle the visitors out for 161, a score which would have been far fewer but for Franklyn Stephenson's hard-hitting 60 down the order. Half-centuries for Haynes, Brown and Emburey then built a massive lead before Tufnell and Emburey secured an innings win by taking nine second-innings wickets between them. It was Middlesex's first innings win since their 1990 victory at Hove which clinched the title.

We recorded earlier that Williams won a solitary Test cap for England, but it's high time we delved a little deeper into his story. He arrived in England with his family aged 13 and like many other cricketers of this era he came to Middlesex via the MCC Young Cricketers programme. He initially refused to play on a Sunday because of his religious faith, but as Cowans explained, that wasn't the only thing to restrict his on-field time in his early days at Lord's.

'Neil and I played together for many years, even opening the bowling together in the second team,' recalled Cowans. 'I remember Neil used to bowl really quick and we were quite a feared attack.

'I don't think Neil really realised how good a bowler he was. He took a while to adjust and believe in himself and to get himself fit as well. He was a very slight guy, very loose as in very stretchy, elastic, but he didn't have the strength to last.

'He was always going off, or playing one game and missing one because of his legs. His upper body was phenomenally strong and loose, but his legs weren't the strongest. He had the potential but just needed to get fit, so he could meet the demands of county cricket.'

Physio Simon Shepard came to Williams's aid, setting him a fitness programme one winter in the early to mid-1980s. This and a few well-chosen words from close friend Cowans got him attuned to the rigours of the county game.

'He got a bit stronger and had a very whippy action which I think was quite deceptive because he didn't have the longest run-up,' continued Cowans. 'He bowled quicker than people thought he would, and so surprised a lot of batters. They'd think from his run-up they were going to be facing a medium-pacer and then the ball would be up around their head.

'Once he started believing in his bowling he became better and better. He was a very good bowler and a little underrated.'

Gatting recalled a one-day game between Middlesex and Somerset where Williams whistled one past the cap of Viv Richards before pitching the next one further up, swinging it and getting the great man's wicket.

'You could see Nellie [Williams] go "Oh my God" having got his hero out sort of thing. It was a great piece of bowling and a testament to Neil. He was another one who would always bowl for you. If they were bowling well it was always, "Yes, I'll have another one," and he kept the quality up.

'I think the fact he got to play for England was a great credit to him. He swung the ball and he and Norman were good competition for each other. He was very hard to play if he started to swing it at that pace.'

Williams would spend one further season with Middlesex before leaving at the end of 1994 to spend four years with Essex before retiring. Sadly, just eight years later he suffered a stroke while coaching back in his homeland of St Vincent. He never recovered, dying three weeks later of pneumonia aged just 43.

With Gatting away on international duty and Carr again in charge, Middlesex raced to the top of the Championship by crushing Derbyshire in two days in a low-scoring game.

Leading by only 25 on first innings, the Seaxes routed their visitors for just 89 at the second time of asking with Fraser, Williams and Emburey all in the wickets.

They were forced to claim the extra half an hour as they chased 65 to win, but Haynes made sure they weren't hanging about for long by belting the first ball of the extended period over the ropes for six to clinch victory by ten wickets.

Rain ruined the draw with Durham, giving Gatting's men little chance to consolidate their position at the summit, but during the rest of June, through July and into the first week of August they established themselves as champions elect with a run of six wins in a row, though the start of that sequence against Somerset at the Recreation Ground in Bath did have an element of fortune about it as the hosts lost two players to injury, neither of whom could bat in their second innings.

With much of the second day lost to rain, declarations were needed to set up a final-day run chase, but even this caused confusion. Acting skipper Carr and his opposite number Chris Tavaré had agreed a chase target prior to the start of play so when Andre van Troost launched a ball into the outfield which was going to fall short, Carr shouted to Haynes to drop it. Haynes, not hearing the call, caught it, giving the umpire no option but to signal out. Therefore, with no other batters to come in, Somerset didn't have as many to defend as planned. Haynes himself led the run chase with a polished century, helping Middlesex to a five-wicket win.

There would be few distractions from the Championship quest as in the wake of the trip to Bath, Gatting's side fell at the first hurdle in the NatWest Trophy, a batting malfunction seeing them demolished by Kent to the tune of 166 runs. There was a similarly early exit in the Benson & Hedges Cup, and the defence of the Sunday League crown – now under the sponsorship of AXA Equity & Law – never got off the ground.

There had barely been time for Middlesex to dust themselves down from their drubbing in the 60-over competition when Surrey crossed the river for the next round of the Championship. The visitors made 322 on the opening day after opting to bat first on winning the toss. Haynes led the response with another cultured century, but when he got out the hosts found themselves potentially looking at a damaging first-innings deficit at 200-6.

They were rescued by a stand of 94 between the redoubtable Brown (80) and veteran campaigner Emburey (65 not out) and by the time they were bowled out on the stroke of stumps on day two they'd edged ahead, albeit by just eight runs.

Four wickets for the in-form Williams on an attritional third day meant Middlesex were left chasing 218 to win, but they lost Haynes before the close and were in trouble again on the final day at 120-6.

For the second time in the game it was Brown and Emburey who came to the rescue, the former demonstrating his ability to make tough runs when they were needed, while Emburey underlined again his development into a top all-rounder at county level.

Looking back, Emburey took time to salute Brown, something of an unsung hero around the corridors of Lord's.

'Keith Brown was a very unorthodox batsman, but gritty, valued his wicket and didn't give it away. He wasn't a pretty player to watch and predominantly an onside player, but one who read the game very well. He was a lovely individual and character, though he could get angry at times.

'He helped win matches for us on bad pitches, or even good ones. If we were four down for 40 or 50 you could bet your bottom dollar he would end up getting 60 or 70 and dig us out of a hole. There were two matches in a row, one against Northants and one against Surrey. He and I put on a big partnership against Surrey when Waqar Younis was coming in firing. Both of us got runs and we ended up winning that game off the back of that partnership.'

Cowans had grown up alongside Brown, who had been his skipper at colts level. He said that calm persona Brown exuded was something he had even as a teenager. And given his gifts for other sports, cricket was lucky to have had him.

'Keith was always a very dependable player from a young age. He captained the colts but was a very unassuming character. He did everything in a calm and steady way.

'He was an underrated batsman and another person who didn't realise how good he was. To see him develop through that time was a joy. He was so much a backbone of Middlesex cricket and a man for a crisis – a great servant to Middlesex.

'I saw him at a reunion a few years ago and he's still the same. One of the biggest pairs of hands you'll ever see – bucket hands. Back in those days we used to have winter jobs, not like now where they get paid all year round. He was a plasterer, so he had these massive forearms and would come back fit as a fiddle.

'He could have played most sports. He was a good rugby player and footballer, an all-round sportsman, but cricket was his first love.'

With Surrey packed off back to south London by four wickets, Middlesex headed west to Cardiff for one of the most remarkable games in the annals of county cricket history.

Having lost the toss, Gatting would have been reasonably content to have the Welsh county 137-3 when he caught Matthew Maynard off the bowling of Feltham. The fall of the wicket brought together an aging Viv Richards with Glamorgan's rising star Adrian Dale. The duo proceeded to bat through the remainder of the first day and most of the second, with Emburey and Tufnell taking their share of the suffering, bowling 80 overs between them for a single wicket. By the time Glamorgan declared, the total had reached 562-3 with Dale and Richards having immortalised themselves in their club's record books, their unbroken stand of 425 a record for any wicket for the county and one highly unlikely to ever be beaten. Surely Middlesex's winning sequence would end at just two? Surely there was no way to win from there – or so everyone thought.

Faced with this mammoth score, Haynes and Roseberry began confidently, raising another century stand and looked set to reach stumps still together before the latter was caught off the bowling of Steve Watkin in the death throes of the day. The decision was taken to promote Emburey to the role of nightwatchman and he dutifully saw the visitors through to the close for no further loss.

Haynes was pinned in front by Watkin early on day three, but with Gatting playing freely from the get-go and Emburey taking advantage of the opportunity afforded him by his nightwatchman duties of the evening before, Middlesex forged on.

The pair would still be together at tea, by which time the follow-on mark was within reach, though given how long Glamorgan had now bowled there was no certainty they would have enforced it.

We've spoken previously of the nature of life in the Middlesex dressing room, a hard school in which only the best survived but an environment where there were high expectations, and where every opinion was valued and everyone allowed voice. It was established under Brearley and further encouraged in the Gatting regime.

Emburey provided insight into the atmosphere and workings of the dressing room in the following tale,'

If someone wasn't pulling their weight or they were pissing around we used to have a big barney in the dressing room. Mike Brearley allowed that to happen and Gatt allowed it too. It felt like those things needed to be cleared up and not allowed to fester. So the dressing room was very volatile and everyone used to get stuck in.

'I remember a time when Gatt had a go at the players one day and the following day he did exactly the same thing. A couple of the young players came to me saying, "We've been told off for this and Gatt has done exactly the same thing."

'So, I got hold of Gatt one lunchtime during that game – again it was a chat in the toilets. I said, "Gatt, I'm going to have a go at you when we get back in the dressing room," and he said, "What about?"

'I said, "You had a go at players the other day for this and that and then did the same." So he said, "Fine."

'So, I had a go at Gatt and all the young players thought, "He's having a go at the captain." Gatt took it and no one knew we'd had a chat beforehand. If Gatt had said "don't do that" I wouldn't have done it as you don't usually openly criticise a captain.

'But it brought everyone together again. We sorted things out like that. We got it done. So we had all those big arguments and barneys in the dressing room. We would climb into someone and if they argued back two or three others would get into them as well.

'By the time we went back on the field, all that aggression was then taken out on the opposition. We'd got it off our chests, so the anger and adrenaline could then be directed at the opposition. It made us a better side and that mentality stayed with us.'

We tell that story here because it helps to explain the goings on in the Middlesex dressing room on that third afternoon in Cardiff.

Gatting had gone into that interval thinking about declaring and setting up a last-day run chase with Glamorgan skipper Hugh Morris. Therefore his opening gambit to his players over their cup of tea was 'OK, how many do we want to chase? Six, seven an over?'

The response was not one he was expecting, 'Not on this wicket.'

Taken aback, Gatting ventured, 'What do you mean, not on this wicket?'

Emburey took it upon himself to explain, 'The ball was turning. Viv Richards was turning the ball, so I said, "Let's carry on batting and we can bowl them out. I'll get five, Tuffers will get five and we can knock the runs off."'

Gatting admitted that he was reluctant, but the rest of the players rallied around their vice-captain, 'Fourth day of the match and you want us to chase six or seven an over on that! No! We're not declaring.'

In a minority of one, Gatting bowed to the inevitable. Stumped by the dressing-room culture he'd cultivated he strapped on his pads once more and went back out to bat, much to the chagrin of the Glamorgan members watching,

'The bloody Glamorgan supporters were ranting and raving on, "You boring gits, why don't you declare."

I thought, "It's not my fault," but I didn't tell them that.'

Emburey and Gatting both fell before the close, by which time Middlesex were still 85 in arrears and therefore the following morning they ran the gauntlet of the cat-calls once more and batted on still further. With each passing over it seemed any chance of a result had gone, especially as by the time they were bowled out Middlesex led by only 22.

Tufnell grabbed a wicket in the short passage of play before lunch which Glamorgan took at 25-1. Any cricket fans who decided the game was dead and found something better to do with their afternoon missed an extraordinary session of cricket in which Tufnell bowled his way to a career-best 8-29, including the wickets of both first-innings centurions, Dale and Richards.

The prize of the former West Indies skipper and batting legend was especially sweet, snaffled for a golden duck.

'He played half forward and the ball leapt up, hit him on the glove or the top of the handle and went to silly mid-off,' recalled Emburey.

Tufnell, never afraid to court a little controversy, went somewhat over the top with his celebrations in the wake of the dismissal, dancing around, jumping up and down and running down the wicket. Richards, to put it mildly was 'not amused', seeing the carry-on as disrespectful and a personal slight.

'Viv got a bit upset when Philip started charging around after getting him out,' revealed Gatting. He said he wanted to see him at the end of the game. He did come in the dressing room, but just said, "Well done, man."'

Tufnell's wizardry meant Glamorgan were all out soon after tea, leaving Middlesex only 88 to win, whereupon Haynes and Roseberry knocked them off without mishap, leaving them victors by ten wickets in a match where they'd conceded almost 600 in the first innings. What an extraordinary game we all love.

With their subsequent Sunday League fixture against Gloucestershire washed out Gatting's men had 11 days to come down off the high of such a victory before heading for Edgbaston to face Warwickshire where John Carr's unbeaten 192 was a class apart from anyone else with bat in hand, securing a winning lead of 150 on first innings. It paved the way for Emburey, who was man enough to admit to being 'hacked off' by Tufnell getting eight wickets to his one in Cardiff, to take 6-61 as the visitors won by nine wickets. Such figures though would serve merely as a prelude to the following week's encounter with Hampshire back at Lord's.

Again, there was little to choose between the two sides over the first two innings. Emburey's four-wicket haul restricted Hampshire to 280, former England skipper David Gower making 91. Gatting's 84 and 44 from Williams secured a slender lead of 30 and then it was time for Emburey to step into the spotlight. Getting some turn and also bounce from the Pavilion End, the off-spinner shared the first four wickets with Tufnell, but then took over as one after another the Hampshire batters fell victim to his wiles. Particularly satisfying for Emburey was getting Mark Nicholas in both innings, the Hampshire skipper having dished out a fair bit of stick to him the previous summer.

Emburey said, 'Hampshire used to block me all the time and Mark Nicholas was always at sea against me.

'Then one year he had a change of thought as to how he was going to play and came down the pitch and hit me over the top. It was not often players would do that to me but he'd obviously had a change of philosophy and thought, "Sod it, I'm not just going to block this old git again."

'I don't think the pitch for my eight-for turned a huge amount. It certainly wasn't a Bunsen Burner. The odd ball would turn and some would go straight on.'

Hampshire were hustled out for 88, leaving Middlesex the formality of scoring 59 to chalk up another win.

According to skipper Gatting, who had a better view than most of the heroics, Hampshire's batters simply froze faced with a spinner of Emburey's class,

'I remember talking to Mark Nicholas about that game. He said they were all shitting themselves the Hampshire boys. The young kids in their team, they'd never seen Embers. By that time a lot of spinners were, I wouldn't say leaving the game, but they were not as good as those from before. There were young guys coming in, but Embers was still there and with people around the bat Hampshire just panicked.'

So it was that within the space of 19 days that July in 1993, two masters of the art of spin bowling each produced career-best figures. They did so in an environment where spinners were prized, their art celebrated, so much so they were bowled in tandem for hours at a time, trusted to play a full part in the attack and a team's bowling strategy.

Sadly, such days appear to have gone. Spinners are rare, counties lucky if they have one, never mind two, and even the one they have is for the most part employed as an afterthought, a last-ditch attempt to buy a wicket perhaps.

There are exceptions of course, Simon Harmer of Essex perhaps the most obvious of those in the modern game. Many now, however, are only found among the seemingly endless circuit of one-day franchise competitions.

Gatting, having worked with three of the best in that golden era, had more reason than most to lament the passing of their influence and was in no doubt the governing bodies are at fault for the demise of the art.

'You don't see spin bowling of that quality [in the Championship] now and it is our own fault sadly because of the way four-day cricket has been played.

'They want it to be played on flat wickets and the ability to play on a turner has gone because young kids don't know how to do it. There are not any spinners around because captains don't know how to handle them. So you get all these medium-pacers playing on green wickets and when you have got seven or eight Championship matches in April and May.

'Admittedly when we played in April and May we played 24 Championship matches, but we still played two spinners because you needed a man for every occasion. We just picked our strongest bowlers and even if it wasn't turning you could get people out bad-pad or lbw. It gave you the ability to have someone around the bat, putting guys under pressure, making them do silly things. There does not seem to be that art any more.

'It is our fault because the ECB weren't strong enough, stopping people just producing seamer-friendly wickets, so spinners never got back into the game and we are still struggling now.

'There is still nothing like a good spinner. You see Adil Rashid come on even in the IPL [Indian Premier League] or t20s. When a spinner like him comes on it is a good contest still. There are so few good spinners around and it's really sad as it's a huge thing to come out of the game.'

Gatting's sentiments are echoed by his former vice-captain Emburey, who said given the nature of pitches at Lord's in the early years of the 2020s, were he playing he'd have had to forge a career for himself elsewhere.'

'It was easier back then than it is now. As a spinner now it is bloody hard work to break through with just the way the game is played, the positivity of batters.

'Lord's isn't such a great place to bowl now because it is not bowler-friendly for spinners.

'You have got to be a different type of bowler to bowl at Lord's now. You literally have five Championship matches there in a season. One is played at Merchant Taylors', another at Radlett. So, you almost play on a fresh pitch every time. They water the bloody surface all the time and they fertilize it, so all grass comes up and all the pitches are green. You don't get the bare pitches we used to have.

'If I was starting my career now, no way would I stay at Middlesex. I would have to go somewhere else.'

If the spinners had been the driving force of much of Middlesex's mid-season winning streak, it was Fraser who stepped in the spotlight for the sixth victory in a row, an innings mauling of Leicestershire at Lord's.

Centuries for Roseberry and Gatting laid the foundation, the duo sharing a stand of 230 for the second wicket after the hosts opted to bat first. Gatting's ton was the 75th of his first-class career but his first against the Foxes, leaving Durham as the only remaining county against whom he'd not reached three figures. He would complete the full set with 171 against English cricket's newest first-class county at Lord's three years later. Ramprakash and Carr weighed in with half-centuries to ram home Middlesex's advantage before they declared with 551-8 on the board.

What followed would be Fraser's best figures in England, a return of 7-40 as he bowled unchanged for 17 overs with Leicestershire hustled out for 114.

Such lengthy stints were not uncommon where Fraser was concerned as once he got into a rhythm it was difficult to prise the ball out of his hand, as Emburey recalled.

'You knew what you were getting from Gus. He wasn't a big five-wicket haul bowler, though he has always said he would have got more five-wicket hauls if it wasn't for me because we used to bowl from the same end at Lord's.

'And if we played away matches we would more often than not want to bowl at the same end. You couldn't get the ball out of Angus's hands. When I felt I wasn't going to get a wicket or that I was getting milked, I would say to Gatt, "Take me off, put me on the other end or bring me back on in 20 minutes," just to break things up a little bit.

'But then Angus didn't want to come off. He would say, "If I come off I'm not going to bowl again because you bowl all day. If you're bowling it means I'm not bowling."

'I would reply, "Yes, but the wicket's dry and turning and you want to bowl when the spinner should be on."

'He was a top bloke, but he used to moan. He used to moan all the time or complain about this or about that.'

Fraser would eventually top this career best with his 8-53 in an England shirt on the 1997/98 tour to the West Indies, the sort of figures which built him a reputation on the international stage with other fast-bowling legends of the game.

I was fortunate to meet several of those stars at a Lord's Taverners gathering around the time Fraser was appointed director of cricket at Middlesex in 2009.

The great and the good of fast bowling were at this gathering including Glenn McGrath, who in my role as a regional journalist I was sent to interview about his own brief spell at Middlesex in 2004.

During the course of our chat at the top of the Warner Stand, I mentioned that an old Ashes adversary of his had become the head honcho at Lord's. The response was memorable.

'Ah, Angus Fraser, great bowler,' he said with his typical New South Wales drawl.

Somehow, I knew he wasn't finished there, so I waited and sure enough he continued, 'Bored everyone to death.'

This was of course a backhanded compliment to Fraser from one of the greats, paying homage to a bowler of relentless accuracy and stamina, who wore down opponents and forced mistakes.

A Lancastrian by birth, Fraser was well and truly adopted by Middlesex, who he served with distinction as a player for 18 years before undertaking a career in written and broadcast journalism. He is a member of Middlesex CCC's Hall of Fame.

Fraser would claim eight more wickets in a rain-affected draw with Yorkshire at Scarborough which brought the Championship leaders' winning run to a halt – but only just.

Rain washed out much of the first day where three wickets for Tufnell left the hosts 89-5. Over the next two days Middlesex built a first-innings lead of 183 before reducing the White Rose county to 110-4 second time around. Rain delayed play on the final day, but even so Middlesex looked set to make it seven wins on the trot when they grabbed Yorkshire's ninth wicket with them still six runs short of saving the innings defeat. However, the last pair scrambled seven runs to edge in front as the overs ran out to force the draw.

Middlesex's one innings here was notable for Gatting's 182 and 140 for Ramprakash, the latter's highest score of the campaign. The pair shared a stand of 321 for the third wicket, a record against Yorkshire which still stands today.

By this time the precocious young talent of the late 1980s was an established member of not only Middlesex's middle order, but he'd made ten Test appearances for England.

Yet he was still in the foothills of a glittering career at county level, underlining the promise that coach Don Bennett had spotted.

'He will be the last person to score 100 hundreds in county cricket. I don't think anybody else will ever do that,' said Gatting, reflecting on his former team-mate.

'If you are talking about a technician, he was better than [Graeme] Hick and if you talk to his contemporaries who he played with and against, they'd say that.'

For one so talented, only two of Ramprakash's centuries came in Tests, something of a mystery. Gatting believed the under-achievement at the highest level was a mixture of a lack of compromise when it came to the need for 'ugly runs' and a temperament which didn't always deal well with the media scrutiny which is inevitably associated with representing your country.

'Ramps was a perfectionist and I just got the feeling in an era that was changing he could have batted all day and done what Geoffrey Boycott did quite easily because his technique was so good,' he continued.

'What I would say is he probably tried to be even more perfect than Geoffrey Boycott. I don't think he knew how to score ugly runs. We talked to him about it a bit, but he wanted to be perfect in everything he did and you can't be like that. I'm not sure he was ever able to get to grips with that.

'We did talk about it a lot, but the trouble is as I found out, you know, the pressure from media and stuff does get at you at times and he could be very fiery, Ramps. I think that might not have helped him. I was able to temper it a bit because I wasn't fussed about it. It was nice to see yourself written up, but even I got to an age where it did hurt because I knew I could do better.

'When you think Ramps got 100 against the West Indies in the West Indies, I was hoping that would open the floodgates like it did for me a bit and that he'd continue on and play Test cricket for a bit longer, but for some strange reason it didn't happen.

'He was intense, but he was just an unbelievable talent. It was great to play with him. He was a lovely man as well, once he'd settled down again having got out. He was very passionate about the game, very passionate and sometimes the passion would overtake other things.'

While Ramprakash's career at Middlesex continued to prosper, the stay of another great of the golden era, Norman Cowans, was coming to an end. However, the paceman returned from injury in time to play a key role in two wins at the back end of the season which all but clinched the laurels.

Their winning streak having been interrupted at Scarborough, Gatting's men headed back to Lord's to face Northamptonshire, naming Cowans in their XI.

Winning the toss and batting, the hosts stumbled to 161-5 only for the trusty middle-order pair of Brown and Emburey to dig them out of trouble as they had done earlier in the season, the latter going on to make 120. It would be the last of his seven first-class hundreds.

With 402 on the board, Middlesex lost Neil Williams to injury early in Northamptonshire's reply so were all the more grateful for Cowans's three wickets in a shade under 16 overs. Two more came when the visitors followed on 170 in arrears, the spinners doing most of the damage, meaning Middlesex required only 11 to win by ten wickets and maintain their charge towards the title.

The honours were all but clinched in the next game with Essex at Castle Park in Colchester, with Cowans again to the fore. The 32-year-old shared eight wickets with new-ball partner Fraser to oust the hosts for 148, though Mark Ilott's six wickets meant Middlesex were all out themselves by stumps having secured only a slim first-innings lead of 19.

Cowans and Fraser, though, regained the initiative on the second morning, two wickets apiece reducing Essex to 60-4. Nasser Hussain held them up with a fine 73, but Cowans finished with 3-26 before Gatting's unbeaten 76 steered them home by seven wickets.

It would turn out to be Cowans's last bowl in a Middlesex shirt as although he was named in the XI for the match with Lancashire, persistent rain meant he never got on the field with ball in hand.

He moved on to Hampshire at the end of that season, spending two years with the southern coast county before retiring.

Like Wayne Daniel and so many other quick bowlers before him, as the decades went by Cowans carried the physical scars of his career and he felt that medical care available to cricketers when we spoke was so much more advanced than it was in his playing days. However, he wouldn't trade the years he spent in the game.

'I'd just come back from a hernia operation, so I was out for quite a lot of that season. I was trying to get back from injury and into the team while having a testimonial year. It was a pretty full-on time and the body was feeling the strain by then.

'I'd had two operations on my groin and back in those days you were pretty much left to your own devices when it came to rehab and that sort of thing. So you didn't get the best treatment really and it was tough, but when I could play I contributed and helped to win a couple of games really. It was quite satisfying in that respect to still be part of a Championship-winning team.

'You look back on what you achieved and the significant contribution you made, and what you go through as a fast bowler as well, with a setup pretty draconian by today's standards, in terms of looking after players. There were no 12-month contracts, so once the season was over you were on your own. You had to fend for yourself and get yourself fit.

'Looking back now you think, "How did we manage to do that?" The game leaves its mark in that you suffer for years afterwards with injuries which maybe could have been treated better or avoided. You are left to mop up the pieces with the injuries picked up during your playing days. The counties now are much better at looking after their bowlers and players, where as fast bowlers you are not having to manage those injuries after you retire.

'You weren't paid a fortune back in the day. You weren't earning the money that warranted the contribution you made. For me I played cricket because I really enjoyed it. It was fun and it was great, but when you become a professional it becomes a completely different game. It becomes a job you know.

'Sometimes when you are at the top of your profession as a lawyer or a doctor you are well rewarded for it but as a cricketer back in the day even playing international cricket you weren't well off. It was a different era and a different time.

'I'm very proud and honoured to have been given the opportunity to be able to play cricket professionally for as long as I did given the ups and downs that go along with being a fast bowler, to play in a great team with great professionals and to represent Middlesex and give them some of the best years of my life really.'

By the time of the near-washout against Lancashire, Middlesex's 12th title had been confirmed and in truth they had long been celebrating. Consequently, when they reached New Road to play Worcestershire in the season finale, their heads were no longer in the game.

They were rolled over for 68 in their first innings and were on the brink of an innings defeat inside two days when last man Tufnell came out to join Fraser at the wicket. Unbeknown to those watching, he'd emerged from the dressing room with the words of Mike Roseberry ringing in his ears.

'Mike had said to him, "I bet you a bottle of champagne you can't hit the first ball for six,"' said Emburey.

Stuart Lampitt was the bowler and at least gave Tufnell the chance to swing with a shortish ball outside off stump and the tailender took up the challenge.

'Tuffers wasn't the bravest, but he was a good timer of the ball when he hit it,' continued Emburey.

'He leant back, latched on to this ball, opened the face of the bat and it flew over cover and went for six. Of course, we all cheered in the dressing room even though we were getting thrashed and the Worcester members sitting in front of us were looking through our window wondering what we were cheering for.'

Fraser was caught by Lampitt off Neal Radford soon afterwards to confirm Middlesex's only Championship defeat of the campaign, but Tufnell ran off still celebrating to make sure Roseberry made good on his bet.

'Phil's six was the only bright spot in the game because we batted shockingly,' admitted Gatting. 'It was sad and unprofessional. We weren't there mentally. We'd won the Championship and we didn't want to be there, I don't think. When you work hard all the way through, fight hard all summer and get to where you do, you sometimes need a release valve.'

Emburey was as certain as he could be that this was the year the frivolity of Tufnell's six-hitting exploit, spilt over into the post-title celebrations later that night.

As vice-captain, Emburey also had the role of social secretary and therefore he organised a bit of a do in their Worcestershire hotel. This one, though, was to take on a more informal nature than most,

Mark Ramprakash – a better technique than contemporary Graeme Hick according to Middlesex skipper Mike Gatting.

'We had a lot of second-team players up at the game at Worcester and I was running the players' pool. So I said we'll all get together and have a meal.

'We'd had dinner in the hotel, but I had a word with one of the Worcester players prior and we got a couple of strippers to come into the hotel which was a bit risky. We had three or four tables and the girls came in dancing and whatever. We had a bloody big night. The

Phil Tufnell – his career best 8-29 won an astonishing game with Glamorgan at Sophia Gardens.

hotel didn't allow us back in after that. We'd been a bit too raunchy for them, so had to go somewhere else.'

This would be the last win of the golden era. Gatting stood down as captain early in 1996 after 13 years at the helm, ceding control to Ramprakash in the hope he'd lead the next wave of success, but it never came. Ramprakash left at the end of the 1999 season to cross the Thames and join Surrey where he would enjoy the best years of his career on the country's best batting wicket. His departure to the rivals, of all counties was, and maybe still is, viewed as an act of treachery by some die-hard Middlesex fans.

Gatting admitted that it was a source of disappointment to him too,

'Ramps went to the best batting pitch in the country at The Oval and just scored "millions" of runs and I didn't expect him to do anything different.

'I was so sad he didn't stay at Middlesex because he might have galvanised one or two of the young guys, but I think he got frustrated.

'I finished in 1996 after three or four games because they had just had enough of me as captain. I'd been doing it for 13 years and we felt Ramps might just get through to his mates and whatever.

'Trouble is sometimes familiarity breeds contempt and I think they all knew Ramps as a very good friend and they couldn't cope with what they needed to do. Ramps could, but because they couldn't in the end he got so frustrated. They were good cricketers, David Nash and people like that. But he got frustrated with them which was sad because they were great mates.'

As a consequence, just as had happened after the wins of the 1920s and post-Second World War years it would be more than 20 years before Middlesex could fly the champions' ensign above the Lord's pavilion again. Some of those were fairly desperate years too including relegation from the First Division in 2006, while only last pair Tim Murtagh and David Burton batting out the final 16 balls of the 2009 season prevented them collecting the Championship wooden spoon for the first time.

They returned to the top flight two years later, but it would be another five years before glory returned on the most dramatic of September days at Lord's.

CHAPTER 11
2016

'I genuinely did not know I'd got a hat-trick,' admitted Toby Roland-Jones. 'I guess that's a good indicator of the occasion and how I was working overtime to keep focused.'

In all fairness, the seamer was by no means alone in blissful ignorance of his individual achievement as Ryan Sidebottom's leg stump rocked back. Many among the thousands of spectators who had gradually filtered into Lord's over the course of that Friday in late September 2016 were initially just as oblivious to the fact that Roland-Jones had captured three Yorkshire wickets in as many balls. They were too enmeshed in the excitement, the emotion and drama of an electrifying climax to the domestic season – and Middlesex's first County Championship title in 23 years.

The match, which had just been settled in Middlesex's favour by 61 runs was in effect a winner-takes-all contest. Both the home side and Yorkshire, county champions for the previous two seasons, knew only victory could secure the coveted pennant. A drawn game would mean disappointment for both teams and raucous celebrations 150 miles to the south-west, where Somerset had already crushed relegated Nottinghamshire by 325 runs to take over at the summit.

For that reason, the showdown in St John's Wood had evolved into a chess match as much as a cricket match. A situation where both Middlesex and Yorkshire were obliged to gamble, risking defeat to maintain their hopes of victory, with negotiating skills brought into play to create a delicate balancing act that kept each side in contention right up until the final few overs of a hard-fought campaign.

Twelve months earlier, the Lord's stage had hosted the same cast to determine the destiny of the title, but with a far lower level of drama. On that occasion, Yorkshire arrived in London for their penultimate game needing only a handful of bonus points to retain their crown and those were safely pocketed on the first day after rolling the hosts for 106. Despite that forgettable start, Middlesex staged an impressive fightback to triumph by a whopping 246 runs – with Roland-Jones hitting an unbeaten century and then claiming figures of 5-27 – as the White Rose slid to their first red-ball defeat in 26 games. Middlesex, meanwhile, had to settle for the runners-up position – although that in itself represented their best performance in the Championship for more than two decades and a growing sense among the squad that they could go one better next time.

'That feeling when we came second was one of what could have been,' recalled Seaxes wicketkeeper-batter John Simpson. 'We hardly ever lost at Lord's and we tried to make it a fortress so that when anyone came there, they'd be thinking, "Middlesex are hot, they're a proper team and they've got all bases covered."' I think that was exemplified when we were so far behind the eight ball against Yorkshire at Lord's in 2015 and ended up asking them to chase 380. When you do that, it gives you a lot of confidence and belief that you can take down a Yorkshire side who were at their peak. We knew we were building something special.'

Little surprise, then, that Middlesex made few changes to their squad in the build-up to the 2016 campaign. Batting all-rounder and former skipper Neil Dexter left for Leicestershire, while the only new face was James Fuller, a pace bowler who had been recruited from Gloucestershire – primarily to bolster the limited-overs side, although he would also end up playing his part in the four-day format. Overseas star Adam Voges, who had led the team at the start of the 2015 season before gaining an unexpected call-up to Australia's Test side at the age of 35, returned as captain. However, former New Zealand all-rounder James Franklin – who had taken over the reins for the rest of that year – would do so again when international commitments took Voges away from Middlesex midway through 2016.

'Adam was the spiritual leader, for want of a better term, and I was fortunate to step into his big boots,' said Franklin. 'He was always in the loop in terms of what was going on and he had a huge amount of respect from everyone in the dressing room, as a bloke and a leader. The side had been settled for a few years and everyone understood their roles in the team.'

According to Roland-Jones, the change of captain was 'pretty seamless'. He observed, 'Both Adam and James have a similar way of working and they got on really well. There was a clear line that had been drawn by Vogesy as captain and James just looked to slip straight on to that and tried to keep things as simple as possible, following similar principles.'

While there was a pleasing consistency in terms of the team's leadership, the consistency in Middlesex's results during the early part of the season was perhaps less satisfying. All of the first six fixtures finished in draws, with spring failing to give way to summer as a significant amount of time was lost to bad weather. Rain was the chief culprit, with two full days of the home game against Nottinghamshire entirely washed out and virtually the same percentage of the fixtures at Hampshire and Durham. In the case of the latter encounter at Chester-le-Street in late April, the players had to contend with more than just a downpour.

'I remember going back out at Durham and there was a light snow drizzle in the air,' said Roland-Jones. 'At that point you're wondering what on earth was going on, to be honest.

'But I think that in the early season, whether we were at our best or not quite on it, we always felt we'd find a way of being competitive enough and not handing games to the opposition. We knew if we stuck to our principles we'd start getting some positive results from the way we were playing.'

Despite the damp – and the snow – there were few rich pickings for Roland-Jones and his fellow pacemen during April and May. In part, that could perhaps be put down to a new rule which had been introduced to Championship cricket since the 2015 season, with all visiting teams now offered the option of bowling first and dispensing with the traditional toss of a coin if they wished. The change had been brought in to address concerns that home sides could prepare playing surfaces to suit their own bowlers – which, as well as providing a clear advantage if the toss went in their favour, also decreased the likelihood of games going the distance.

Roland-Jones reflected, 'In that year, the rule change definitely led to teams safeguarding away from losing the game in the first session if the pitch did a little too much. Certainly they were more aware of not making pitches too bowler-friendly so that a team could come and have first use and take a stranglehold on the game. I feel that part of the rule was a good introduction, but there were some other iffy sides to it as well.

'I remember it being one of the better years in terms of the pitch at Lord's and the balance between bat and ball. It definitely had consistency – we've seen in the last few years that it's proved difficult to prepare long-lasting pitches there.

'We had some games where it felt like hard work and there was a decent number of runs – at the same time we felt that as a bowling unit we should have a good chance of taking 20 wickets on our home ground.

'I recall [off-spinner] Ollie Rayner having a huge hand in a good number of home games – and you wouldn't always stereotype Lord's as being a spinner's ground. That generally tells you the pitches were a bit harder-wearing than they have been at times.'

Whatever the reason, bat tended to dominate ball during that initial period of the 2016 season and Middlesex's chief beneficiary, certainly at Lord's, was opener Sam Robson. The right-hander, who had played seven Tests for England two years earlier, took a particular and immediate liking to the surfaces at HQ as he amassed 231 – at that time his career-best performance – in the Seaxes' opening fixture against Warwickshire at Lord's and followed it up with a century in the second innings. Robson posted three figures again in Middlesex's next home game, the rain-ruined encounter with Nottinghamshire, and by then it was becoming evident that the county had unearthed another promising talent to partner him at the top of the order.

Left-hander Nick Gubbins, having emerged in the wake of Chris Rogers's switch to Somerset, had now begun to establish himself in the team at the tender age of 22. While the Leeds University graduate had already shared two century partnerships with Robson before Rogers returned to Lord's with his new team-mates at the end of May, he had also endured a few near misses when it came to the personal landmark of posting three figures. Curiously enough, two of those had already occurred against the men from the West Country – he was run out for 95 at Uxbridge, in only his second Championship appearance, and then hit 92 in Middlesex's five-wicket win at Taunton the previous summer. Gubbins had chalked up yet another excursion into the 90s only a week earlier, when the team fought out the fifth of those six draws against Surrey at The Oval.

This time, the young opener would finally reach his target against the Somerset bowling attack. After Rogers had anchored the visitors' total of 376 with a century of his own, Robson and Gubbins put on 198 for the opening wicket and this time it was the right-hander who fell just short of his hundred. Gubbins, however, cruised on to reach his maiden ton on the third morning and maintain a vein of form that would propel him to a total of 1,409 runs for the season and at a healthy average of more than 60. Only Keaton Jennings, soon to be selected for England's tour of India, outranked him in the pecking order of Championship runs during the summer.

With Robson and Gubbins providing a strong base at the top of a batting order that also featured Voges and the stylish Dawid Malan, there was little danger that Nick Compton's absence for a chunk of the middle part of the season would cause disruption. Compton had featured in the first four Championship games of the summer before joining England's Test squad to take on Sri Lanka, but a string of low scores in that series prompted him to take a complete break from the game until August. Middlesex's strength in depth, though, proved to be more than adequate and that also applied to the seam attack, where the frontline trio of Roland-Jones, Tim Murtagh and Steven Finn were ably backed up by James Harris, Fuller and 21-year-old west Londoner Harry Podmore.

'Gubbo had a magnificent season,' said Simpson. 'He got well over 1,000 runs, which was a hell of an effort and played some fantastic innings over the summer. Dawid got very close to 1,000 as well.

'Bowling-wise, Murts gave you control and then you had the excitement and youth of Finny and Toby as well as Ollie Rayner spin-wise. We also had a really good slip cordon. I got close to 50 victims in the Championship, but we had Vogesy or Robbo at first or third, Ollie at second and then Dawid or Compo as well.

'My abiding memory is that everybody stood up at certain stages of every game, whether that was to move the game forward into a position where we could win or a position where we couldn't lose it.'

Ensuring they couldn't be beaten was something the Seaxes had successfully managed to achieve throughout those first six games. Sooner or later, however, the players were well aware they would have to conjure up methods of converting draws into victories if the title challenge that had been envisaged was to become a reality.

'It was frustrating at that stage but we felt we'd played some really good cricket, we just couldn't break teams down,' Simpson recalled.

'Lord's had been pretty flat in that period and it was Vogesy's idea to sit us all down and say, "Right, if this is the way the season's going to pan out and the wickets are like this, how are we going to change the way we think? Whether it's to get the ball reversing or something else, can we do something different to change and adapt?"

'We had a real honest conversation about what we could do that was different, without affecting the really good stuff we were already doing with bat, ball and in the field. We tried to open it up and come up with some ideas.'

Although they were yet to put a win on the board, the sequence of six draws had certainly not left the men from Lord's lagging hopelessly off the pace. The twin issues of bad weather and unresponsive pitches had been in evidence throughout the country and, as Middlesex went into that Somerset home game in late May, Lancashire were the only Division One side to have mustered more than a single victory. Champions Yorkshire had picked up one win to date, an innings success against Surrey at Headingley, while Somerset's run of consecutive draws was identical to that of their opponents at Lord's.

Nevertheless, Voges was keen to kick-start the Seaxes' championship challenge before he departed London to re-join the Australia squad for their Test series in Sri Lanka. The one remaining opportunity to do that would be available when the team faced Hampshire at Merchant Taylors' School, a picturesque countryside setting on the Hertfordshire border where Middlesex were staging a four-day fixture for the third time. So far, they had been less than fortunate in terms of the weather – not a ball was bowled when Sussex visited the school in 2014, while the loss of a day's play the previous season had ultimately scuppered the home side's chances of forcing a win against Somerset.

The captain certainly led from the front against Hampshire, whom he had represented nine years earlier, by winning the toss and opting to bat – and then digging Middlesex out of early difficulties with a masterful unbeaten 160, his first and only century of the campaign. With both openers gone and a meagre 14 on the board, Voges and Malan proceeded to flay the Hampshire attack to the tune of a 279-run partnership – the Australian unruffled despite being on the receiving end of a beamer that earned Tino Best an official warning. Malan struck 147 before Simpson weighed in with an undefeated 100 of his own from just 125 balls, ensuring a torrid second morning for the Hampshire bowlers and Voges promptly declared as soon as his partner had reached three figures. With the Middlesex total at a commanding 467-3, it was now a case of handing over to the seamers the responsibility for pressing home that advantage.

Ominously, the capricious weather had already begun to intervene, making it clear that the home side's best chance of victory would be to bowl Hampshire out cheaply and enforce the follow-on. With Murtagh and Roland-Jones picking up four wickets each, that was exactly what they did and second time around, it was the turn of Fuller – drafted in to make his red-ball debut for the county with Finn away on England duty – to sample the limelight.

Sixth-wicket pair Jimmy Adams and Adam Wheater had threatened to hold Middlesex up on the final day, putting together a stubborn partnership, but once Franklin had removed the opener leg before for 78, Fuller quickly cut into the tail. The debutant completed a five-wicket haul before Rayner captured the final Hampshire wicket to wrap up proceedings and ensure that, for the first time in the summer, the team's victory song could be afforded an overdue, boisterous airing.

'Having finished second to a very good Yorkshire side in 2015, we'd gone out with the belief that, if we could play some tough, uncompromising cricket and be in the top half of the table, we could look to really mount a challenge for the title,' said Franklin.

'Everyone knew their roles in the team and, halfway through the season, we were in a position where we could try to win the Championship. Games along the way then started to instil that belief even more and nothing fazed us.'

The schedule, however, meant there was no immediate opportunity for Middlesex to build on the momentum of their innings victory over Hampshire. The very next day, in fact, six of the triumphant XI were back at Merchant Taylors' School, having shed their whites in favour of the county's more eye-catching pink outfits to take on Gloucestershire in the early rounds of the T20 Blast. The annual tournament had brought little, if any joy for the Seaxes since their Finals Day success eight years earlier. On the contrary; a losing streak in the shortest format had frequently tended to spill over into red-ball performances – something Middlesex could ill afford if hopes of a title challenge were to become a reality.

In 2016, thankfully, there was to be no Blast-fuelled collapse – largely because Middlesex's T20 campaign proved to be their most successful since winning the trophy in 2008. Now led by Malan and featuring limited-overs specialists such as England's white-ball captain Eoin Morgan, former New Zealand skipper Brendon McCullum and big-hitting opener Paul Stirling, the team won half of their group fixtures to qualify for the quarter-finals. Despite a seven-wicket defeat at the hands of eventual champions Northamptonshire, there was a general feeling that Middlesex had finally made genuine progress in white-ball cricket.

In the meantime, what of their bid for the Championship crown? In the midst of the Blast campaign, the team recorded yet another draw on a lifeless Lord's track against Lancashire. Keen to strengthen their title credentials by seeing off the side who were topping the table at that stage, any realistic prospect of Middlesex achieving that evaporated once the Red Rose had racked up a first-innings total of 513. Nevertheless, the Seaxes batted their way to safety in relative comfort, with Gubbins highlighting his class once again by registering an undefeated double hundred, supported by a maiden Championship century from his friend and fellow rookie Stephen Eskinazi. The young batting duo's second-wicket partnership of 208 helped to ensure their side made up two bonus points on Lancashire before a final-day downpour put paid to any lingering chance of a result. However, with Middlesex precisely halfway through their 16-match programme – and with only three of the remaining eight fixtures on home turf – it was clear that their upcoming trips to Yorkshire and Somerset, in successive weeks, were likely to be critical.

The picturesque North Marine Road ground at Scarborough, high on the list of favourite venues for ground-hopping county cricket lovers, was also seen as a formidable bastion of strength for Yorkshire. The defending champions rarely endured defeat at their seaside out-ground and had crushed both Worcestershire and Durham by heavy margins during their title-winning campaign the previous year. So the task facing Middlesex as they headed north on the train from King's Cross was a daunting one.

'Scarborough is not the easiest place to go to and get results, or at least it certainly wasn't at the time,' Roland-Jones recalled. 'It's a pretty unique ground with a special feel to it.

'We respected that Yorkshire team hugely. They set a really high bar that we were trying to jump over, so we went up there knowing they were the ones to try and take down.'

Roland-Jones and his fellow seamers battled hard to rein in the home side on the first day and a half, with Gary Ballance's century underpinning the Tykes' total of 406. Middlesex's response with the bat, however, was patient and effective as Eskinazi followed up his ton in the Lancashire game by taking another against their Roses rivals – a career-best effort of 157 compiled over the best part of seven hours. With Compton still taking time out from the game, Middlesex had bolstered their batting line-up by signing Australia's George Bailey to replace compatriot Voges – and the newcomer made his mark immediately. His debut knock of 62 provided a base for Eskinazi, who went on to share a partnership of 172 with Franklin and earn the visitors a slim lead of 64 with two wickets standing, going into the final day.

Also slim, it seemed, were Middlesex's prospects of forcing the pace sufficiently to drive themselves into a winning position. But Roland-Jones and Murtagh, the not-out batters at stumps on day three, had other ideas.

'We needed a lot of things to go our way and I do remember having a lot of fun on that final morning!' said Roland-Jones. 'It was a case of seeing how far we could take it and we felt, if we could get 100 runs in front, we could make something happen in the game.

'Sometimes when it comes out of the blue, it's hard for the batting side to get their mental state right, knowing they're suddenly batting to save the game rather than just meandering towards a draw.'

Never mind extending their lead to 100 overall – instead, Middlesex added over another 100 to the total in just 40 minutes of utter carnage on the final morning. Roland-Jones slammed three successive balls from Jack Brooks over the rope, while Azeem Rafiq's first over of the day cost him 20 runs and the visitors' advantage mushroomed. The free-scoring pair put on 107 from only 58 deliveries, with Roland-Jones unbeaten on 79 and Murtagh missing out on a half-century by just three runs as the Seaxes posted 577, the county's record total against Yorkshire, to leave their hosts somewhat shell-shocked.

With that said, opening pair Adam Lyth and Alex Lees made rapid inroads on the deficit of 171, adding 41 from the first 11 overs of their second innings before Roland-Jones achieved the breakthrough with his first ball, edged to third slip by Lyth. From then on, the scenario evolved into a race against the clock, with Roland-Jones, Murtagh, Finn and Rayner all picking up wickets at regular intervals as the Yorkshire total grew steadily – raising the possibility that they might clamber up to 171 with time running out. Tim Bresnan took on the role of chief obstacle in the path of Middlesex's success – one he would reprise at the season's climax – as he held firm with a stubborn 39 until Murtagh eventually pierced his defences with a ball that skidded through. Yet Yorkshire's last pair, Rafiq and Brooks, clung on for a nerve-shredding 35 minutes, nudging their side to within one boundary of making Middlesex bat again before Murtagh sealed the win by having Brooks caught in the slips. It was the first time the Scarborough crowd had ever witnessed an innings defeat for Yorkshire in a County Championship fixture. But, just as significantly, the result lifted Middlesex to the top of the table for the first time that summer and, in psychological terms, gave the jubilant squad a collective shot in the arm.

'I've got hugely fond memories of that game,' added Roland-Jones. 'There were a lot of strong individual performances. But it was also a nice way to do it, with everyone being on the train together following a great win to share the moment and being able to celebrate as a squad.

'Those are the little things that start to bring together a bigger picture in terms of savouring success together and having that time to reflect on what we'd done rather than everyone going off separately in their cars. It felt like a pivotal moment in the season – but as Yorkshire showed afterwards, they didn't go anywhere too quickly and they were always in the hunt.' Literally speaking, however, Middlesex were on the move again very soon. Just three days after their Scarborough triumph they faced another lengthy journey – this time in a westerly direction to Taunton, where Somerset had recently chased down a 300 target in the fourth innings to overcome Surrey. With international commitments claiming the services of Murtagh and Finn, and Roland-Jones in need of a rest, the visitors travelled to Taunton shorn of their three main seamers. Consequently, on arrival at the ground, there was something of a surprise awaiting them, as Simpson remembered,

'We did wonder which wicket we were playing on, because there wasn't one marked out. There were two training nets towards the far end of the pitch, so a few of the guys just put their bags down on what later turned out to be the match wicket.

'All of a sudden, someone asked, "Oh, can you move the bags? We're going to play on this wicket on the far side." There were three wickets marked out and then they picked the one that hadn't been rolled or marked out or anything!

'That immediately screamed "interesting" and it threw us a bit of a curveball. But I knew exactly why that was – it was the greenest wicket they had and they'd realised we didn't have Murts playing.

'As it turned out, that wicket actually played pretty well, although I got a second-ball duck in the first innings, caught behind walking down to James Allenby.'

Initially, Somerset's ploy backfired. What they had viewed as a 'green' bowling attack made the most of a green surface, with Podmore taking 4-54 on his Championship debut and Harris and Fuller sharing the other six wickets to dismiss the home side for 236. Harris and Fuller then displayed their capabilities with the bat as the pitch began to dry, compiling a ninth-wicket stand of 162 on the second evening to earn the Seaxes a handy first-innings advantage. So far, so good – and Middlesex seemed squarely on track for victory when Podmore picked up three more wickets second time around to leave their hosts four down and still in arrears.

Peter Trego, a Middlesex man at one stage of his career, had frequently proved a thorn in the side of his former employers since returning to Taunton a decade earlier. The popular all-rounder filled that role again, digging Somerset out of trouble with an intrepid century as he and Marcus Trescothick built a steady lead with their partnership of 181, and by the final morning it was clear that Rogers would be asking Middlesex to chase an awkward target.

That target transpired to be 302 from 46 overs and the visitors started well, with Gubbins hitting a brisk 76, but once he and Bailey fell in quick succession to Tim Groenewald and Allenby trapped Franklin in front of his stumps, it was down to Simpson – celebrating his 28th birthday – to try and steer his side home.

'Groenewald was bowling around the wicket, it was swinging away and they had three slips and a gully,' Simpson recalled. 'I remember thinking it was going to be a trickier chase than we'd realised but I had to not get suckered into what they wanted – playing a big loose drive outside off stump and getting caught.

'So, it was a case of taking time out of the game, because he wasn't going to bowl forever, then trying to capitalise later on. I remember the conversation I had with James Fuller when he came out – he said, "I'm going to look to take the game on, you just play your way and we'll go from there." Straight away he ran down and hit a six to put some impetus back into the innings and I kind of piggy-backed off that with a few boundaries. I remember everyone leaving, thinking we were shutting up for a draw, but we got so much momentum from that partnership, we were always going to have a go towards the back end.'

Fuller's knock of 36 from 18 balls was exactly what his side needed and, with the pair adding a quickfire 86, those spectators who had written off the contest as an inevitable draw and headed home missed a thrilling climax. When the eighth wicket fell and Harris made his way out to join Simpson at the crease, Middlesex needed ten runs from nine deliveries. The new batter saw out the over with a two off Groenewald and, with eight more needed,

Simpson took guard against the medium-paced Allenby, who was preparing to send down the final over.

'I remember thinking, "Right, what are my options here?" I felt running down to Allenby was probably my best option as he kept bowling it down the leg side,' said Simpson. 'So, I thought if I could pick it up and middle the ball, it should sail a long way.'

Allenby's first three deliveries yielded two runs and Simpson put his plan into action on the fourth. He connected squarely and the ball disappeared into the car park, leaving the left-hander unbeaten on 79 and wrapping up a scintillating two-wicket win with just two balls to spare.

'It's what dreams are made of, really,' he added. 'To chase 300 down really set the tone we needed towards the back end of the season. Being my birthday as well, it was nice to have a few drinks with the boys and celebrate that.

'Then we had a day off and the next day we beat Somerset in a T20 as well. It wasn't too often teams went down there and did that, so it was a pretty good week and it gave us a lot of belief.'

Franklin confirmed that assessment, reflecting, 'Winning at Scarborough – a place where Yorkshire were notoriously hard to beat – along with the win at Taunton, really started to say to the group, "We can win this thing."'The Championship games against Yorkshire during 2015 and 2016 were excellent games of cricket, some of the best I ever played in, and all things pointed towards a game that was going to be winner takes all – a showdown at Lord's.'

Rewinding by ten weeks or so, confidence in the camp was clearly building and, although the ledger charting victories at Lord's remained empty as August approached, back-to-back home fixtures against Surrey and Durham represented opportunities to remedy that situation. In the first of those, a Middlesex win was never on the cards – the brown-capped visitors seizing the initiative on day one and maintaining it right up to the final afternoon, when Bailey's dogged unbeaten century and a partnership of 174 with Franklin secured a draw. Again, the team's stubborn streak had come to the fore to stave off defeat – but when they lined up against Durham, the characteristics on show were ruthlessness rather than obduracy.

Ruthless, it's probably fair to say, was not an adjective often associated with Ollie Rayner during his career. Yet the tall, easy-going spinner, a member of the Sussex side that had claimed successive titles almost a decade earlier, was more than capable of being a match-winner and so it proved, with overall figures of 9-102 steering the Seaxes to an innings victory inside three days. Rayner would finish the campaign with an impressive haul of 51 wickets at just over 23.5 runs apiece, a more parsimonious average than any of Middlesex's other regular bowlers that summer. Ironically, Roland-Jones – the only one of his team-mates to surpass Rayner's total of wickets – ended the Durham match with none at all against his name. His main contribution came with the bat, another belligerent knock of 66 as he and Franklin put on a century partnership to follow individual hundreds from Gubbins and Compton.

'Funnily enough, those matches sometimes stick out more than the ones you do well in!' Roland-Jones admitted. 'I remember being about as frustrated as I've ever been in that game, trying to find a way through.

'There were games where conditions were in Ollie's favour but his ability to break partnerships, on pitches that weren't offering as much, was as valuable as anything. We knew how good a spinner he could be when there was a bit of bounce and something to aim at and it felt like he had both sides of his game really on point that year.

'He could really impact the game when it wasn't doing as much in the first innings and the Durham game was a perfect example.'

Finally, then, a win at Lord's – but it would be another five weeks before Middlesex returned to base, in which time plenty of water could be expected to have flowed under a plethora of bridges. As it turned out, Trent Bridge would be the most significant of those – the venue for the second of three consecutive games on the road and the only one to witness a positive result, sandwiched by rain-affected draws at Edgbaston and Old Trafford. While Scarborough and Taunton had both developed into intense races against the clock, Trent Bridge was a tightly fought, high-stakes scrap spread across three and a half tension-filled days. Not only were Middlesex in desperate need of another victory to keep Yorkshire at arm's length, Nottinghamshire had by now reached a 'win or bust' scenario in their battle to avoid relegation. That meant the league leaders, having taken up their option of bowling first and dismissed Nottinghamshire for 241, faced an unwelcome half an hour or so with the bat as the autumn shadows fell across the Trent Bridge pavilion and home seamer Jake Ball tore in like a man possessed.

Ball had Robson caught in the slips with his third delivery. Rayner, sent in as nightwatchman, was leg before to the next. Then the partisan home crowd became impatient. 'I remember those wickets going down that first evening and Compo [Nick Compton] was next in, but he didn't have any pads on!' Simpson recalled. 'There was a delay and we had to quickly get him strapped up to go out there.

'All the Notts fans started giving us a load of grief, "Come on, get on with it, time him out!" and all that sort of thing. Then Compo was out to the hat-trick ball and it put us in quite a precarious situation. We had to absorb some pressure and set it up.'

With Gubbins compiling a patient 75, Middlesex managed to eke out a slender first-innings lead of six and then pegged back the home side from 106-1 to 240 all out second time around, with Rayner collecting four wickets. Just seven runs, therefore, spanned the totals of the first three innings of the match and Middlesex would have to muster a similar one in the fourth – but yet again they needed to try and survive against the fiery Ball in the evening twilight. Once more, the Nottinghamshire paceman wrecked their top order, with Gubbins, Robson and Dawid Malan back in the pavilion and just 25 on the board as the locals sensed their team might just keep those survival hopes alive. On this occasion, Compton was padded up in good time and he and Eskinazi steered Middlesex to the close but, with Yorkshire well on the way to victory against Durham at Headingley, the pressure was very much on.

Yet despite the lingering effect of his Test disappointment earlier in the summer, Compton coped admirably with that pressure on a tense final morning. Blunting Ball's relentless assault, he advanced to a gritty 63 – only to be run out attempting an ambitious single – but by then the platform had been built for Simpson and Franklin to share an unbroken stand of 89 and seal a five-wicket victory in mid-afternoon.

'To be there at the end with Frankie was special and it carried on the momentum we'd gained from scraping over the line at Scarborough as well as Taunton,' said Simpson.

'Throughout the season we kept finding a way to get over the line and that was testament to what we'd been building and what a good team we were. Guys stood up to be counted when the chips were down.'

There would be another twist to the title race in the penultimate round of fixtures, but not at Old Trafford, where Middlesex had to settle for another draw against Lancashire. On the other side of the Pennines, Somerset romped to a ten-wicket victory at Headingley – not only ensuring that the champions would go into their final game nine points adrift of Middlesex, but also upgrading the contest into a three-horse race. If the Taunton team could round off their campaign by overcoming Nottinghamshire, which the form book indicated was an extremely likely outcome, a simultaneous stalemate at Lord's would deliver them that long-awaited maiden county title.

'Playing Yorkshire last, it had always felt like we'd have to be a long way in front for it not to play a part,' said Roland-Jones. 'But the way we'd been playing, with a positive mindset, it seemed like an advantage to be up against them.

'If it had only been a two-horse race, we'd certainly have felt confident it could go in our favour. There was non-stop jostling for position during the game and circumstances were changing all the time.'

While the points advantage lay with Middlesex, the toss rule ensured it was the visiting side who got to make first use of the ball in typical autumnal seamer-friendly conditions. With Jack Brooks claiming three early wickets, the Seaxes were soon in difficulty at 57-3.

'Everything you didn't want, we got on that first morning,' Franklin observed. 'It was overcast, the wicket had a green tinge to it and we had a real battle on our hands but we had to hang in, just stay in the game.'

Maintaining the role he had frequently filled during the summer, it was Gubbins who held the innings together with a valiant hundred and, although Brooks returned to clean up the tail, Middlesex posted a respectable 270. Up to a point, Yorkshire's reply mirrored their innings as a trio of wickets fell to Roland-Jones before Tim Bresnan led the counterattack, hammering an undefeated 142 to keep his side in the hunt for a third consecutive title. With Somerset already coasting towards victory at Taunton, it became critical for the White Rose to reach 350 in their first innings and secure a fourth batting bonus point – leading to a tense period on the third day when that objective hung in the balance. If Bresnan, in tandem with last man Ryan Sidebottom, failed to nudge Yorkshire over the threshold, it would not only scupper their championship prospects but wipe out any genuine incentive for them to win the game. Inevitably, in that scenario, it would also become far harder for Middlesex – already facing a first-innings deficit with around a day and a half left – to force a victory.

That being the case, there must surely have been heartfelt sighs of relief in both camps when, after an untimely delay for rain and bad light, Bresnan and Sidebottom edged their way past 350. Less so from the Middlesex perspective once the last pair had added another 40 and they went out to begin their second innings, trailing by 120 – only to lose Robson and Compton cheaply inside the first four overs.

'I was sitting with our batting coach Dave Houghton on the third evening and when we lost those two quick wickets, I looked at Houghts and thought, "Oh no, this might be it,"' Franklin admitted.

Simpson provided similar memories of that evening session on the penultimate day, adding, 'I'd be lying if I said there weren't a few nerves around. We needed a partnership to consolidate and get through to the end of the day.

'Gubbo and Mala soaked up the pressure brilliantly – they didn't look in any trouble and played fantastically well to set the game up for us. I remember waking up the next morning excited, nervous and not really knowing what would happen.

'By then, Somerset had won down at Taunton but we felt the game at Lord's was going to go one way or the other.'

Although Gubbins and Malan had guided Middlesex to stumps, they were still 39 behind their rivals. A flurry of dismissals in the morning would clearly increase the likelihood of a Yorkshire triumph, so the first task facing the not-out pair was still to keep their wickets intact before concerning themselves with acceleration. All four results remained possible as the final morning of the 2016 season dawned – but two of them would be no use whatsoever to anyone bar the Somerset players, already showered, changed and readying themselves for an anxious day's TV viewing.

'We still knew we had hard work to do on that fourth morning,' said Franklin. 'It didn't seem likely we could contemplate doing anything to try and win the game until teatime.

'If we'd lost another couple of quick wickets at that point, they could end up chasing about 150 in 50 overs. But Nick Gubbins played really well, on the back of an amazing season, and then Dawid Malan scored a fantastic hundred.

'I believe that helped Dawid's cause in terms of getting into the England team. To do it under pressure in a big game on TV was an innings that might have just confirmed it.'

Progress on that final morning was steady rather than spectacular, with Gubbins missing out on his century by seven runs after giving Azeem Rafiq a return catch, but Malan and Eskinazi continued to stretch Middlesex's advantage after lunch. It was fast becoming a question of who would blink first in this battle of brinkmanship and, according to Simpson – who was padded up at the time – initial overtures about negotiating a target were made by Yorkshire captain Andrew Gale.

'It was just a case of "keep batting and let them try and force the issue". We knew when we were looking to pull out but we thought, if we could hold our nerve a little bit longer than them, then hopefully we'd get something favourable,' he said.

'It was quite an interesting period. Gale had gone running off the pitch and asked Frankie [James Franklin] what was happening and while they were negotiating in the toilets I was just trying to keep focused.

'Gale's first attempt got rebuffed, then a couple of overs later he went off again and tried a second time. You could see the Yorkshire players were getting quite frustrated from their body language.'

There was just as much eagerness among the Seaxes' camp for a deal to be struck, even if – as the batting side – they were able to conceal that from their opponents far more easily. Roland-Jones reflected, 'It was on a bit of a knife edge. Both sides had what you might call their entitlements, if you like, as to what they thought was right and fair and gave an even game.

'I didn't say very much – basically, "I don't care. Whatever it is, we've got a chance and let's take them on." That was the sentiment of the squad and looking back, I think it left a perfectly valid chase. It certainly wasn't the easiest pitch to score fast on, but I felt it opened up an avenue for both teams.'

A third attempt at negotiation was needed before Gale and Franklin eventually settled on an equation that would determine the destiny of the County Championship pennant. Yorkshire would attempt to score 240 in 40 overs, exactly a run a ball, with the understanding that the chase would continue come what may. Now they just needed to ensure Middlesex would be in a position to set them that target – paving the way for an extraordinary nine-over passage of play in front of a steadily expanding Lord's crowd.

While Adam Lyth could certainly be classed as a useful part-time bowler, it would be hard to say the same of Alex Lees and his gentle leg-breaks. That scarcely mattered as the Yorkshire pair proceeded to serve up a strict diet of buffet bowling, with the batting side tucking in to the tune of 120 runs. Yet Lees managed to collect two of his three first-class wickets during that bizarre period – those of Malan and Simpson, who had clubbed 31 from just nine deliveries before being castled by the part-timer. Franklin followed him to the crease, smacking 30 off 14 and sending the gentlest of catches looping up into Lyth's hands to signal the declaration.

'When Dawid got out and I went out in that weird situation, I don't think I'd ever had any lob-ups before, to be honest,' Simpson recalled.

'It was probably not my finest moment, getting out bowled by Alex Lees. He was almost bowling double bouncers – you couldn't hit them! Then Frankie just chipped one back to Adam Lyth and walked off.'

Phoney war over, it was game on. Yorkshire launched their chase at around four an over, but Roland-Jones made the initial breakthrough by having Lyth caught in the slips, and Lees and the dangerous David Willey followed suit, both falling to Murtagh. That ushered in the man who Middlesex knew might take the game away from them – first-innings centurion Bresnan, whose pugnacious mood was in evidence once again as, in tandem with Gary Ballance and then Gale, he pressed his foot on the accelerator.

'Bresnan was in good form and had been all season,' said Franklin. 'He looked dangerous again but we always knew that, if we could just keep chipping away and get wickets, they would keep attacking.

'It was the old cliché of, if you put one or two wickets on their score, you're right back in the game. I don't think there was any point in that innings where we didn't feel we had our noses in front, it was more on Yorkshire to take risks and we had to hold our nerve.'

Even if that pressure rested more heavily on the visitors, Franklin still needed to be skilful in manipulating the ongoing game of cat and mouse. As Simpson recalled, there was a stage of the innings when Bresnan – observing several fielders stationed in the deep – indicated he was prepared to call the Seaxes' bluff and all but dispatch the title to Taunton.

'We'd set a pretty standard field – two slips and a gully – but then about halfway through that final session we had a lot of men out,' said the wicketkeeper.

'Bresnan was a thorn in our side again and I remember him turning around to me and saying, "Simmo, if Frankie's going to keep this field, I'm going to tell whoever's coming in to shut up shop."' I'm not sure whether it was an idle threat, but I told Frankie what Bres had said and he brought a few fielders in to see whether he wanted to take it on.'

Bresnan did want to take it on. He clubbed his way to 55 from 47 balls, bringing the target into double figures, and although the asking rate had risen above eight per over, Middlesex knew the title could be slipping away. With 11 overs left and six wickets still needed, it was time to bring back Roland-Jones for what Franklin – and everyone connected with the club – desperately hoped would be a decisive second spell.

'At that point Toby was immense for Middlesex,' stated Franklin. 'He'd bowl eight- or nine-over spells and get two wickets and it was almost the longer the spell went on, the quicker he bowled.

'I look on it as another moment like with Dawid Malan, where Toby really put his name up in lights for the England selectors and the next summer he did really well in the Test side before that horrible stress fracture.'

Turning to the most prolific wicket-taker he had available – at that stage, Roland-Jones was actually two behind Rayner, who was not playing in the match – paid off immediately. The seamer's fifth ball pinned Bresnan in front of his stumps and, with that moment, Yorkshire's hopes of retaining their crown all but evaporated. Gale followed in Roland-Jones's next over, then Rafiq to the last ball of the next, skying one into Simpson's gloves before Finn bowled Steven Patterson to leave the visitors eight down with five overs remaining.

The first ball of Roland-Jones's next over was straight and Andrew Hodd swung and missed, with the inevitable clatter of stumps leaving Middlesex one wicket from glory as Sidebottom strode to the crease.

'It was a really good test, an example of not just pressure, but the emotion of the situation and knowing what the outcome would be of getting Sidebottom out,' Roland-Jones looked back.

'Maybe people perceive you as looking calm or whatever – you're not, you're trying to keep a lid on things. I remember asking James Franklin what ball he thought was best, so I could be clear we were in agreement when I ran in – and I missed by two stumps!

'If anyone thought I was aiming at leg stump, that's very generous of them, but I'm afraid not. Thankfully it was the right side and you can see in the footage of the celebrations, I'm not pre-empting anything.

'Essentially, I didn't know what to do, and in some ways that's the nicest way to celebrate – let the occasion take over. When Rob Key interviewed me for Sky afterwards, he mentioned the hat-trick in passing.

'I sort of brushed over it, then I walked off thinking, "Did he just say I got a hat-trick?" I knew it was three in three from a team perspective, but it was a bit of blur. Maybe it was better to find out that way!'

Cue scenes of exhilaration and celebration – on the pitch, then in the home dressing room and relocating a few hundred yards to the Tavern later in the evening. As a climax to any league competition, it had been a gripping spectacle for supporters of both teams and any lover of cricket, bar those of a Somerset persuasion who felt hard done by at the contrived finish. As Simpson observed, though, 'Obviously, those Somerset boys were not particularly happy with what was going on – but they'd have done exactly the same.'

In reality, while Somerset merited praise for their late run, it had been abundantly clear that the two best teams in the country – not only during 2016 but also in the previous season – were Yorkshire and Middlesex. The home side had completed the campaign undefeated and their triumph brought a 23-year hiatus to a close – not quite as lengthy as the wait between

Middlesex v Yorkshire scorebook, 2016.

Middlesex CCC v Yorkshire	Played At: Lord's	Result: Middlesex CCC Won By 61 runs
Specsavers County Championship	Tuesday, September 20 2016 (10.30)	
Innings of Middlesex CCC (1st innings)	Yorkshire won toss and decided to field	Man of the match: TT Bresnan

	Batsman	Time In/Out	Mins Balls	Batting Analysis	4s 6s	50 100	How Out	Bowler	Runs
1	SD Robson*	10:27 / 10:42	14 / 15		0 / 0		lbw	JA Brooks	0
2	NRT Gubbins	10:27 / 11:07	370 / 274		15 / 1	94 / 191	c A Lyth	TT Bresnan	125
3	NRD Compton	10:43 / 11:17	33 / 24		1 / 0		lbw	JA Brooks	8
4	DJ Malan	11:18 / 11:44	26 / 24		4 / 0		bowled	DJ Willey	22
5	SS Eskinazi	11:45 / 13:27	64 / 45		2 / 0		bowled	JA Brooks	12
6	JA Simpson	13:28 / 15:02	93 / 76		3 / 0		lbw	TT Bresnan	15
7	JEC Franklin*	15:03 / 11:26	150 / 106		8 / 0		c AJ Hodd	TT Bresnan	48
8	OP Rayner	11:08 / 12:25	76 / 54		1 / 0		not out		15
9	TS Roland-Jones	11:27 / 12:00	33 / 19		1 / 0		c A Lyth	JA Brooks	7
10	TJ Murtagh	12:01 / 12:16	14 / 8		0 / 0		c AW Gale	JA Brooks	0
11	ST Finn	12:16 / 12:25	8 / 7		1 / 0		c A Lyth	JA Brooks	6
			652 Balls Received					Batsmen Total	258

Fall of Wickets

Wicket	1	2	3	4	5	6	7	8	9	10
Score	11	33	57	97	154	229	244	254	258	270
Bat Out	1	3	4	5	6	2	7	9	10	11
Not out Score	7 [2]	21 [2]	23 [2]	50 [2]	87 [2]	36 [7]	3 [8]	6 [8]	9 [8]	15 [8]
Partnership	11 (22)	22 (48)	24 (34)	40 (98)	57 (141)	75 (212)	15 (25)	10 (46)	4 (16)	12 (10)

15.2 50 total runs 92 deliveries 67 mins (9 4s 0 6s)
33.2 NRT Gubbins: 50 runs 94 balls 140 mins (9 4s 0 6s)
35.3 100 total runs 213 deliveries 151 mins (16 4s 0 6s)
54.2 50 Partnership : 125 deliveries 83 mins (6 4s 0 6s); NRT Gubbins 34 runs (56); JA Simpson 11 runs (69)
55.4 150 total runs 335 deliveries 231 mins (23 4s 0 6s)
66.2 NRT Gubbins: 100 runs 191 balls 272 mins (14 4s 1 6s)
72.4 200 total runs 437 deliveries 298 mins (28 4s 1 6s)
76.6 50 Partnership : 120 deliveries 74 mins (5 4s 1 6s); NRT Gubbins 31 runs (68); JEC Franklin 20 runs (52)
101.2 250 total runs 609 deliveries 411 mins (34 4s 1 6s)

Extras

No balls		2
Wides		0
Byes		4
Leg byes	1211	
Penalties prev inn	0 this inn	0
	Provisional score	12
		270
Penalties awarded following innings		0
	Total for innings	270
	Wickets (all out)	10
	Target	

Middlesex CCC v Yorkshire	Played At: Lord's	Result: Middlesex CCC Won By 61 runs
Specsavers County Championship	Tuesday, September 20 2016 (10.30)	
Innings of Middlesex CCC (1st innings)	Yorkshire won toss and decided to field	Man of the match: TT Bresnan

Bowling Analysis

	Bowler	Wides	No balls	Balls	Overs	Mdns	Runs	Wkts	Ave
1	RJ Sidebottom	0 (0)	0 (0)	132	22.0	12	29	0	-
2	JA Brooks	0 (0)	0 (0)	141	23.3	2	65	6	10.83
3	DJ Willey	0 (0)	0 (0)	96	16.0	1	71	1	71.00
4	SA Patterson	0 (0)	1 (2)	103	17.0	9	32	0	-
5	TT Bresnan	0 (0)	0 (0)	138	23.0	7	48	3	16.00
6	A Rafiq	0 (0)	0 (0)	42	7.0	1	15	0	-
7									

106.5 JA Brooks 5 wickets in innings

	Wides	No balls	Balls	Overs	Mdns	Runs	Wkts
Bowling totals	0 (0)	1 (2)	652	108.3	32	260	10
less wides / fielding extras						10	0
Provisional score			652	108.3	32	270	10
Penalties in following innings						0	
Final score						270	10

Umpires: RT Robinson RJ Bailey	Match Referee	Scorers: DK Shelley JT Potter

	Middlesex CCC v Yorkshire	Played At: Lord's		Result: Middlesex CCC Won By 61 runs
	Specsavers County Championship	Tuesday, September 20 2016 (10.30)		
	Innings of Yorkshire (1st Innings)	Yorkshire won toss and decided to field		Man of the match: TT Bresnan

Yorkshire Batting

	Batsman	Time In/Out	Mins Balls	Batting Analysis	4s / 6s	50 / 100	How Out	Bowler	Runs
1	A Lyth	13:03 / 14:15	72 / 54	1•••1••••44•••••44••4•1••••41••4••••••12••••••••••4•4w»	9 / 0		bowled	ST Finn	43
2	AZ Lees	13:03 / 13:26	22 / 17	••••••••••••••w»	0 / 0		bowled	TS Roland-Jones	0
3	GS Ballance	13:27 / 13:43	16 / 4	•••w»	0 / 0		c OP Rayner	TS Roland-Jones	0
4	AW Gale*	13:44 / 13:47	2 / 2	•w»	0 / 0		c OP Rayner	TS Roland-Jones	0
5	TT Bresnan	13:48 / 15:44	452 / 293	•••1L'••••••••••1••3•4•••••••••••••••1••4411•••••1••2•••341•••1•11•1•••• •1•4•••••L'1••1•••••2•4•••••1•○•••2••••1••••••1••••••1••••••L'•• •11••1•41••••••••••1•1141L'••1•2••••••••••44••••••1••1111•1••4•••1••1• ••••21••11•L'•31•1•1••••1•••••••1•••••4•1•••11••1•••1••••1••••• •4•116••111121•1	12 / 1	107 / 222	not out		142
6	AJ Hodd+	14:17 / 17:00	142 / 104	•••••••••1•••41•2•3•••1•4••114••••1••1•21••1••••4•••••••2•1••4••••211 •11•1••1•••4•L'•2•••1•••4••••••1w»	7 / 0	79 /	lbw	TS Roland-Jones	64
7	DJ Willey	17:01 / 17:40	39 / 27	L'••1••••4••1••6••••••6•i••w»	2 / 0		lbw	TJ Murtagh	22
8	A Rafiq	17:41 / 12:04	125 / 97	•••••••4••4•••4••4••1••1••••1•••••••••4••1•4411••••••1•1••1○•14••1•1• ••L'1•••••4•••••••••6••141••w»	10 / 1	78 /	bowled	TJ Murtagh	65
9	SA Patterson	12:05 / 13:07	22 / 20	1••••1•••••3•2••○4w»	0 / 0		c OP Rayner	ST Finn	11
10	JA Brooks	13:07 / 13:11	3 / 4	•••w»	0 / 0		c NRT Gubbins	TJ Murtagh	0
11	RJ Sidebottom	13:12 / 15:44	85 / 80	•1••••••••••1'••••••••••••••••••••4•••••1••••4••••1•4•••••••••• •111•w»	4 / 0		bowled	OP Rayner	23
			702 Balls Received					Batsmen Total	370

Fall of Wickets

Wicket	1	2	3	4	5	6	7	8	9	10	Extras		
Score	14	32	32	53	169	204	318	333	334	390	No balls	222	8
Bat Out	2	3	4	1	6	7	8	9	10	11			
Not out Score	14 [1]	32 [1]	32 [1]	6 [5]	54 [5]	62 [5]	106 [5]	108 [5]	109 [5]	142 [5]	Wides		0
Partnership	14 (34)	18 (22)	0 (2)	21 (38)	116 (214)	35 (57)	114 (166)	15 (33)	1 (5)	56 (131)	Byes		0

15.5 50 total runs 95 deliveries 71 mins (9 4s 0 6s)
28.4 100 total runs 172 deliveries 115 mins (15 4s 0 6s)
29.4 50 Partnership: 82 deliveries 56 mins (6 4s 0 6s); TT Bresnan 23 runs (41), AJ Hodd 27 runs (41)
41.2 AJ Hodd 50 runs 79 balls 99 mins (5 4s 0 6s)
43.2 150 total runs 260 deliveries 180 mins (20 4s 0 6s)
43.6 100 Partnership: 168 deliveries 108 mins (11 4s 0 6s); TT Bresnan 42 runs (82), AJ Hodd 56 runs (86)
44.6 TT Bresnan 50 runs 107 balls 142 mins (5 4s 0 6s)
59.5 200 total runs 360 deliveries 252 mins (24 4s 2 6s)
72.2 250 total runs 435 deliveries 302 mins (33 4s 2 6s)
73.1 50 Partnership; 73 deliveries 48 mins (10 4s 0 6s); TT Bresnan 19 runs (28), A Rafiq 33 runs (45)

Leg byes		11141111			14
Penalties	prev inn	0	this inn	0	0
					20
Provisional score					390
Penalties awarded following innings					0
Total for innings					390
Wickets (all out)					10
Target					

	Middlesex CCC v Yorkshire	Played At: Lord's		Result: Middlesex CCC Won By 61 runs
	Specsavers County Championship	Tuesday, September 20 2016 (10.30)		
	Innings of Yorkshire (1st Innings)	Yorkshire won toss and decided to field		Man of the match: TT Bresnan

Bowling Analysis

	Bowler		Wides	No balls	Balls	Overs	Mdns	Runs	Wkts	Avg
1	TJ Murtagh		0 (0)	0 (0)	192	32.0	4	96	3	32.00
2	TS Roland-Jones		0 (0)	0 (0)	174	29.0	5	73	4	18.25
3	JEC Franklin		0 (0)	1 (2)	55	9.0	1	32	0	–
4	ST Finn		0 (0)	2 (4)	182	30.0	4	105	2	52.50
5	OP Rayner		0 (0)	0 (0)	99	16.3	1	70	1	70.00
6										
7										

Bowling totals	0 (0)	3 (6)	702	116.3	15	376	10	
	less wides	0	fielding extras		14			
Provisional score			702	116.3	15	390	10	
Penalties in following innings								
Final score						390	10	

Umpires: RT Robinson RJ Bailey | Match Referee: | Scorers: DK Shelley JT Potter

Middlesex v Yorkshire scorebook, 2016.

Middlesex CCC v Yorkshire	Played At: Lord's	Result: Middlesex CCC Won By 61 runs
Specsavers County Championship	Tuesday, September 20 2016 (10.30)	
Innings of Middlesex CCC (2nd Innings)	Yorkshire won toss and decided to field	Man of the match: TT Bresnan

	Batsman	Time In/Out	Mins Balls	Batting Analysis	4s 6s	50 100	How Out	Bowler	Runs
1	NRT Gubbins	16:03 12:24	262 200		9 1	147	c A Rafiq	A Rafiq	93
2	SD Robson+	16:03 16:07	4 3	••w⟩⟩	0 0		c AZ Lees	RJ Sidebottom	0
3	NRD Compton	16:08 16:20	11 8	•1•••••w⟩⟩	0 0		bowled	JA Brooks	1
4	DJ Malan	16:21 14:17	319 246		14 0	131 203	c JA Brooks	AZ Lees	116
5	SS Eskinazi	12:25 14:56	97 63		10 4	65	not out		78
6	JA Simpson	14:18 14:23	4 10	4144444•6w⟩⟩	6 1		bowled	AZ Lees	31
7	JEC Franklin*	14:24 14:40	16 14	464•4+•••44•4•w⟩⟩	6 1		c A Lyth	A Lyth	30
8	TS Roland-Jones						Did Not Bat		
9	OP Rayner						Did Not Bat		
10	ST Finn						Did Not Bat		
11	TJ Murtagh						Did Not Bat		
		564	Balls Received					Batsmen Total	349

Fall of Wickets

Wicket	1	2	3	4	5	6	7	8	9	10
Score	1	2	200	265	303	359				
Bat Out	2	3	1	4	6	7				
Not out Score	1 [1]	1 [1]	98 [4]	47 [5]	54 [5]	78 [5]				
Partnership	1 [6]	1 [18]	198 [386]	38 [12]	56 [32]					

27.2 50 Partnership: 140 deliveries 92 mins (5 4s 1 6s); NRT Gubbins 28 runs (71); DJ Malan 23 runs (69); 50 total runs 164 deliveries 111 mins (6 4s 1 6s)
45.4 100 total runs 275 deliveries 173 mins (9 4s 1 6s)
46.4 DJ Malan: 50 runs 131 balls 158 mins (6 4s 0 6s); 100 Partnership: 257 deliveries 158 mins (10 4s 1 6s); NRT Gubbins 45 runs (126); DJ Malan 51 runs (131)
48.6 NRT Gubbins: 50 runs 147 balls 185 mins (5 4s 1 6s)
57.3 150 total runs 346 deliveries 222 mins (16 4s 1 6s)
57.4 150 Partnership: 323 deliveries 204 mins (16 4s 1 6s); NRT Gubbins 62 runs (155); DJ Malan 80 runs (168)
67.6 200 total runs 409 deliveries 260 mins (20 4s 1 6s)
70.3 DJ Malan: 100 runs 203 balls 252 mins (11 4s 0 6s)

Extras		
No balls		2
Wides		1
Byes		1
Leg byes	411	6
Penalties prev inn 0	this inn 0	0
		10

Provisional score: 359
Penalties awarded following innings: 0
Total for innings: 359
Wickets (dec): 6
Target:

Middlesex CCC v Yorkshire	Played At: Lord's	Result: Middlesex CCC Won By 61 runs
Specsavers County Championship	Tuesday, September 20 2016 (10.30)	
Innings of Middlesex CCC (2nd Innings)	Yorkshire won toss and decided to field	Man of the match: TT Bresnan

Bowling Analysis

	Bowler	Wides	No balls	Balls	Overs	Mdns	Runs	Wkts	Ave
1	RJ Sidebottom	0 (0)	0 (0)	78	13.0	0	36	1	36.00
2	JA Brooks	0 (0)	0 (0)	90	15.0	5	48	1	48.00
3	TT Bresnan	0 (0)	1 (2)	73	12.0	3	33	0	-
4	SA Patterson	0 (0)	0 (0)	84	14.0	5	40	0	-
5	DJ Willey	0 (0)	0 (0)	60	10.0	3	21	0	-
6	A Rafiq	0 (0)	0 (0)	108	18.0	3	46	1	46.00
7	A Lyth	0 (0)	0 (0)	47	7.5	0	77	1	77.00
8	AZ Lees	1 (1)	0 (0)	25	4.0	0	51	2	25.50
	Bowling totals	1 (1)	1 (2)	565	93.5	19	352	6	
	Provisional score		less wides	1		fielding extras	7	0	
	Penalties in following innings			564	93.5	19	359	6	
	Final score						359	6	

Umpires: RT Robinson RJ Bailey	Match Referee:	Scorers: DK Shelley JT Potter

Middlesex CCC v Yorkshire
Specsavers County Championship
Innings of Yorkshire (2nd Innings)

Played At: Lord's
Tuesday, September 20 2016 (10.30)
Yorkshire won toss and decided to field

Result: Middlesex CCC Won By 61 runs
Man of the match: TT Bresnan

Batsman	Time In/Out	Mins Balls	Batting Analysis	4s 6s	50 100	How Out	Bowler	Runs
1 A Lyth	14:58 15:22	23 16	1•4•1••1••4•2••w»	2 0		c SD Robson	TS Roland-Jones	13
2 AZ Lees	14:58 15:40	41 31	•4•2••1•4•••1•2••••1121••1••w»	2 0		c NRT Gubbins	TJ Murtagh	20
3 DJ Willey	15:23 15:50	26 21	••••15••••••••4•1•w»	1 0		c SS Eskinazi	TJ Murtagh	11
4 GS Ballance	15:41 16:28	47 39	1••1•1•11111•4••••1•1•11•6•112••••12w»	1 1		c SD Robson	ST Finn	30
5 TT Bresnan	15:52 16:59	67 48	•••1•••14••••6111•1211112••2•1•6411124•11111•4w»	4 2	44	lbw	TS Roland-Jones	55
6 AW Gale*	16:29 17:09	39 28	•1••1•4••1•41••1•1•4•L'1111•w»	3 0		bowled	TS Roland-Jones	22
7 AJ Hodd+	17:00 17:27	26 19	•••11•211224•••111w»	1 0		bowled	TS Roland-Jones	17
8 A Rafiq	17:09 17:20	10 5	•211w»	0 0		c JA Simpson	TS Roland-Jones	4
9 SA Patterson	17:20 17:25	4 4	11•w»	0 0		bowled	ST Finn	2
10 JA Brooks	17:26 17:29	3 0		0 0		not out		0
11 RJ Sidebottom	17:28 17:29	1 1	w»	0 0		bowled	TS Roland-Jones	0

212 Balls Received | Batsmen Total | 174

Fall of Wickets

Wicket	1	2	3	4	5	6	7	8	9	10
Score	27	39	48	98	153	160	174	178	178	178
Bat Out	1	2	3	4	5	6	8	9	7	11
Not out Score	14 [2]	6 [3]	4 [4]	24 [5]	20 [6]	5 [7]	15 [7]	17 [7]	0 [10]	0 [10]
Partnership	27 (36)	12 (27)	9 (13)	50 (58)	55 (45)	7 (12)	14 (13)	4 (6)	0 (1)	0 (1)

13.1 50 total runs 79 deliveries 55 mins (5 4s 0 6s)
22.1 50 Partnership; 57 deliveries 35 mins (2 4s 2 6s); GS Ballance 26 runs (30); TT Bresnan 24 runs (27)
22.4 100 total runs 136 deliveries 92 mins (7 4s 2 6s)
28.6 TT Bresnan 50 runs 44 balls 63 mins (3 4s 2 6s)
29.1 50 Partnership; 41 deliveries 26 mins (5 4s 1 6s), TT Bresnan 27 runs (18), AW Gale 19 runs (23)
29.4 150 total runs 178 deliveries 120 mins (13 4s 3 6s)

Extras

No balls		0
Wides		0
Byes		0
Leg byes		4
Penalties prev inn 0 this inn 0		0

Provisional score	178
Penalties awarded following innings	0
Total for innings	178
Wickets (all out)	10
Target	240

Middlesex CCC v Yorkshire
Specsavers County Championship
Innings of Yorkshire (2nd Innings)

Played At: Lord's
Tuesday, September 20 2016 (10.30)
Yorkshire won toss and decided to field

Result: Middlesex CCC Won By 61 runs
Man of the match: TT Bresnan

Middlesex CCC v Yorkshire / Specsavers County Championship / Innings of Yorkshire (2nd Innings)

Bowling Analysis

Bowler	Wides	No balls	Balls	Overs	Mdns	Runs	Wkts	Ave
1 TJ Murtagh	0 (0)	0 (0)	48	8.0	1	28	2	14.00
2 TS Roland-Jones	0 (0)	0 (0)	74	12.2	0	54	6	9.00
3 OP Rayner	0 (0)	0 (0)	30	5.0	0	32	0	-
4 ST Finn	0 (0)	0 (0)	60	10.0	0	60	2	30.00
5								
6								
7								

35.1 TS Roland-Jones 5 wickets in innings
35.2 End; TS Roland-Jones hat trick 10 wickets in match

	Wides	No balls	Balls	Overs	Mdns	Runs	Wkts
Bowling totals	0 (0)	0 (0)	212	35.2	1	174	10
	less wides	0	fielding extras	4			
Provisional score			212	35.2	1	178	10
Penalties in following innings						0	
Final score						178	10

Umpires RT Robinson RJ Bailey   Match Referee   Scorers DK Shelley JT Potter

Scoreboard says Middlesex are champions!

1949 and 1976, but nevertheless the heroes of 2016 sensed they had forged a new link in that chain of Middlesex tradition.

'When you spend any time with Gus [Angus Fraser], Gatt [Mike Gatting], Embers [John Emburey], Rad [Clive Radley], Selve [Mike Selvey] – they talk about the glory days, when Middlesex were the best in the country, winning all those titles,' Simpson reflected.

'You see the names on the honours board, you hear the stories from them and suddenly those feelings they had when they were winning a lot of trophies resonate with you.

'When Gus took over [as managing director of cricket], we were languishing in Division Two. To turn things around and get us to where we wanted to be was testament to his hard work and ideas, bringing in the right people and the right characters.'

Roland-Jones, the man whose individual achievement will forever be entwined with the county's 2016 title triumph, concurred. He said, 'Even with the numbers you get at T20 and Test matches, that's still the best atmosphere I've played in at Lord's.

'It was a really special feeling to see the stands filling up and you knew it meant a lot to Middlesex members. I think that was a big part in making it feel like a real moment in history.

'We're very fortunate in that a lot of the great Middlesex players are still around and connected to the club. You wanted to feel part of the history they created and part of a Middlesex team that ended a wait which had been too long.'

ND - #0307 - 270225 - C0 - 234/156/12 - PB - 9781780916484 - Gloss Lamination